Bullying in Youth Sports Training

Based on an extensive national research project with global relevance, this pioneering volume draws on unique data on bullying in youth sports training collected from both athletes and coaches using a variety of methodological approaches. Nery, Neto, Rosado and Smith use this research to establish a baseline of the prevalence of bullying among young male athletes, offering evidence-based strategies for prevention and providing a solid theoretical basis for the development of anti-bullying intervention programmes.

Bullying in Youth Sports Training explores how often bullying occurs, how long it lasts, where and when bullying takes place, the coping strategies used by victims, and the individual roles of victims, bystanders and bullies. It provides new insights into theories of youth sports bullying and highlights the particular characteristics specific to bullying in sport. The backgrounds of bullies and victims are also explored, as well as the consequences and practical implications of sustained bullying. The book provides both theoretical and practical approaches to bullying in youth sports training, providing anti-bullying guidelines based on the results of the research.

The book is essential reading for scholars and students in child development and sport sciences as well as sports coaches and professionals in mental health, education and social work.

Miguel Nery is a clinical psychologist and psychodynamic psychotherapist. He is currently a researcher at the Motor Behaviour Laboratory in the Faculty of Human Kinetics, Lisbon University, Portugal. He is responsible for a Portuguese Government funded intervention project about bullying in sport, Red Card to Bullying.

Carlos Neto is Full Professor at the Faculty of Human Kinetics, Lisbon University, Portugal. He is a member of the Motor Behaviour Laboratory.

António Rosado is Full Professor at the Faculty of Human Kinetics, Lisbon University, Portugal. He is a member of the Sport and Exercise Psychology Laboratory.

Peter K. Smith is Emeritus Professor of Psychology at Goldsmiths College, University of London, UK. He is editor of *Making an Impact on School Bullying: Interventions and Recommendations* (Routledge, 2019).

Bullying in Youth Sports Training

New Perspectives and Practical Strategies

Miguel Nery, Carlos Neto, António Rosado and Peter K. Smith

First published 2020
by Routledge
2 Park Square, Milton Park, Abingdon, Oxon OX14 4RN

and by Routledge
52 Vanderbilt Avenue, New York, NY 10017

Routledge is an imprint of the Taylor & Francis Group, an informa business

© 2020 Miguel Nery, Carlos Neto, António Rosado and Peter K. Smith

The right of Miguel Nery, Carlos Neto, António Rosado and Peter K. Smith to be identified as authors of this work has been asserted by them in accordance with sections 77 and 78 of the Copyright, Designs and Patents Act 1988.

All rights reserved. No part of this book may be reprinted or reproduced or utilised in any form or by any electronic, mechanical, or other means, now known or hereafter invented, including photocopying and recording, or in any information storage or retrieval system, without permission in writing from the publishers.

Trademark notice: Product or corporate names may be trademarks or registered trademarks, and are used only for identification and explanation without intent to infringe.

British Library Cataloguing-in-Publication Data
A catalogue record for this book is available from the British Library

Library of Congress Cataloging-in-Publication Data
A catalog record has been requested for this book

ISBN: 978-1-138-10608-6 (hbk)
ISBN: 978-0-367-89388-0 (pbk)
ISBN: 978-1-315-10170-5 (ebk)

Typeset in Sabon
by Swales & Willis, Exeter, Devon, UK

Printed in the United Kingdom
by Henry Ling Limited

Contents

List of figures vii
List of tables viii
Preface ix
About the authors xi

Introduction 1

PART I
Conceptual issues **7**

1 Research on bullying 9

2 History of sport, violence in sport and issues in youth sports training 34

3 The Portuguese context 65

PART II
Research on bullying in youth sports training **75**

4 Methods 77

5 Frequency of bullying behaviours 97

6 Circumstances of bullying episodes 105

7 Narratives of the athletes 124

8 Narratives of the coaches	146
9 Narratives of the ex-elite athletes	161

PART III
Conclusions and practical implications — **177**

10 Discussion and conclusions on athlete–athlete bullying	179
11 Coach abuse	213
12 Practical implications, and guidelines for athletes, parents and coaches	230
References	265
Appendices	283
Index	300

Figures

2.1	Ecological Systems Theory applied to bullying in youth sport	57
3.1	Map of Portuguese national territory divided into districts	68
3.2	Portuguese youth sports organizational chart	69
3.3	Geographical distribution of sports clubs	73
5.1	Percentages of different roles of athletes involved in bullying episodes	98
12.1	Levels of intervention based on the Ecological Systems Model	232

Tables

1.1	Summary table for multi-level approach contributions to understanding bullying	30
2.1	Description of the micro-system in relation to sports clubs	55
2.2	Description of the meso-system in relation to sports clubs	56
2.3	Description of the exo-system in relation to sports clubs	56
2.4	Description of the macro-system in relation to sports clubs	57
3.1	Description of the geographical areas	67
3.2	Contents of the coach courses (levels 1, 2 and 3) and workload per topic	71
3.3	Description of the sports studied	72
5.1	Analysis of victimization frequency by number of good friends	103
5.2	Frequency of bullying types and feelings towards bullying for victims, bystanders and bullies	104
6.1	Frequency, duration, location, activities and number of athletes involved in victimization episodes	106
6.2	Victimization frequency by victimization duration and activities in which victimization occurred	109
6.3	Victimization duration by activities and location	110
6.4	Victims' employed communication and coping strategies	111
6.5	Victims' communication by coping styles and frequency of victimization	113
6.6	Victims' family support by frequency of victimization	114
6.7	Summary of main results for bullies	115
6.8	Type of bullying by frequency of bullying episodes	118
6.9	Bullies' communication per number of athletes involved in bullying episodes	119
6.10	Summary of main results for bystanders	120
6.11	Bystanders' feelings by bullying reasons and reactions towards bullying	122
7.1	Reasons for bullying occurrence	131
7.2	Coping strategies used by victims and bystanders	138

Preface

This book is a product of a research project on bullying in youth sports training carried out over several years in Portugal, on a national basis. It provides a comprehensive picture of the nature of bullying in youth sports training; how often it occurs; how long it lasts; where episodes take place and in what activities; what kind of behaviours are considered; if bullying is individual or group; the feelings of victims, bystanders and bullies towards bullying; the communication about bullying episodes (who do victims speak with, and who approaches perpetrators when bullying occurs); and the coping strategies used by victims to address it and their support sources. Besides the circumstances of bullying episodes, the profiles of bullies and victims are also considered, and the consequences and practical implications are described. The book provides both theoretical and practical approaches to bullying in youth sports training, by providing anti-bullying guidelines based on the results of the research.

With this research, we establish a baseline of bullying among young male athletes in Portugal. As it is a barely studied topic, we contribute with some new insights which may help to reformulate and improve the actions of stakeholders, providing them with more useful strategies concerning both prevention and intervention, not only in Portugal but internationally. The results of this research should also help provide a solid theoretical basis for the development of anti-bullying intervention programmes.

This book will be informative for students, educational and mental health professionals in general and, more specifically, for sports professionals. Decades of international research on school bullying have shown that it is an important issue worldwide, which concerns educational and mental health professionals. Being involved in bullying episodes has severe consequences for athletes and for the sports community. By accessing a detailed description of the particular characteristics of bullying in youth sports training, and based on the guidelines provided, readers will be able to deal more effectively with this form of peer aggression, and contribute to a healthier sports environment and better opportunities for young athletes to fully develop their sports and social skills.

Postscript

There has been increasing interest by sporting and educational organizations about the well-being of young athletes, especially in recent years. This endeavour includes the development of research, campaigns and intervention programmes to tackle issues such as violence, abuse and discrimination in sport. Although much has been done, research on bullying in sport is still limited.

In this book, we have described four studies carried out in Portugal about bullying in sport. We also made a review of the limited literature about this topic internationally. We also included a consideration of abusive coaching practices, as well as sexual harassment and abuse in sport, which we included under the concept of *coach bullying*. Here, we summarize some important issues.

- Bullying among young male athletes is not infrequent, and it is definitely a cause for concern. We estimate that around 1 in every 10 athletes has been victimized, and the rates we report may be underestimated due to the normalization of some forms of aggression in sports settings;
- It is important to consider the sports ethos in order to understand bullying behaviours among athletes. Although bullying episodes may be observed in any social setting, its prevalence and characteristics are influenced by the norms and beliefs of that setting;
- Athletes who are victimized often remain silent about it, and being a target of bullying contributes to early drop out of sports practice;
- The coach has a key role in the prevention of bullying among athletes. However, some coaches get involved in abusive coaching practices, and may become the perpetrators themselves. It's therefore important to raise awareness about bullying among sports stakeholders;
- There is an urgent need to develop evidence-based prevention programmes. These should include different levels of intervention, and the whole sports community.

About the authors

Professor Miguel Nery is a clinical psychologist, psychodynamic psychotherapist and professor of psychology. His main research interests are human development, psychopathology, human aggression, play and sport. He has participated in international conferences about bullying and written articles and book chapters about bullying in youth sports training. He was the Project Manager of the Portuguese Government funded projects *Cartão Vermelho ao Bullying* (Red Card to Bullying) and *Desporto sem Bullying* (Sports without Bullying) to prevent and tackle bullying in youth sport, and coordinated a campaign against violence and discrimination in sport. He is also a clinical psychologist in private practice, and works as a professor and research coordinator at the Faculty of Health Sciences and Sport (Universidade Europeia).

Professor Carlos Neto is a Full Professor at the Faculty of Human Kinetics (FMH) of Lisbon University, Portugal. He is the Portuguese representative of the International Play Association (IPA) and the coordinator of the Master in Child Development of FMH. He was the founder of the Portuguese Association of Physical Education. Between 1998 and 2013, he worked as the coordinator of the Lisbon team of the international project TMR Network Project "Nature and Prevention of Bullying: The Causes and Nature of Bullying and Social Exclusion in Schools, and Ways of Preventing Them". He has also collaborated with various Portuguese-speaking universities as a consultant. He is the author of several books, for example *Jogo e Desenvolvimento da Criança* (Play and the Child's Development), *Motricidade e Jogo na Infância* (Human Movement and the Play in the Infancy) and *Tópicos em desenvolvimento na Infância e adolescência* (Developing Themes in Child and Adolescent Development).

Professor António Rosado is a Full Professor at the Faculty of Human Kinetics (FMH) of Lisbon University, Portugal. He is a member of the Sport and Exercise Psychology Laboratory. He is involved in a series of studies related to the development of models and methods in the fields of sport pedagogy and sport psychology. His current research interests include toughness and resilience in sport, sport and inclusion, and developing life skills in sport. He has published many book chapters and articles in peer-reviewed journals. Among other books he has published *Métodos e Técnicas de Investigação qualitativa* (Qualitative Research Methods and Techniques) (with I. Mesquita and C. Colaço) (Cruz-Quebrada: FMH-UTL Edições, 2012) and *Pedagogia do Desporto* (Sport Pedagogy) (with I. Mesquita) (Lisboa: FMH-UTL, 2002).

Professor Peter K. Smith is Emeritus Professor of Psychology, Unit for School and Family Studies at Goldsmiths College, University of London, UK. He has published *Understanding School Bullying: Its Nature and Prevention Strategies* (Sage Publications, 2014), *Understanding Children's Development* (with H. Cowie and M. Blades) (6th ed., Wiley-Blackwell, 2015), *Adolescence: A Very Short Introduction* (Oxford University Press, 2016), and *The Psychology of School Bullying* (Routledge, 2019). His edited books include *School Bullying in Different Cultures: Eastern and Western Perspectives* (Cambridge University Press, 2016), *Bullying, Cyberbullying and Pupil Well-being in Schools: Comparing European, Australian and Indian Perspectives* (Cambridge University Press, 2018), and *Making an Impact on School Bullying: Interventions and Recommendations* (Routledge, 2019). In 2015 he was awarded the William Thierry Preyer Award for Excellence in Research on Human Development, by the European Society for Developmental Psychology.

Introduction

Human aggression is a passionate research topic and writing about bullying is a great challenge, especially in the particular social setting of sport, in which some forms of violence may be tolerated and, in some cases, even valued. In sports settings, athletes compete with each other by symbolically attacking their opponents, from whom they have to defend themselves and avoid being defeated. The genesis of sport was to prepare men for war, and in many domains it has been considered a predominantly male field; although much has changed and is changing in this respect.

Sport is an ancient phenomenon which plays a very important role in modern life and in human development and education. Sport is considered by many as a way of promoting the development of young people. It is not usual to dwell on the negative side of it, because it is typically thought of as a social good (Vertommen et al., 2016). However, a straightforward relationship between sports practice and a positive effect on youth development cannot be accepted without qualification. Although sport practice may result in many positive outcomes for physical and psychological health, it can also have a negative effect on youth development depending on the quality of the involvement in the activities, and the quality of the relationships established with others. Bullying, overtraining, doping, sexual harassment or even sexual abuse are a few examples of what can contribute to make the sport experience negative. However, there has been little study about systematic peer abuse in sport settings.

In the school setting, bullying has been studied for some three decades and has been recognized as a problem internationally (Smith, 2014). It has been studied to some considerable extent in Portugal (Carvalhosa, Moleiro & Sales, 2009; Pereira et al., 2004), with many researchers describing it and developing intervention programmes. Some of these programmes have been tested and found to be effective (Carvalhosa, 2008). There are several Portuguese researchers who are integrated in important international networks and part of research projects involving different countries.

However, research on bullying in sport settings is lacking in Portugal, just as it is internationally. Bullying in sport has been a taboo. The sports setting differs considerably from school and other social settings studied, due to its unique features: the sports setting is characterized by a particular culture, based on a tough mentality, which contributes to the perception of some aggressive behaviours as being just normal sport aggression rather than bullying (Volk & Lagzdins, 2009). It also contributes to the silence of the athletes regarding bullying, because breaking silence is often considered a sign of weakness (Stirling et al., 2011). Bullying is a sensitive topic and the organizational structure of sport raises new challenges, which makes bullying more difficult to study.

Considering the importance of sport in child development, topics like peer aggression cannot be ignored, and understanding of bullying should be part of the training of sport specialists. The particular nature of sports settings may increase the risk of labelling and bullying behaviours. Bullying in sport is not a new phenomenon, but it has only started to be studied in recent years. The sports clubs and professionals who work with young athletes are beginning to be more focused on their emotional development instead of focusing only on sport performance.

Bullying is a public health subject and research is needed in order to design better and more effective intervention programmes. These have proven to be economically beneficial because taking preventative measures early on can spare many future interventions. The victims of bullying in sport suffer from many negative consequences. This includes abandoning sports practice prematurely; many children and adolescents may be deprived of access to a positive sport experience for many years.

Overview of the book

This book is divided into three parts and 12 chapters.

Part I concerns conceptual issues.

Chapter 1 is introductory and provides a theoretical overview of bullying, considering the conceptual and methodological changes which have taken place over the last four decades of research, as well as referencing some key authors in the development of bullying research. We discuss the general issues and theories about bullying, including translation issues, taxonomy of bullying behaviours, the roles of those involved in bullying episodes, and age and gender differences. Although much research has taken place on school bullying, social settings other than the school have also been studied. The main findings of bullying behaviours in these social settings are described and discussed. For bullying in sports, we present a multi-level understanding of bullying, which includes an analysis of the social environment of sports, an individual traits approach, and also the influence of group dynamics on bullying behaviours. We end by describing the coping strategies used by the victims, and the consequences of bullying.

In Chapter 2, we review a fairly limited literature on bullying in youth sports training. Starting with the history of sport and its importance in youth development, we consider the problem of violence in sport and the relative lack of research on bullying in sport. We consider aggressiveness, sexuality and sexual stereotypes for the understanding of violence in sports settings, and discuss the definition of bullying in this particular social setting, considering its special features. We describe the main studies and highlight their results. We also consider the research difficulties associated with the sport context, and the interplay between school and sports club settings. We suggest an application of Ecological Systems Theory to the youth sports setting. We refer to the major types of bullying, the location where episodes occur, who victims speak with about bullying (if they do), the influence of the coach on the prevalence of bullying behaviours, and the consequences of bullying for those involved in bullying episodes, with a special focus on victims. We finish with a brief reflection on the use of sports for youth development, but also its limitations.

Chapter 3 provides a framework of the Portuguese sport context. Our research was nationwide, exploratory and descriptive. We provide a brief description of the previous research on bullying conducted in Portugal, as well as some geographical and demographical information that is useful for readers. We also describe how sports are organized in Portugal, alluding to the major sport governmental entities, and how these interplay with each other, considering sport activity in both schools and sports clubs. The contents of the educational programme for coaches are described, and the different sports studied are also considered and described individually and by category.

Part II of the book focuses on the four studies made, with the methods and the results obtained.

Chapter 4 describes the methods used in the various studies, which together involved a combination of quantitative (Study 1) and qualitative (Studies 2, 3 and 4) approaches. A description of the participants is given. The variety of participants involved (athletes, coaches, ex-elite athletes), characterized by different experiences and perceptions about bullying in sport, provide complementary perspectives, resulting in deeper insights about bullying in youth sports training. We describe the different instruments employed, the validation processes which were used, and the data analysis procedures. We first consider the quantitative part of the project, Study 1, which was a nationwide survey of youth in sports training. We describe detailed processes related to instrument and methodological validation and data treatment. We then summarize the methods used in the qualitative parts of the project, composed of Studies 2, 3 and 4. We explore the validation procedures, the process of content analysis and the thematic organization of the final results. In Study 2, young athletes were interviewed regarding their perceptions about bullying in sport. In Study 3, the participants were coaches. Study 4 is a recall study, in which ex-elite athletes were interviewed about their involvement in bullying episodes when they were young athletes.

In Chapter 5, some of the main findings from the large quantitative survey in Study 1 are presented. We focus on general findings, in order to give the reader a global overview of bullying behaviours in youth sports training. We show results about the frequency of victims', bystanders' and bullies' involvement in bullying episodes, and consider some general variables such as the different types of sport, geographical area, and the number of good friends they have inside the peer group within the sports club. We consider the athletes' participation in bullying episodes as victim, bully and/or bystander in relation to the types of bullying and feelings towards bullying episodes, providing important information about the social dynamics of bullying incidents.

Chapter 6 continues the survey findings, describing the circumstances around bullying episodes. We start by analysing the relation between some variables of victimization: the age of the victims; the frequency and duration of bullying episodes; and the activities, location and number of athletes involved in bullying episodes. We also analyse who victims speak with (if they do) about bullying episodes, their support sources and the coping styles they use when targeted. The effectiveness of family, coach and peer support is considered within this framework. These results tell us about the way victims deal with bullying, and give some insight into how to intervene to help victims. The athletes' involvement in bullying episodes as bullies is also considered, by analysing the age of the perpetrators, the relation between the types of bullying, the frequency of behaviours and the number of athletes involved, and who spoke with the perpetrators (if someone did) about their bullying behaviours.

We also focus attention on the bystanders of bullying episodes. The variables considered for analysis are the reasons ascribed for bullying episodes, the reactions of the bystanders towards bullying episodes, and their feelings about these. We show the reciprocal influence of these variables, and provide some insights about the bystanders' participation in bullying episodes.

In Chapter 7 we start presenting the qualitative data. In Study 2, 127 athletes from 9 different sports were interviewed and asked about their participation in bullying episodes. We divide the narratives into three groups: (1) those athletes who did not think that bullying existed in sport at all; (2) those athletes who never got involved, but still thought that it can happen; and (3) those athletes who got involved in bullying episodes as victims, bystanders and/or perpetrators. For group 3, the results are organized into three major themes: bullying circumstances, roles and implications. A discourse analysis of athletes who got involved in bullying episodes as victims, bystanders and/or bullies is made, providing further understanding of bullying dynamics, and some suggestions about intervention strategies.

In Chapter 8, the findings of Study 3 are presented. This followed the same method as Study 2, but the participants were coaches instead of athletes. Altogether, 32 coaches from 9 different sports were interviewed about bullying in youth sports training. We divide the narratives into two groups: (1) those coaches who considered that bullying did not occur in sports settings, and (2) those coaches who acknowledged the existence of bullying among athletes. The results for group 2 are again organized into three major themes: bullying circumstances, roles and implications. The narratives are analysed and major findings are reported. These are explored and compared with the athletes' perceptions of bullying.

In Chapter 9 we present findings from Study 4. This was a retrospective study in which nine elite athletes (one for each sport studied) were interviewed about their participation in bullying episodes when they were young athletes. We divide the participants into two groups: (1) those ex-elite athletes who considered that bullying did not occur in sports settings, and (2) those ex-elite athletes who considered that bullying happened in sport and had been involved. The results for group 2 are also organized into the three major themes: bullying circumstances, roles and implications. The narratives are analysed and major findings are reported and explored.

Part III of the book discusses the findings and their practical implications, and provides guidelines for athletes, parents and sports coaches.
In Chapter 10 we provide an in-depth discussion of the results of all four studies. We start by focusing on the conceptual issues of bullying, and then analyse the prevalence of bullying behaviours, including the different types. The profiles of the victims and the perpetrators are described, as well as their age. We also analyse the bullying episodes, by considering their location, the number of athletes involved, the reasons for their occurrence, the transition to an older peer group, the prevalence of victimization and perpetration in different social settings, and the role of the coach in athlete-to-athlete bullying. We finally analyse who victims speak with, who approaches the bullies, and who bystanders speak to about what they have seen. The coping strategies used by victims and bystanders are described, and also the consequences of bullying. These studies provide different perspectives, and we compare their various findings. We

articulate the major theoretical contributions and their applicability to the findings presented. After this, the main conclusions are summarized.

In Chapter 11, we consider some forms of coach abuse which can be included in the definition of bullying. A conceptual discussion is provided, followed by the description of the nature of the behaviours. Here, we also consider sexual harassment and abuse in sports. The results presented in this chapter derive from previous studies conducted by other researchers.

In Chapter 12, we describe the practical implications for coaches and trainers, as well as for young athletes themselves and their parents. Initially, we use an ecological systems approach to address bullying in sport, in which we describe the aims and targets of several levels of intervention, and provide some possible interventions. We end with guidelines for athletes, parents and coaches; these are relevant for both general and specific contexts, as well as for those who may be directly involved in bullying episodes (athletes and coaches) and those who may have a more indirect but still strong influence over the expression of bullying behaviours among young athletes (parents, other sports professionals). These guidelines should be helpful to coaches, parents and young athletes, and may assist the reader to act on the problem.

Part I

Conceptual issues

Chapter 1

Research on bullying

We start by reviewing some of the major topics in bullying research, to provide the reader with an historical and theoretical framework. We describe some methodological advances and major contributions made over several decades of research and intervention. Much, but not all, of this research has been on school bullying. In the final part of this chapter, we give a general description of bullying and the characteristics of those involved as bullies or victims.

There is a definition of bullying that is largely accepted by researchers. This describes bullying as *an intentionally aggressive behaviour among peers, with repetition, and a power imbalance between victims and aggressor such that it is difficult for victims to defend themselves* (Olweus, 1999). Another possible definition provided by Smith and Sharp (1994, p. 2) is that bullying is "the systematic abuse of power". This is succinct and potentially more comprehensive.

However, what may seem quite a clear concept, commonly accepted, is still a topic for theoretical disagreements. Some researchers raise questions about the criteria in the standard definition by Olweus given above. For example, taking the repetition criterion, is it really necessary for bullying to be repeated over time (more than once)? Some research has shown that individuals victimized once or repeatedly may suffer the same consequences (Escury & Dudink, 2010; Evans, Adler, MacDonald & Cote, 2016). When can the abusive relation be considered a repeated pattern?

Intentionality of the bullying can also be considered a questionable criterion. There are many factors which contribute to bullying others. Peer pressure is one strong influence; individuals behave according to some social norms and standardized behaviours accepted in a specific social setting. This may lead individuals to act based on the need for acceptance (among others), sometimes without reflecting on the consequences of their behaviours. It does not mean that the individual cannot be considered responsible for their behaviours, but only that their intention may be to safeguard their own social standing rather than specifically to harm the victim. These arguments, among others, may raise some questions about whether bullying behaviours are always intended to cause hurt.

Bullying face-to-face or offline is now often referred to as "traditional" bullying, while online – using mobile phones and the internet – is often referred to as cyberbullying. The standard definition has had critics particularly with regard to cyberbullying. Here, the criteria of repetition and imbalance of power are more complex and debatable (Smith, 2014). As a result, some researchers prefer terms such as "cyber aggression", or "digital victimization" (for example, Hamby et al., 2018).

Despite these reservations, the standard definition of bullying is still quite widely accepted and used (Olweus & Limber, 2019).

Historical framework

Some level of aggressive behaviour can be perceived as normative throughout life, and something to be coped with. But bullying differs from this normative aggressive behaviour and raises special concerns, being a systematic abusive relationship (Smith, 2014). Nevertheless, for many years bullying was considered a normal part of human relationships (Trautmann, 2008), based on the argument that power imbalance in human relations has always existed, and people will be tempted to take advantage of this. Although this is true, and abusive behaviours have always been a part of human relationships, it does not justify bullying or make such behaviours acceptable.

Systematic research on school bullying started in Scandinavia, during the 1970s. The psychologist Dan Olweus worked on this, first in Sweden and then in Norway. Widespread concern and action was sparked when three 14-year-old youngsters in Norway committed suicide due to systematic peer abuse in school (Olweus & Limber, 2010). This sad incident drew attention to the consequences of school bullying and the need to develop research and intervention programmes, resulting in the first nationwide campaign against bullying in Norway.

Among Eastern countries, there is also a long tradition of research, notably on *ijime* in Japan (Morita, Soeda, Soeda & Taki, 1999) – *ijime* being the corresponding Japanese word to *bullying*. Over the last 40 years bullying research has expanded greatly, in terms of the number of publications, contexts and international coverage. Smith (2014) argued that the historical development of this research programme can be divided into four major periods, which correspond to major theoretical and practical developments, as well as to the conceptual changes.

First wave: origins

The first wave, from the 1970s until around 1988, covered the origins of the research programme. One of the major events in the history of bullying research occurred in this period: the publishing of Olweus's (1973/1978) book *Hackkycklingar och översittare. Forskning om skolmobbning/Aggression in Schools: Bullies and Whipping Boys*. This book was a landmark work on bullying, and it can be considered the first brick of a future major construction. It was the product of the first large-scale research undertaken by Olweus. Besides giving a definition of bullying (Olweus, 1986, 1993), Olweus developed a self-report questionnaire, and later worked on the first nationwide campaign in Norway to produce a whole-school anti-bullying programme.

First bullying definition

Mobbning (Swedish; mobbing in Norwegian) was the concept originally used in Scandinavian languages and referred to a group of children who attacked the same single victim by repeatedly harassing that person. Heinemann (1972) described mobbing as a situation in which an entire (or at least a majority) group of peers attacked a deviant individual. However, Olweus rejected using the term "mobbing" because he considered bullying episodes to often also occur in one-to-one or small-group situations. He defined bullying as "A student is being bullied or victimized when he or she is exposed, repeatedly and over time, to negative actions on the part of one or more other students" (Olweus, 1993, p. 9). It was also made clear that it was difficult for the victim to defend him/herself.

Although at that time the emphasis was on physical and verbal forms of bullying, Olweus did mention indirect forms of bullying in the 1980s (Olweus, 1986). However, this received more attention in the 1990s and early 2000s, in particular from a gender perspective (see below in "Reformulation of the bullying definition"). Although some scholars have emphasized other aspects of bullying, Olweus's definition has by and large been widely accepted. There is a considerable level of consensus about bullying being characterised by repeated and intentional aggressive behaviours, based on power imbalances between perpetrators and victims; these can be physical, verbal, relational or (more recently) cyber.

Olweus's questionnaire and anti-bullying programme

Olweus developed the first self-report questionnaire, which is still widely accepted and used. This instrument was designed to collect data from large samples, allowing for the establishment of general descriptions about bullying and baselines of bullying prevalence.

Olweus's perspective was mostly based on quantitative data, and he was seeking to identify causes, predict occurrences and develop an evidence-based programme. Many other measurement instruments were developed in the following years in order to fit new research needs.

Early surveys showed that many children suffered from bullying, social exclusion, peer rejection and neglect in school (Whitney & Smith, 1993). Ten years after publishing the first book about bullying in 1973, the first national anti-bullying campaign occurred in Norway, in 1983. The period 1983–1985 saw the development of this school-based intervention into the Olweus Bullying Prevention Program (Olweus, 1999, 2013), and the success of this in Norway inspired the next phase of research. The model of school bullying developed by Olweus emphasizes the profiles of the perpetrator and the victim. However, besides this micro-analysis, it also includes other important factors in the understanding of bullying such as the group climate, home conditions or background factors. As a result, the Olweus Bullying Prevention Program comprises interventions at the school, classroom and individual levels.

Second wave: establishing a research programme

The second wave corresponded to the period between 1989 and the mid-1990s. The Norwegian national campaign, and the good results achieved through the use of Olweus's school-based programme, resulted in other researchers becoming interested in the topic. Another reason for the growth in interest was the advent of international networks on bullying and increasing cooperation between different countries. Although research on school bullying started in Scandinavia, it soon spread to many countries in Europe, and to Australia, New Zealand and Canada. The USA engaged in these international networks some years later. Large surveys and campaigns were carried out in many other countries, beyond Norway. There was also a long tradition of work in Eastern countries such as Japan and South Korea. The international partnerships allowed the comparison of data collected in different parts of the world. During this period, some methodological and conceptual shifts occurred. Peer nomination methodology was developed and started being used in some studies. In addition, the definition of bullying (as with aggression generally) expanded to include relational and indirect forms, notably social exclusion and rumour spreading.

Peer nomination methodology

The most used instruments to measure bullying prevalence are self-report questionnaires and peer nomination techniques (Smith, 2014). Peer nomination is a sociometric method, in which peers nominate who among their colleagues or classmates shows specific behaviours. By using it, the researcher is able to identify perpetrators (bullies), victims and bystanders. The peer nomination technique brought an important new contribution for research on bullying, and started being used by many researchers (Björkqvist & Österman, 2000). As it relies on multiple informants, it can be argued to be more valid than self-report data from questionnaires (Pellegrini, 1998a). It can also identify perpetrator-victim dyads or perpetrator-victim-bystander triads, and has more recently been extended for social network analysis (Huitsing & Veenstra, 2012).

Reformulation of the bullying definition

The early definition of bullying needed some revision, which occurred mostly during this period. A major contribution came from Kaj Björkqvist in Finland, who broadened the definition of bullying to emphasize indirect types of bullying. This resulted from research conducted on gender differences in bullying, which highlighted less approached types of aggression (indirect aggression). These strategies were more often used by girls than boys. Indirect bullying is characterized by no direct confrontation between perpetrator and victim. It is linked to the idea of a person being made uncomfortable in his or her social networks. A similar concept is relational bullying, where the main objective of a bully is to damage another's social standing or reputation, or to exclude them from a social group (Crick & Grotpeter, 1995). Primary examples of these kinds of behaviour are rumour spreading and social exclusion.

Third wave: an established international research programme

The third wave, from the mid-1990s to around 2004, is marked by the creation of an international research programme. Cooperation among different countries increased greatly, and researchers in the USA became highly involved (e.g. Espelage & Swearer, 2004). Surveys and intervention work were reported from many countries around the world. Bullying behaviours may be observed in different cultures, races, ethnic groups and socioeconomic statuses, from which one may infer its universal character. Nowadays, research on bullying is spread all over the world (Campbell & Bauman, 2018; Jimerson, Swearer & Espelage, 2010; Smith, Kwak & Toda, 2016; Smith et al., 2018).

This period also saw the development of participant role scales by Christina Salmivalli and colleagues, including the defender role (someone who helps the victim). These roles are described in detail shortly. The sociometric status of the children was found to be connected to their participant roles. Also, whereas boys have a higher tendency to be in the bullying roles, girls tend to more often take the role of defender (Salmivalli et al., 1998).

This early research was mainly focused on children in school settings. Although many other settings and populations have been studied since then, the school is still the social setting in which most research has been done. The characteristics of those involved and of situational factors have been examined using a variety of methodological approaches and theoretical frameworks

(Scott, 2018; Smith, 2014). There is a considerable tradition of research on workplace bullying (Einarsen et al., 2003), and some research in other contexts such as residential homes, pre-school (Alsaker & Nägele, 2008), army settings (Ostvik & Rudmin, 2001), prisons (Ireland, Archer & Power, 2007), and the related phenomena of abuse in the family. Another related topic is elder abuse. The edited volume by Monks and Coyne (2011), *Bullying in Different Contexts*, brought together reviews of such studies. Interestingly, however, there was no contribution on bullying in sport, and "sport" does not appear in the book's index.

The increasing volume of research on bullying led to more knowledge and the possibility of designing more effective anti-bullying programmes. These have become increasingly evidence based and adapted to different countries and settings, according to their targeted population (Campbell & Bauman, 2018; Smith, 2019a, 2019b). Nowadays, bullying is being studied all over the world, by specialists from different scientific areas, who share their knowledge and theoretical contribution when gathered together in national and international congresses.

Although bullying is now understood and discussed worldwide, discussion and reformulation of its theoretical concept is ongoing. Different authors consider and emphasize different aspects of bullying, which is reflected in their diverse approaches. For example, some authors focus more attention on indirect types of bullying, the role played by the bystanders and their contribution to bullying maintenance, as well as the influence of peer pressure and group dynamics to explain bullying behaviours. Other authors include teacher-to-pupil relationships of systematic abuse as bullying; although the peer-to-peer criterion is not fulfilled, the power imbalance, the abusive nature and repetition of the behaviours are present. However, in this book the concepts adopted regarding peer-to-peer and coach-to-peer systematic abuse have different labels and are considered in more detail in Chapter 10.

Fourth wave: cyberbullying

The last of the four periods described started in around 2004 up until the present time of writing. The main topic which characterizes it is research on cyberbullying, resulting from the development of technology and new forms of communication, especially the generalized access to and use of the internet, and the spread of smartphones, in the last decade or so. Although cyberbullying has origins prior to 2000, awareness of the issue and most press reports and academic study date from around 2004, initially with text message and then email bullying, but now taking many forms.

The traditional forms of bullying kept being studied; however, cyberbullying brought many new challenges to bullying research. For example, it is still being debated whether cyberbullying should be considered a new and very different type of bullying, or whether it is simply just another way to bully others, not so different from traditional forms (Wolke, Lee & Guy, 2017). The difficulty in identifying the bullies in these cases, and the fast and generalized spread of abusive videos, messages and/or photos on the internet, can have very severe consequences for the victims and raises new challenges concerning intervention.

This historical framework helps us to understand the evolution of bullying research and the consequent theoretical and practical developments which have taken place in recent decades. Next we describe some general topics of bullying.

Final notes

The waves scheme described here aims to help readers to understand the evolution of bullying research. However, it doesn't mean that each wave gives new understanding which makes findings from an earlier wave outdated in some way. In some cases, the results from older waves are still relevant and useful.

General issues and theories about bullying

Translation issues

There are some difficulties regarding the translation of the concept of *bullying* due to cultural and linguistic differences among countries. This makes it difficult to find a common term across languages. Considerable effort has been made by many scholars to adopt a label comparable to *bullying*, based on their own idiom. This endeavour resulted in the identification of several labels, used in a variety of countries (Smith et al., 2002, 2018), for example:

- UK: bullying, harassment, teasing, intimidation, tormenting, picking on;
- Italy: *violenza, prepotenza, aggressività, cattiveria, scorretto, approfittarsi, fare il duro*;
- Spain: *maltrato, egoismo, abuso, rechazo, meterse con*;
- Portugal: *provocação, violência, abuso, rejeição, insulto*;
- Japan: *ijiwaru, iyagarase, ijime*.

However, any translation of the word *"bullying"* may lead to a conceptual bias, or slight change of meaning, such that it may be easier to adopt the original term. In Spain the term *"bullying"* is commonly used, and in Italy *il bullismo*. In Portugal, although some of the terms above may be used, when referring to systematic peer abuse, we usually now call it *bullying*.

Taxonomy of bullying behaviours

Bullying behaviours are often put into different categories (Smith, 2014). Here we present some possible labels, and examples of the behaviours associated with each.

TRADITIONAL BULLYING

- Physical (physical abuse, hitting, intimidating, being taunted, tortured, beaten up);
- Verbal (mocking, insulting, teasing, putdowns, cruel criticism, calling names, using sarcasm to be mean);
- Social/relational (spreading nasty rumours, encouraging others to avoid a certain person).

Some researchers also separate out categories of damaging belongings; and extortion.

CYBERBULLYING

- Cyberbullying: (obsessively sending messages to a person or cyber stalking; sending mean emails, texts or messages; posting hurtful things about someone on social media; spreading rumours or gossip about someone online; password theft; making fun of someone in an online chat; attacking or killing a character in an online game constantly and on purpose; pretending to be another person by creating a fake online profile; threatening or intimidating someone online or in a text message; using vulgar and abusive language with the intention of starting a fight with the victim; taking an embarrassing photo or video and sharing it without permission; and proxy attacks).

All of these types above may be involved in what is often called bias bullying or prejudice-based bullying.

BIAS BULLYING OR PREJUDICE-BASED BULLYING

This is bullying against groups defined by some particular aspect of identity.

- Race – victims are targeted because of the colour of their skin, the way they talk or their ethnic grouping;

- Gender – the use of sexual language, gestures or violence aimed to degrade and/or single someone out; sexual harassment refers to unwelcome sexual advances, requests for sexual favours, and other verbal or physical harassment of a sexual nature. Girls are more prone to becoming victims of this, often involving appearance or reputation. Perpetrators can be other girls or boys;
- Sexual orientation – behaving or speaking in a way which makes another feel bullied because of their actual or perceived sexual orientation. Examples of homophobic bullying are derogatory comments about actual or inferred sexual orientation. People may be targeted due to their appearance, behaviour or because they have friends or family who are lesbian, gay, or bisexual. Homophobic bullying usually appears more prevalent and severe for boys;
- Sexual identity – affecting people who are trans, but also those questioning their gender identity or those who, despite not being trans, do not conform to conventional gender stereotypes;
- Disability – being bullied because of mental or physical disability or special needs;
- Faith/religion – being targeted due to religious belief, or being in a particular religious or faith group.

Some authors also consider other types of bullying not mentioned here; in the scientific literature, the reader may find further taxonomy of bullying behaviours. We focused our attention on the types of bullying most cited and considered important. However, besides the types of bullying described above, other more general taxonomy, which divides bullying into two main categories, should also be mentioned.

One contrast is between direct vs. indirect bullying:

- Direct: bullies and victims are directly involved with each other (share the same space and can identify each other);
- Indirect: there is no direct confrontation between perpetrator and victim. In these cases, the victims may find difficult to identify the perpetrators.

Another contrast is hostile vs. instrumental bullying:

- Hostile: bullying is used to attack another without a specific purpose beyond hurting them;
- Instrumental: bullying has other specific purposes and is a means of reaching them (e.g. bullying as a way for bullies to achieve social status in a peer group).

A further contrast is pro-active vs. reactive bullying:

- Pro-active: the bully initiates bullying by him/herself spontaneously;
- Reactive: bullying results from a previous attack suffered by an individual.

A final contrast is individual vs. group bullying:

- Individual: one-to-one situation, between a bully and a victim. Bystanders may be involved, and observe, but do not act directly;
- Group: bullying episodes are performed by a group of bullies, against a single victim. In these cases, bystanders may be involved and become assistants or reinforcers (see "Roles", below).

Despite these various contrasts, when bullying episodes occur, they often include multiple and combined types, rather than just one type of bullying (Gutiérrez et al., 2008).

Roles

There are different roles in bullying episodes (Salmivalli et al., 1998). Besides bullies and victims, bystanders play a major role in bullying episodes, and can be divided into several sub-types. There is also a category of bully-victims. Here we present one possible categorization and description of the types and sub-types of participants in bullying episodes.

- Bullies: those who attack others. These can be subdivided into:
  - Ringleader bullies: who instigate the bullying;
  - Assistants or reinforcers: who passively accept, instigate, encourage and/or join in the bullying.
- Victims: those who are attacked by the bullies. Victims can be divided into two types, depending on the frequency of involvement:
  - Victims: those who are targeted by the bullies;
  - Provocative victims (or bully-victims): those with features of both victims and bullies. These individuals may be in both roles at different times. Some bully-victims bully other more vulnerable peers, as an attempt to escape from victimization themselves.
- Bystanders: those who watch bullying episodes. Bystanders can either contribute to the problem or to the solution, depending how they act when involved in bullying episodes. These findings lead to the categorization of bystanders according to some sub-types:

- Defenders: directly intervene and/or get help for the victim;
- Outsiders: merely observe without taking any action. (Some researchers distinguish between bystanders, who witness the bullying but do nothing, and outsiders, who do not witness the bullying).

The profiles of bullies, victims and bully-victims, as well as the description of their families' relational dynamics, are provided in detail later in this chapter, when describing the Individual Traits Approach to the understanding of bullying behaviours in sport.

Age differences

The prevalence of bullying behaviours tends to vary with age. Younger children are more prone to be victimized and, as youngsters get older, the prevalence of being bullied tends to decrease (Barrio et al., 2008), due in part to the development of social and coping skills. However, at these later ages, those bullying episodes that do occur tend to be more severe and result in more serious consequences (Gonzalez, 2008).

The types of bullying and patterns of aggressive behaviour change over time: in young children, aggressive behaviours are mostly physical, becoming more verbal and relational with the acquisition and development of verbal skills (Björkqvist, Lagerspetz & Kaukiainen, 1992).

Physical bullying is quite prevalent among children from 7 to 12 years old. Up to the age of 8, the capacity to perform indirect bullying is not completely developed (Björkqvist, Österman & Kaukiainen, 1992) and both victim and bully roles are not yet clearly defined and stabilized. Bullying behaviours tend to peak around the age of 13, and then gradually decrease during later adolescence (Björkqvist, 1994). Österman et al. (1998) argue that until the age of 13, the prevalence of verbal and physical bullying are very similar. Physical bullying, which is easily spotted and sanctioned, then decreases and, by the age of 15, verbal bullying is more prevalent than physical bullying. Physically aggressive behaviour is usually socially rejected, leading to the development of less overtly obvious strategies to perform aggression by the perpetrators. Indirect aggression enables the perpetrator to attack the other person without being identified, avoiding a possible counter-attack. Children who continue to use more physical aggression are relatively lacking in social and verbal skills (Björkqvist & Österman, 2000; Björkqvist, Österman & Kaukiainen, 1992).

Nevertheless, the most severe acts of physical violence are often committed by adolescents. Anti-social teenagers are not isolated; they are part of a social network of similar peers. According to Pepler, Craig and Roberts (1998), these teenagers may be at risk not due to the lack of social skills, but mostly due to the influence of peer pressure on their behaviour.

Adolescence is considered by many researchers as being from around 10–18 years, and socially can be marked by increasing independence from parents, and increasing importance of the peer group. As adolescents become more independent from their parents, they spend more time with same-sex and later opposite-sex peers, from whom they seek social support and identity. Peer friendships differ widely from relationships with parents, as they are more mutual and reciprocal, more easily allowing the expression of divergent opinions and the discussion of new ideas (Smith, 2016). Although adolescents eventually become more resistant to peer influence, the influence of the peer group at this stage of life is considerable, and many adolescents fear peer group rejection (Blakemore & Mills, 2014).

Gender differences

There has been considerable focus on gender differences regarding bullying behaviours. There are gender differences concerning the types of bullying mostly used by perpetrators. Boys usually resort to direct physical and verbal bullying, which is more effective in establishing physical dominance, while girls tend to engage more in indirect or relational bullying (Björkqvist & Österman, 2000; Björkqvist, Österman & Kaukiainen, 1992).

Boys tend to be involved in bullying episodes more often (Pereira et al., 2004), and to victimize other boys, although girls may also be targeted; while girls usually restrict bullying to other girls (Björkqvist, 1994; Pellegrini & Long, 2002). The reason for bullying occurring more often among same-gender individuals may be that it is based on competition between them, with individuals seeking to achieve a high status inside same-gender peer groups. However, bullying among individuals from the opposite gender also occurs quite frequently (Pellegrini, 2003). Girls usually value being the centre of interpersonal networks, while boys seek more to achieve dominance and popularity among peers (Pellegrini & Long, 2003). This may partly explain why bullying episodes tend to occur in the presence of bystanders. Although bullying can occur in a one-to-one situation, usually bullies want or need an audience when bullying someone.

Victim rates tend to be rather equal between boys and girls. Although boys more often tend to be victims of traditional bullying, some studies, especially in recent years, find more girls to be victims of cyberbullying (Smith, López-Castro, Robinson & Görzig, 2019).

Males and females generally differ in their aggressive patterns (Fry, 1993, 1998). Besides physical characteristics, other aspects related to culture strongly influence the type of aggressive behaviours adopted by each gender. According to Seixas (2009), when analysing gender differences in bullying behaviours, one should consider the gender development differences according to three axes: biological (physical characteristics), psychological (gender identification) and cultural (sexual stereotypes), and also consider the interplay between them. Each of these axes exerts an influence on bullying behaviours.

Multi-level approach for the understanding of bullying

Here we focus on reviewing the literature concerning the understanding of the underlying reasons for bullying occurrence. We divide the theoretical contributions into three complementary approaches: social environment, individual traits and group dynamics. These different approaches have a direct influence on the research methods chosen (see Chapter 4).

Social environment approach: school ethos

There are several important school-related factors that influence peer group relationships and bullying. Here we briefly explore the influence of the norms and values, school climate, peer influences, academic pressure, the teacher–student relationship and risk factors for victimization.

NORMS AND VALUES

The norms and values on which a school is based exert an influence on bullying (Giroux, 2001). To prevent bullying, it's important to address the culture of bullying (Rigby, 2005), which allows and normalizes these behaviours.

SCHOOL CLIMATE

The school ethos influences the prevalence of bullying among students (Wang, Berry & Swearer, 2013). A positive environment facilitates positive peer relations and reduces bullying (Allodi, 2010; Smith, 2003). Espelage and Swearer (2003) highlight school factors for the understanding of bullying, such as social climate and classroom management and discipline. The former was also described by the students who participated in the study of Bibou-Nakou et al. (2012), in which 90 secondary school students, divided into 14 focus groups, discussed the nature of bullying behaviours at school.

Developing strong bonds with school that foster prosocial behaviours among peers is a protective factor against bullying. These students are less likely to get involved in bullying episodes (Catalano et al., 2004; Cunningham, 2007). Students are more likely to report bullying if the school climate is perceived as positive (Unnever & Cornell, 2004).

PEER INFLUENCES

In classrooms in which peer norms support bullying, these behaviours are more likely to happen (Salmivalli & Voeten, 2004). The influence of peers has received much attention in recent years, and peer support has become an important component to consider in preventing bullying (Salmivalli, Kärnä & Poskiparta, 2010).

ACADEMIC PRESSURE

The pressure of academic achievement is also a factor that may contribute to bullying among school students (Sullivan, Cleary & Sullivan, 2003). Some studies find that academic competition may increase bullying among students (Rigby, 1996; Yoneyama & Naito, 2003).

TEACHER–STUDENT RELATIONSHIP

The teacher–student relationship has also been referred to as a school-related factor that influences bullying (Olweus, 1993). Teachers have a key role in prevention; they need to be role models, and contribute to creating a social environment of respect in school. Poor teacher–student relationships are linked with more bullying (Bacchini, Esposito & Affuso, 2009; Richard, Schneider & Mallet, 2011), as is a lack of teacher support (Barboza et al., 2009), or inappropriate responses from teachers to students. Besides peers, teachers are a key factor in preventing and tackling bullying. This should therefore be considered in anti-bullying programmes.

RISK FACTORS

There are some risk factors concerning victimization, mainly derived from studies in school settings. Although these risk factors are related to characteristics of the victims, here we have included them under the social environment approach, because the individual traits approach has to do specifically with the personality traits of bullies and victims. The risk factors described here regard other characteristics of the individuals which make them more prone to becoming victims in a specific social setting.

Besides personality, there are other characteristics of young people which can potentiate victimization: having a disability (Mishna, 2003) or any other physical difference, can lead to rejection by peers; however, compensatory and adaptive defence mechanisms may develop in order to cope with it. Other groups who are identified as being at higher risk of suffering bullying are immigrants (Anabel & Anna, 2009), people who change their usual social environment and haven't yet learned the rules and codes of conduct of the new context (Gonzalez, 2008), people with autism spectrum disorders, due to their difficulties in understanding the social norms (Van Roekel, Scholte & Didden, 2009), and boys with a feminine appearance, and those of different sexual orientation, who are often rejected and attacked in adolescence and adulthood (Mora-Merchán, 2006). However, individual risk factors don't necessarily mean victimization. More important than the individual's appearance is the way a child relates with peers, in order to be accepted and cope with difficulties. Some of the risk factors described here overlap with the ones previously mentioned for sport, linked mainly to the idea of being perceived somehow as different.

Individual traits approach: profile of the victims, bullies and bully-victims

Although bullying behaviour can partly be explained by environmental factors, individual personality traits should also be considered and this is still a very insightful approach. Early explanations of the aggressive behaviours of children who have bullied others, tended to emphasize their aggressive personality patterns (Olweus, 1978). This perspective considered behaviours to be independent from the social setting, and emphasized the influence of personality traits on bullies' and victims' behaviours. The individual traits approach helps to explain some important topics, like the tendency of victims and perpetrators to behave in that way in different social settings. Since the family is the primary origin of social development, and family interactions strongly influence the development of the personality of individuals, we also describe here the type of families associated with bullies, victims and bully-victims.

The victims and the bullies differ in several domains, namely in self-concept, sportive behaviours, romantic behaviours, and global self-esteem and self-confidence. Despite this apparently clear division between different roles, in reality these differences tend to diminish, because a number of children are both bullies and victims (the bully-victims). Considering the lack of information about the profiles and families of victims and bullies in sports settings, the descriptions provided are mostly derived from research on school bullying. The considerable overlap between the sports and school settings reported by Escury and Dudink (2010) suggests that victims, and bullies, have similar profiles in school and in youth sport. This topic will be explored more in the final discussion (Chapter 10).

Below we provide profiles of the characteristics of victims, bullies and bully-victims. These are of course generalizations; not everyone conforms to the same role profile. However, they are commonly found characteristics that have been confirmed in a number of research studies.

Profiles of the victims

In childhood, the roles played in bullying episodes tend to extend beyond the school setting. Individuals who were bullying victims during childhood are more prone to also becoming victims in adulthood, which suggests a stabilization of the roles defined during childhood, in school (Tilindiene, Rastauskiné, Zalys & Valantiniené, 2008). Children also tend to adopt the same role as their parents (Mora-Merchán, 2006), suggesting some degree of transgenerational transmission.

Victims tend to avoid risky behaviours, are characterized by low aggressiveness and assertiveness (Olweus, 2010), and by having a positive attitude towards work and study. This is often reflected in good academic performance; however, victims tend to perceive themselves as not good enough, even at an academic level (Mora-Merchán, 2006).

Victims of bullying tend to be socially inept, more physically fragile than peers, with low stature and lower ability for sports activities. They are often described as being sensitive, shy, inhibited, submissive, insecure, introvert and characterized by an attitude of conflict avoidance (Olweus, 1995; Salmivalli & Isaacs, 2005; Schwartz et al., 1998). They also tend to lack friends or at least popular friends. Besides this, victims suffer more often from social rejection and exclusion (Bond et al., 2001), resulting in being frequently isolated from peers (Olweus, 2010). These characteristics reflect their difficulties in developing social protection skills, such that they are easy targets for bullies (Anabel & Anna, 2009). Victims tend to blame themselves for bullying, and often cry when attacked by the bullies, starting a cycle of aggression which is hard to break (Trautmann, 2008). They often present internalization behaviours and physical symptoms, being anxious, having low self-esteem, poor self-concept and a negative perception of their physical appearance (Debarbieux, 2004; Olweus, 1995, 2010). Poor social skills when dealing with peers, and low self-esteem, may be both a cause and a product of the involvement in bullying episodes. According to Due et al. (2005), the experience of being bullied is responsible for a lack of engagement and attachment, and limited development of victims' social skills.

Profiles of the bullies

Bullies tend to be extrovert and confrontational. They are also described as having good communication skills, being exhibitionist and highly self-confident (Olweus, 1995). However, concerning self-esteem, there is no general consensus among researchers; some consider bullies to have high self-esteem, while others consider their behaviours cover a defensive structure, and that perpetrators are characterized by having low self-esteem (Gonçalves & Matos, 2007). Boys who are perpetrators tend to exhibit behaviours based on the underlying stereotype of masculinity. They are usually more physically active (Roberts, 2008), more powerful (Olweus, 1995) and have a higher athletic status among peers.

Bullies often show a lack of guilt concerning their aggressive behaviours and empathy or concern for the victims (Jolliffe & Farrington, 2011). However, lack of affective empathy does not necessarily mean a lack of social skills. Despite often being described as controversial and socially rejected, bullies can be perceived as very popular among peers (Pellegrini, 1998b), especially in social environments in which aggressive behaviours are valued (Martins, 2005). Perceived popularity should not be confused with sociometric popularity or peer approval: bullies can be perceived by their peers as popular and as having high status, but this is not the same as actually being liked or chosen by others as a friend (Juvonen, Graham & Schuster, 2003; Olthof & Goossens, 2008).

In their relationships with others, bullies need to feel control and dominance (Anabel & Anna, 2009). They manipulate their victims and use their skills for their own benefit and anti-social purposes. They may have difficulties in making and developing friendships, which results in superficial relationships. They may blame others for their personal failures, and are often characterized by a lack of capacity to take responsibility for their actions, and low tolerance to frustration (Olweus, 1995; Trautmann, 2008). They may show defensive egotism – reacting angrily to minor threats to self-esteem (Salmivalli, Kaukiainen, Kaistaniemi & Lagerspetz, 1999). In sports settings, whereas victims usually present difficulties in their relations with peers, bullies report conflicts in their relations with coaches (Evans, Adler, MacDonald & Cote, 2016).

Bullies show more externalization behaviours, and risky behaviours, such as a higher tendency for drug consumption or weapon carrying (Seixas, Coelho & Nicolas-Fischer, 2013). They tend to have a more positive attitude towards violence and delinquency (Moral, 2005), which may start to express itself in adolescence, and extend into adulthood (Losel & Bender, 2011). They tend to behave aggressively within their family context, as well as other social settings in life such as school or later at work (Pellegrini, 1998a). Persistent perpetrators have a higher tendency to commit crimes and become offenders, which means they are more prone to becoming problematic adults who keep bullying their peers and subordinates in work settings. Persistent bullies more often become bad workers/employers, who have difficulties in maintaining a stable job and contributing positively to society (Ttofi, Farrington & Losel, 2011).

Although these findings are well documented by researchers, the personality features of bullies may be quite adaptive in some social settings. Examples are business or politics settings, which often strongly value those who are confrontational, who have the capacity to be manipulative/seductive and to do whatever it takes to achieve their personal goals. In these types of social settings, strongly ruled by power dynamics, having these characteristics of bullies may result in positive outcomes for the individual (despite often negative outcomes for those around them and for the organizations they work in). These individuals are often perceived by many as more intelligent, powerful, courageous and unbeatable opponents. This perceived image and their usually coercive styles of leadership may be promoted and considered a role model for functioning in such settings.

Profiles of the bully-victims

There is less documented information about bully-victims, but generally they present characteristics of both victims and bullies, namely excessive internalizing and externalizing behaviours (Olweus, 2010). They tend to be characterized by psychological and physical discomfort, and high levels of depression and loneliness. Bully-victims tend to be anxious, impulsive, aggressive, and to suffer from hyperactivity and lack of attention. They are often described by peers as being annoying, suffer from social rejection and have a high risk of psychosocial maladjustment (Juvonen, Graham & Schuster, 2003). This happens because bully-victims often provoke and insult their peers, leading to conflicts which they cannot resolve or defend themselves from adequately, due to their lack of social skills. They may adopt bullying behaviours and attack more vulnerable colleagues as an attempt to escape from being a victim but, at the same time, are victimized by powerful perpetrators (Olweus, 2010), which results in a strong and generalized rejection from peers (Fontaine, 2003). Bully-victims consider that the best way to defend themselves is by attacking others first (Pellegrini, 1998a). This combination of a lack of social competence, their aggressive behaviour towards victims, and being victimized by other bullies, contributes to them being especially rejected and isolated.

Families

Children are usually raised within a family, and are dependent on their parents for care and emotional support. The relationships established with parents, siblings and other relatives, as well as the dynamics within the family, have a strong impact on the construction of the individual personality. Healthier relations within the family promote children's capacity to establish relationships with others (including peers) based on trust and cooperation, and to cope with frustrating situations more easily. On the other hand, more pathological relationships result in less healthy and adaptive styles of interaction.

The development of aggressive patterns of social interaction with others is one of many possible outcomes. When parent–child interactions are based on the prevalence of punishment over play/praise, and the punishments are arbitrary, based on the unpredictable state of humour of the adult rather than on clear rules and boundaries, they often result in, among other things, the development of aggressive behaviours. Inconsistent discipline combined with a lack of positive affect interferes with the development of the capacity to solve conflict through dialogue.

FAMILIES OF THE BULLIES

The families of children who bully others are often characterized as problematic, closed, cold and with dysfunctional parents who fail in monitoring their children and frequently punish them, oscillating from overprotection to neglect and hostility. The relationship of bullies with their mothers is often too permissive, lacking clear rules and boundaries between them, and at the same time with low emotional involvement from the mother. The mother–child relational pattern is also characterized by frequent criticism, rather than positive reinforcement and encouragement.

In these families, violent relational patterns are often accepted without constraints due to the lack of discipline, and physical punishment is frequent, resulting from the parental incapacity to cope with conflicts in a healthy way and to discuss them. The maternal hostility leads to child aggressiveness. These relationship patterns are learned, and tend to be enacted in other social settings besides the family. The aggressive environment which often characterizes the families of bullies contributes to serious impairments in their social development, and is directly connected with some of the personality features described earlier.

Altogether, the parental lack of monitoring, excessive permissiveness, lack of limits on aggressive behaviours, abusive and inconsistent discipline, and rejection lead to a lack of social and emotional competence and a high level of aggressive behaviours in these children (Gonzalez, 2008).

FAMILIES OF THE VICTIMS

The analysis of the family network of the victims described these as usually being strict regarding the norms. The parents' educational style is based on restriction and overprotection (Lereya, Samara & Wolke, 2013), resulting in the promotion of dependency and inhibition of children. Overprotection and lack of monitoring can both result in equally negative outcomes for child development.

Overprotected children are less confident in exploring their social environment. Being autonomous is felt by victims as bad behaviour, and being disappointing to their parents, especially their mother.

The parents of the victims are often intrusive and demanding. Intrusiveness is frequently observed as excessive control of the youngster's behaviour, which promotes a childish and dependent functioning. A circle of overprotection establishes, leading to children not learning how to behave like an autonomous adult in the future. This frequently results in the child of a grown-up victim becoming a new victim (Mora-Merchán, 2006). The parents of the victims may justify the occurrence of bullying based on their children's characteristics, resulting in an increasing sense of guilt in the victims, and a negative self-perception due to their reinforced incapacity to cope with problems.

FAMILIES OF THE BULLY-VICTIMS

The families of the bully-victims are generally characterized by attributes of both bullies' and victims' families (Cook et al., 2010); similar to bullies' families, these families also have a high prevalence of manipulation. The parental figures are dysfunctional, and these individuals are generally distant from their families, which are characterized by lack of supervision, affection or emotional support, and are considered particularly problematic (Schwartz et al., 1998, 2001). Besides low emotional involvement, often felt by children as aggression and rejection, bully-victims frequently suffer from other forms of neglect and abuse.

Group dynamics approach: peer pressure

A considerable amount of research on school bullying has demonstrated the importance of approaching bullying as a "group process" for a deeper understanding of bullying behaviours; namely, individuals' motivation to bully, the lack of support provided to victims and more effective interventions to deal with bullying. The group members perform different roles, driven by their individual attitudes and motivations, and interventions to deal with bullying should also be targeted at the peer group level (Salmivalli, 2010).

Peer relations can promote adaptation, but can also become dysfunctional (Pepler & Craig, 1995): the peer group is external to the family, and provides a social setting in which youngsters have opportunities to learn to defend their points of view, to respect others' perspectives, to negotiate problem resolution and to develop behaviours accepted by peers, in a setting characterized by equality, reciprocity and informality, cooperation but also competition. The peer group promotes the construction of a collective conscience, through critical and creative processes.

Bullying episodes tend to occur within a group situation. Besides victims and bullies, bystanders also play a very important role in the process. In the early stages of peer group formation, when each member's social role and their position in the status hierarchy is still being defined, bullying prevalence tends to increase. The affiliative bonds between the members are still fragile but, as time passes and peers continue to interact with each other, the social roles inside the peer group become more firmly established, and the attachments become stronger.

This early stage, characterized by the creation of social status and definition of each member's role, is when the occurrence of bullying episodes is particularly likely, according to analyses by Pellegrini and colleagues

(Pellegrini & Bartini, 2000; Pellegrini & Long, 2002). This is because bullying can be used to seek dominance over other peers, as a way to achieve high social status in the peer group. These processes are particularly evident in school transitions, when new peer groups are formed. When children are being integrated into a new and unknown social environment among older peers, the younger children lose their previous social status, and more easily become bullying victims of older peers, who are already integrated into this setting (Pellegrini & Bartini, 2001). So, in the early stages of school transition, bullying behaviours tend to increase, and later tend to decrease as social roles become more established. Some teenagers have an extreme need to feel accepted by peers, and may therefore adopt aggressive behaviours with the purpose of seeking peer approval, even if these are not in accord with their usual ways of behaving.

From this perspective, bullying is a pro-active and goal-oriented form of aggressive behaviour (Coie, Dodge, Terry & Wright, 1991), driven by status goals. Social status concerns the individual's standing in peer hierarchy, which is assigned by the members of the peer group. The use of bullying to achieve their goals shows that bullies are not socially unskilled (Salmivalli, 2010). This is especially so in adolescence, a period in which popularity and status among peers are particularly important. Girls tend to organize in dyads or small friendship groups; this type of relation facilitates discussion of emotions and relationships, and status relates to reputation. In contrast, boys tend to belong to wider and larger groups, and to develop looser social bonds (Björkqvist & Österman, 2000); status is often related to physical strength and also sports prowess. These differences are reflected in the different kinds of bullying tactics typically used by girls (more relational), and boys (more physical).

A summary of the three complementary approaches (individual traits, group dynamics and social environment) is given in Table 1.1.

Theoretical framework for bullying in youth sport: Ecological Systems Theory

According to Ecological Systems Theory, people are in constant interplay with their social environment: the developing individual modulates and recreates the social environment in which he or she is integrated, and the social environment exerts a direct influence on the individual's development. This interplay between agent and social environment is mutual and continuous (Brofenbrenner, 1979, 1996).

Brofenbrenner (1979) describes four different developmental settings: the micro-, meso-, exo- and macro-systems. Ecological Systems Theory helps with understanding the multiple influences on bullying behaviours, and effective intervention strategies require an understanding of the social ecology (Hong &

Table 1.1 Summary table for multi-level approach contributions to understanding bullying

	Bullying		
Approach	Individual traits	Group dynamics	Social environment
Main theoretical contributions	Profiles (bullies and victims)	Group processes	Risk factors for victimization
Description	**Victims** Passivity Less confident Submissive Insecure Conflict avoidance **Bullies** Impulsivity Confrontational Extroversion Activity Exhibitionism	Age transitions (groups) Social status pursuit Dominance Peer pressure	Low performance Lack of engagement in sports activities Belonging to an ethnic minority Being disabled Being gay/lesbian/bisexual Not conforming to conventional gender stereotypes Body issues (physically weaker, physically different, overweight, lower weight) Age (being younger) Being clumsy Having a feminine appearance

Espelage, 2012). More on this will be described in Chapter 2, specifically applied to the sports setting.

Coping strategies employed by victims

Some research has focused on how victims attempt to cope with bullying. Coping can be defined as the cognitive and behavioural efforts made by an individual in order to deal with adverse and frustrating situations. It can be divided into two main styles: coping focused on emotion, and coping focused on problem solving, which differ in their characteristics and degree of effectiveness (Lazarus, 1991). Coping focused on emotion consists of cognitive efforts to regulate the emotions produced by the stressor and act on the perceptions of the problem rather than the problem itself. Coping focused on problem solving consists of efforts by an individual to change the stressor situation (Folkman & Lazarus, 1985).

Research on coping strategies used by victims of bullying has been considerable (Naylor, Cowie & Del Rey, 2001; Smith, 2014). The most used strategies are ignoring, talking with the bully and telling him/her to stop, keeping quiet without reacting, and talking with someone and seeking help (from friends, teachers or family). A coping strategy used less often is to confront the bullies (Mora-Merchán, 2006).

Seeking help is often useful for victims; however, when bullying episodes occur, victims tend to remain silent about it (Fontaine, 2003). When this happens, it can increase the confidence of the perpetrator and contribute to the maintenance of the bullying (Anabel & Anna, 2009). The silence of the victims is mostly due to their fear of retaliation, feeling shame and/or the belief that the support systems cannot provide an adequate solution to the problem. When youngsters talk about the experience of being bullied and share their thoughts and feelings, they feel stronger and more capable of coping with the situation effectively (Naylor, Cowie & Del Rey, 2001). In school settings, the main support sources are parents and teachers, whose response can only be effective if the support provided is consistent (Barrio et al., 2008).

Adolescents are less likely to seek help from adults than in earlier childhood, which makes peer support schemes especially important at this stage (Smith, 2014). More socially competent children use more active coping strategies, namely problem resolution and seeking support (Zimmer-Gembeck, Lees & Skinner, 2011).

Consequences of bullying: results from research in school

So far as school bullying is concerned, much research conducted internationally has found negative effects of being victimized (Arseneault, 2018). These effects can be substantial and long term (Farrington, Loeber, Stallings & Ttofi, 2011; Kerr, Gini & Capaldi, 2017; Wolke & Lereya, 2015).

A major consequence of being victimized is depression (Losel & Bender, 2011; Ttofi, Farrington & Losel, 2011). Meta-analyses of many longitudinal studies (Ttofi, Farrington, & Losel, 2011) showed that even after adjustments for a range of other factors, victims at school were at greater risk of later depression. The most tragic end is suicide; although rare, this can be an outcome to which experiences of being victimized can be a significant contributor (Kim, Leventhal, Koh & Boyce, 2009). According to Wolke and Sapouna (2008), being a bullying victim during childhood is strongly associated with muscle dysmorphia, anxiety, obsessive-compulsive symptoms and low self-esteem in adulthood.

Although consequences of bullying are more often described for victims, the bullies also suffer negative outcomes from being involved in bullying episodes. Children involved in bullying others are at greater risk of depression as well (Ttofi, Farrington & Losel, 2011), but are more significantly at greater risk of later offending (Farrington, Lösel, Ttofi & Theodorakis, 2012). It is widely agreed that bully-victims are highly maladjusted, frequently more so than children who are only victimized (Schwartz, Proctor & Chien, 2001).

Children who bully others tend to engage in anti-social behaviour in other social settings and to perform poorly in school. They may have difficulties in establishing long-lasting and positive relations with peers. Their maintenance of aggressive behaviour patterns in different social settings increases the risk of anti-social behaviour and delinquency (Farrington, Loeber, Stallings & Ttofi, 2011).

Bystanders or witnesses of bullying can also be adversely affected (Nishina & Juvonen, 2005; Rivers, Poteat, Noret & Ashurst, 2009). The considerable research developed about the consequences of bullying at school has shown that bullying frequently results in negative outcomes for children involved individually, as well as the peer group itself. When involved in bullying episodes, the passive bystanders often report anxiety, feeling impotent to act, and being afraid of becoming the next victims of the perpetrators (Francisco & Libório, 2008).

Why study bullying in youth sport?

The examination and understanding of power dynamics in sport is crucial for sports coaches and practitioners who work with athletes, and who should care about their welfare (Fisher & Dzikus, 2010). Research on violence in sport has been developed in different sports, countries, and concerning different types of aggression, but there has been relatively little specifically on bullying (Escury & Dudink, 2010; Evans, Adler, MacDonald & Cote, 2016). Bullying in sport appears to have often been considered as a taboo topic (Kirby & Wintrump, 2002) or else treated as regular sports aggression. It can be harder to undertake solid research on bullying in sports settings than in schools, due to particular aspects such as the tough mentality encouraged in many sports, and because sports clubs are less organized than schools (Stirling, Bridges, Cruz & Mountjoy, 2011). Nevertheless, it is important to develop research and intervention on bullying in youth sports training. Bullying in sport has potential short- and long-term negative consequences for those involved, including early drop out of sports practice by many victims (Escury & Dudink, 2010; Evans, Adler, MacDonald & Cote, 2016). More fundamentally, bullying behaviours are considered a breach of human rights, and contrary to the values and ethical concerns that underpin youth sports training, including inclusion and equality.

The limited research does indicate a considerable prevalence of bullying in youth sports training. Anti-bullying programmes are starting to appear in sports clubs but many are directly adapted from the school setting, not considering the specificity of sport, and not based on scientific research. It is very important to educate sports professionals about bullying (how to identify it, consequences, provide action guidelines, etc.), and it is necessary to develop more research on bullying in sport in order to design more efficient anti-bullying programmes.

The rationale for our research

Our research tries to shed some light on bullying in youth sports training. Its main purpose has been to describe and analyse the prevalence of bullying behaviours in youth sports training athletes, in male athletes and in different sports in Portugal, and to provide theoretical and practical contributions for research. To do so, we used both quantitative and qualitative approaches. In the quantitative approach, we used a self-report questionnaire. This nationwide data functions as a baseline on bullying prevalence in sports settings in Portugal. In the qualitative approach, we used interviews for data collection. Besides athletes, we also analysed the narratives of their coaches' perceptions about bullying episodes in their group of athletes. Finally, we interviewed ex-elite athletes, one from each of the nine sports studied, who retrospectively described their involvement in bullying episodes when they were young athletes.

This mixed methodological approach not only provided research methodological strength but also allowed deeper insights. The data obtained in the four complementary studies has allowed us to develop the guidelines that feature at the end of the book.

Chapter 2

History of sport, violence in sport and issues in youth sports training

Sport: an ancestral phenomenon

Sports activities as we see them today are a product of an evolutionary path across many centuries of other activities. So, before analysing sports as they are known at present, it is useful to go back to their roots, based on *play* and *rituals*. We consider the meaning of sport in the ancient civilizations of Greece and Rome, and the development of the Olympic Games. Following this historical analysis up to the present day, we consider the issues of violence in sport and the influence of sexual stereotypes. Sport is generally considered as a social good, but bullying can occur in sport and we review the limited research on this topic, focusing on youth sports training. We consider conceptual issues in this area, and discuss Ecological Systems Theory as a useful theoretical framework.

Play and rituals

When defining play in terms of child development, Pellegrini (2009) divides it into four major domains: social play, locomotor play, object-directed play and pretend play. Play is characterized by being non-functional and not purposefully directed towards a well-defined and practically attainable goal. Rituals are also ancestral and have a major role in human societies (Renfrew, 2017). As play, rituals have multiple definitions. It was defined by Rappaport as "the performance of more or less invariant sequences of formal acts and utterances not entirely encoded by performers" (Rappaport, 1999, p. 24). Depending on the definition considered, rituals may be considered present among other animals or restricted to humans. There is a considerable overlap between rituals and play, because rituals also appear to be non-functional. However, rituals are more highly structured than play, and are sometimes accompanied by the use of ceremonial artefacts.

Both rituals and play require considerable resources of time and energy, and are transformative in social terms; their transformative power lies in introducing humans to a new social reality. The similarities between play and rituals raises some interesting questions, such as to what extent rituals fall within the category of play, or within the special subcategory of play labelled "games". Some rituals are considered play, including sport events, and games include several domains of play. It is directly from the behaviours designated as play that many games engaged in by human adults clearly develop; many sports are simply systematized domains of play, which are structured in a competitive and/or agonistic format.

When games are performed, these may be playful competition, or they may be depicted in a ritual context. Examples of this are the Mesoamerican ballgame, a form of play which took place in a ritual context, or the Panhellenic Games in ancient Greece, which were played at the greatest sanctuaries of the gods (Renfrew, 2017).

The characteristics of animal play suggest that sports are rooted in play. The rough and tumble play among juvenile mammals (including humans) is particularly characteristic of males, and has important physical and psychological effects in the development of the youngsters. Besides physical practice, it also allows them to assess others' skills and physical strength (Humphreys & Smith, 1987). According to Lombardo (2012), sports are rooted in play and began as a way for men to develop the skills needed in primitive hunting and warfare. Further developments over the centuries that followed led to it becoming a scenario in which athletes could display their skills, and spectators had the opportunity to evaluate the qualities of potential allies and rivals.

Modern sports are based on these more primitive and ancient forms, whose main purpose was to prepare men for action. There are many ancient historical records of sports activities spread all over the world. Here, we provide a brief review of some of the most important cultural contributions to sports as we know them today.

Evidence of health building activities in China have been traced back to over 4,000 years ago. According to Zhang and Pan (2011), sports in China have existed for more than 10,000 years. The first known sports emerged in the Zhou Dynasty in the 11th century BCE. The traditional culture of ancient China influenced sports and their development in that country (Yao, 2009). The traditional Chinese sports aimed to enhance bodybuilding, preserve health and were focused mostly on entertainment purposes. However, many things changed over time due to cultural and social developments, and in modern times Western sports almost entirely replaced the traditional ones in China. Nowadays, Chinese sports are mostly the same as those in the Western world (Zhaojin & Aiping, 2015). In Japan, Sumo is the most popular sport, and is among the oldest ones in this country. There is evidence of sumo combats taking place many centuries ago (Cuyler, 1979).

The culture of ancient Egypt had a strong influence on the development of sports worldwide. Initially, these were closely linked to religion

(Hamed, 2015). Evidence suggests that many of today's sports were already practised by the ancient Egyptians. A mural dated 3000 BCE contains illustrations of Pharaoh Zoser the Great participating in a running event held at a festival (Elgammal, 2008). Illustrations of sports activities inside the temples of the pharaohs can be traced to around 1200 BCE, and suggest their participation in and encouragement of them. For example, the tomb of Tutankhamun, the Egyptian pharaoh who was crowned around 1347 BCE, strongly suggests he was a sportsman. It contained many items of sports and recreational equipment, including artefacts for fowling and hunting. There is historical evidence that he learned various sports during his primary education, and several sporting scenes were found in the tombs of Theban Nobles (Habashi, 1976).

There is considerable recognition among scholars that the cultural development of Western civilization was largely influenced in the past by the Eastern civilizations of Mesopotamia and Egypt. Phoenicia played a major role by sending skilled engineers, artisans and entrepreneurs by sea to the Mediterranean territories, who promoted the exchange of goods and ideas, resulting in civilizational development of these territories. The shipping, mercantile and cultural activity of the Phoenicians reached its peak during the Greek early Archaic period, especially the Orientalizing phase in 750–650 BCE. This activity appears to have had some influence on Classical Greece (Scott, 2018). Many sports activities which flourished in Egypt later spread to Greece, Rome and other parts of the world. Combat sports are strongly represented in different forms by the ancient Egyptians (Hamed, 2015). The particular sport of fencing was widespread throughout Asia and was quite popular among the Romans who used it as preparation for war (Cohen, 2002). The Phoenician culture was also strongly influenced by sporting activities, which were held as worship rites, near religious temples. The economic and cultural trades between Phoenicia (nowadays Lebanon) and Mediterranean countries may have had some influence on the development of sports, including the Olympic Games in ancient Greece.

The ancient Olympic Games in Greece were rituals in which athletes competed to serve the gods, and the victories achieved were perceived as according to their will (Guttman, 2004). This belief contributed to competition winning athletes being considered heroes, and the immortalization of their achievements with artistic productions of that time, such as paintings and other art forms (Justiciano, 1998). In this period of history, sport was perceived in its purest form, and its advantages for human development were acknowledged and promoted. So, not surprisingly, in the 6th century BCE, sport was a common and institutionalized practice in Greek society (Raposo, 1976).

However, things changed when sports started being perceived as a potentially profitable activity. The focus on competition and entertainment around sport also resulted in other outcomes: the specialization of athletic skills led to a rise in professional activity, and some athletes started being paid to dedicate themselves exclusively to sports activity in order to strongly improve their performance (Guttman, 2004). These individuals could now fully dedicate themselves to training, in order to improve their skills and to win competitions. Both professionalization of sport and the rupture of the bond between sport competition and religion strongly contributed to the moral decline of the ancient Greek Olympic Games, because it created a gap between its original underpinnings and the current motivations of the athletes for its practice. Athletes started seeking to win at all costs to achieve social status through money and fame, rather than perceiving themselves as serving the gods (Justiciano, 1998). Other important factors which also contributed to this decline were the invasion of Greece by the Macedonians and Romans, which was accompanied by the growth of corruption and violence in sport (García Ferrando, 1985, 1987).

The Romans tended to perceive sports differently from the Greeks: they believed that the purpose of physical activities lay in war, which led them to focus their attention on combat events, especially gladiatorial combat. The Greek principles related to body beauty and gracefulness were disapproved of by the Romans, and labelled as feminine in a derogatory way. In the Roman Empire, sports were associated with politics, which contributed to the increased prevalence of various types of violent behaviours. Although the bureaucratization of sport started in Greece, it increased greatly under the Romans; they organized sports in a very similar way to modern sports, characterized by a logic based on standardization and quantification of achievements (Guttman, 2004). Some impressive monuments dedicated to sports built by the Roman Empire, such as the Colosseum in Rome, illustrate the importance of sports.

There are historical artefacts which serve as evidence of the spread of Greek and Roman culture to the eastern shores of the Mediterranean. Examples include coins, inscriptions, the writings of ancient historians and the physical remains of facilities (Kilby, 1976). The Roman Empire had a strong influence outside Europe and the Mediterranean, such as in its African and Middle Eastern territories. Its later decadence, along with the barbarian invasions, led to social instability, which made it difficult to continue sporting activities in the ways known then.

The end of the Roman Empire had repercussions in sport and marked the beginning of a new era in Europe. The sporting activities of the Middle Ages did not have any direct connection with the ancient Greek Olympic Games. During this period (5th–15th centuries), physical activities were endorsed mostly on the basis of recreation purposes rather than sports. The Greek educational ideal of using sports as a tool to promote human development was abandoned in the Middle Ages. Only later during the Renaissance (15th and 16th centuries), was it revived, when school physical training restarted (Demirel & Yıldıran, 2013), and physical activity and sport were again perceived as a type of play, and their contribution to human development and promotion of health was once again acknowledged (Hernández & Recoder, 2015).

In the Middle Ages, there was a transition from mostly individual sports to team sports. The prevalent idea was to develop several skills, rather than focusing on specialization (Guttman, 2004).

Many sports created in the 19th and 20th centuries have clear links to the Middle Ages. An example is provided by Renson (1976), who describes the evolution of archery, from elite troops in the 13th century to an Olympic sport nowadays. Renson describes how, by the end of the 13th century, there was a group of elite troops among the urban militia of the Flemish city states. These soldiers were important and powerful. However, in the 15th century, the introduction of firearms seriously affected the usefulness of these groups of soldiers whose main pursuit became official representation and recreational purposes. However, the historical influence cannot be ignored, and today archery clubs can be found in almost every Flemish town. These vary from conservative closed societies, to modern Olympic sport archery clubs.

More modern ages also brought new developments to sports activities, especially once the Industrial Revolution had occurred in Europe. In the mid-19th century, the first national sports organizations were founded in England. These kinds of organizations, aimed at promoting and regulating sport practice, started to spread across many countries. This eventually culminated in the creation of the International Olympic Committee. Modern sports were born in the final part of the 19th century. According to García Ferrando (1985), some of the reasons to explain the increasing engagement of the general population in sport and its increasing importance in society were the reduction of labouring hours in work schedules, the reformulation of educational systems, the general increasing focus on health and well-being, as well as political support for the organization of sport events. The number of amateur athletes increased greatly, and sports started being perceived as an educational tool, generally practised by individuals of different ages and social standards (Raposo, 1976).

An important landmark in modern sports history was the 23 July 1894, when the Olympic Games were re-established by Pierre de Coubertin, aiming to promote the idea of peace in Europe, and to mitigate the social class struggles in process then (García Ferrando, 1985). The first modern version of the Olympic Games took place in 1896, and the main ideas were to promote the importance of positive relations between humans, and also between individuals, their society and nature. Considering these objectives, there was an attempt to go back to the roots of the ancient Olympics: the main focus was to compete with dignity, rather than winning medals at all costs, and sports were perceived as a way to modulate human behaviour, to contribute to the union of people and to promote peace all over the world (Braz, 1998).

Since the re-establishment of the Olympic Games and until today, many important changes have occurred. Although the Olympic Games were consistently held in the 20th century, exceptions were made in 1916 (originally scheduled in Berlin and cancelled due to the tensions around World War I), and in 1944 (not held due to the devastating effects of World War II). Also, more and more sports have become included within the scope of the Olympic Games. These and other transformations have had a direct impact on how the Olympic Games have come to be perceived.

Nowadays, the Olympic Games are extremely commercialized, and serve as a theatre of political and ideological affirmation. They may be perceived as a stage upon which to enact struggles between different nations. There is an involvement of huge crowds, who are attracted by technological evolution and media transmissions, giving the press enormous power and contributing to a rise in consumerism (Raposo, 1976). Nowadays, the selection of the athletes is based exclusively on performance, and competitive pressure can block democratic access to sport participation (Braz, 1998).

Many factors have contributed to making sports activities a source of enormous profits, and to dividing sports clubs into "big" and "small", based on their financial capacity and power (Raposo, 1976). Sports clubs became sports companies, resulting in a profound shift away from the original sporting social values, and the restriction of access to only the best athletes. There is an increasing number of sports clubs and sport federations and, currently, there is huge specialization in sport which also reflects the investment made throughout recent decades. Considerable support systems have been developed, including coaches, referees, scientists and other experts, with the creation of specialized sports departments and training academies. Scholars also began focusing their attention on sports, resulting in a scientific research field created around them, and research studies being published in specialized journals (Guttman, 2004).

Although the Romans started converting sports achievements into numbers, this task has become highly developed in more recent times. A special feature of modern sport is how every athletic achievement is converted into numbers, in a bid to measure and quantify everything, and later perform statistical analyses. The quantifying idea, along with the wish to win, led to the creation of records in sport. This concept relied on the idea that progress in performance is a linear concept, and that every single achievement can be defeated. This concept results in the extension of sport competition throughout space and chronological time. The egalitarian philosophy is no longer the focus of attention, and it has been substituted by the achievement of reaching new records (Braz, 1998). The record is the main feature of modern sports, and can be considered the modern form of immortality. The athletes who achieve it are still remembered and evoked as the champions, even when their sporting careers are finished (at least until someone achieves a better result and becomes the new champion) (Guttman, 2004). According to Constantino (1998), it is important to resist this perspective and look at sport from educational and cultural points of view. Sport should not be restricted to athletes, and its main purpose should be to promote ethics and respect in all members of society.

Violence in sport

The practice of sport does enact aggressive behaviours. In fact, many aggressive behaviours are allowed and even rewarded within sports settings, with a high social status conferred on athletes who act in such ways (Smith, 1976). When the social setting allows these kinds of behaviours, there is a tendency for violence to increase (García Ferrando, 1987). According to Marivoet (1998), unethical behaviours can be observed in all sports, and there is an overall need to win at all costs.

Any violent behaviour betrays a lack of ethical responsibility, and it is important to reflect on the ideals underlying sport practice. Many governments all over the world have been focusing their attention on violence in sport and have created organizations to carry out research on it and reduce it (Ibañez, Marco, Pablo & de Elejalde, 2012). Besides the work developed locally by national organizations in each country, international networks and projects have also been created to tackle violence, abuse and harassment in sport all over the world. Websites with information about these topics and with recommendations can also easily be found. Here we mention some of these organizations and projects, and provide a brief description of their actions.

The International Olympic Committee (2007) has focused on abusive behaviours in sport and produced a Consensus Statement on Sexual Harassment and Abuse in Sport, which covers issues such as bullying, hazing, and physical and psychological abuse in sport. The European Commission has promoted a considerable number of campaigns and projects, aiming to humanize sport, prevent violence and abuse, and enhance the good practices of stakeholders. The international network within the European project Prevention of Sexualized Violence in Sports – Impulses for an Open, Secure and Sound Sporting Environment in Europe (2012), has written a report entitled "Prevention of Sexual and Gender Harassment and Abuse in Sports: Initiatives in Europe and Beyond", which describes some actions taken by several organizations in different countries. Other initiatives have also been promoted by the European Commission, such as the PsyTool project, which aims to use sports psychology as a strategic tool for preventing violence and abuse in sport, and enhance good practices by providing information and pedagogical tools to sports agents.

The United Nations has also focused on violence and abuse in sport and initiated some important actions regarding these topics. UNICEF (2005, 2010) have collected data about violence against children in sport, described different types of aggressive behaviours in youth sport in several countries and provided guidelines and recommendations for action. The Brunel International Research Network for Athlete Welfare (BIRNAW) has worked with UNICEF to develop research on violence and abuse in sport and provided documents with guidelines. Some other organizations have also focused on youth sport. In the UK, the NSPCC has been developing important work on preventing child abuse in sport, although their activities are not restricted to sports and also include other settings of children's lives. Interventions are being made in England, Northern Ireland, Scotland, Wales and Jersey. In Portugal, the intervention project *Desporto sem Bullying* (Sports without Bullying) sensitizes the sport community to interpersonal violence and bullying in youth sport, provides pedagogical materials for free download and runs campaigns against violence and abuse in sport. Besides the action being developed by the Portuguese Olympic Committee and other sports organizations, the Portuguese Government has recently created the *Autoridade Nacional contra a Violência no Desporto* (National Authority Against Violence in Sports), which reflects a concern about improving the quality of sports and tackling violent and abusive behaviours.

Research studies on violence and abuse have been undertaken in many sports, focusing on different types of violence (Dunning, 1999), and aiming to understand the nature and prevalence of these behaviours, in order to prevent them and more efficiently reduce their occurrence. Many types of violent behaviour may be observed in sport. Research suggests that the frequency, nature and intensity of violent behaviours vary across different forms and levels of sport (Fields, Collins & Comstock, 2010; Guilbert, 2004; Pedersen, 2007). The acceptance or rejection of aggressive and dominant behaviours depends on the characteristics of the social groups and settings, and cultural aspects should also be considered (García Ferrando, 1987, 1990). Violence in sport can be observed in team, individual and combat sports (Guilbert, 2009) and many of these behaviours are based on the perceived idea of being macho. This underlying tough mentality of sport promotes the enactment of aggressive behaviours. However, sports differ from one another, and the special features of each one should be considered when analysing aggressive behaviours.

According to Marivoet (1998), professional adult sport is dominated by the need to win above all and by strong economic interests, which contribute to ethical conduct being easily ignored in order to achieve competitive goals. This makes it much more difficult to implement the ethical ideals of sport in adult competition, although it seems reasonable to believe that a different and much more positive scenario can be created in youth sport. Although much has already been done, even in professional adult sport, in order to enhance the ethical standards of sports agents, much still needs to be done and sport performance remains the main focus. Considering that youth sport aims to promote human development (learning social skills, tolerance, promoting inclusion), unethical behaviours must be addressed and safe environments for children should be a top priority. Violence in sport distorts the ethical ideals that it has the potential to foster, and it is the responsibility of sports agencies and governments to act in order to improve this situation. We believe much can be changed in youth sport, and sports agents must care about the athletes' welfare. A long path must be followed to reduce the prevalence of the different types of violence in sport, and to make it a more inclusive and healthy activity for youngsters.

Discrimination in sports settings

For many years, different types of exclusion were more commonly accepted in Western societies, and obviously in sport as well. The international sports organizations have been developing a continued effort to make sport increasingly inclusive, with the aim of enabling everyone to benefit from it and enjoy its practice. Here, we explore the inequalities between women and men in sport, homophobia in sport, the participation of disabled persons in sports competitions and racism, based on an historical perspective.

Inequalities between women and men in sport

Biological differences between the sexes

There has been considerable increased participation of women in sport in recent decades. Although some female athletes were widely known (e.g. Maria Bueno – tennis), they were an exception. A landmark development in the equality movement between men and women in sport was the work achieved by the tennis world star Billie Jean King – considered by many as the female athlete pioneer for gender equality and social justice in sport – in her struggle against inequalities between men and women in sport. Nowadays the participation of women in sport is higher, and there are many more female sports stars.

However, and despite measures to include other sets of populations in elite sport competition besides highly skilled men, these changes are relatively recent, and inequalities still exist. Besides the influence of the cultural roots of sport (Messner, 2011), when it comes to the inequalities between men and women, we think that anatomical issues have some influence here; generally, men are stronger and faster than women, and benefit from other physical skills that are very adaptive in the majority of the most popular sports (e.g. football, rugby). Females usually have other more developed skills that serve them well, especially in other sports (e.g. gymnastics, netball, volleyball). However, these sports are often considered less popular, and receive less attention than the mainstream ones.

Many sports separate male and female competition, and adapt their standards (e.g. number of sets in tennis) due to the biological differences between sexes. To win elite competitions, women have to train as much as or even harder than men. However, the general focus of the audience who consume sports is on how strong and skilled the athlete is (despite his or her sex), rather than how much a person needs to overcome him/herself to achieve such results. In many sports, men have an advantage due to their biological characteristics.

Here we provide an example of a sportive competition in which men and women compete together, and men benefit from a biological advantage. The Ironman is a very tough and demanding triathlon competition, in which athletes often fail to finish due to the tremendous effort needed to do so. The label of this sport refers to someone who has an extreme endurance capacity, far beyond the average. Daniela Ryf was the best female athlete competing at the 2019 Ironman World Championship. She made the best time among the female athletes. However, when compared to the overall classification, she stood at 25th place. This result doesn't necessarily reflect any lower effort by this athlete, but biological differences that benefit male athletes in this kind of competition.

There are some sports in which men and women compete together because biological differences don't seem to influence their performance. Here, the differences of popularity between men and women may be reduced. An example is horse riding; in this sport, many elite female riders compete with elite male riders on an equal basis, and achieve equally good results. Also, there are sports in which female athletes benefit from their biological differences when compared to men. "Female" sports such as gymnastics are mostly dominated by women; however, the media coverage of these sports is often lower, which makes them less popular among the public in general.

The bodies of female and male athletes are perceived differently by stakeholders and the general public. Caster Semenya is an athlete with higher physical capacity than her female opponents; the body differences led to the International Association of Athletics Federation to force her to take medication to lower her testosterone levels (www.theguardian.com/sport/2019/jun/18/caster-semenya-iaaf-athletics-guinea-pig). She wasn't allowed to compete along with other female athletes, due to her natural biological advantage. However, the incredible sporting achievements performed by male athletes such as Michael Phelps (swimming), Usain Bolt (athletics) or Cristiano Ronaldo (football), are considered superhuman, and their body shapes are admired. Caster Semenya's inherent physical ability was perceived as not natural and needed to be "fixed" so competition could be fair, while other male athletes who benefit from special characteristics of their bodies that increase their sport performance (Michael Phelps is a good example), are admired and considered role models within their sport setting.

Differences in media coverage of male and female competitions

Evidence suggests that more men than women of all ages practise sports activities and also consume sport by watching it (Dietz-Uhler, Harrick, End & Jacquemotte, 2001; Stubbe, Boomsma & De Geus, 2005). Despite a higher profile of women in some sports recently, most of the main sports personalities are still men (athletes, coaches, stakeholders). The media focus their attention mostly on masculine athletes, which tends to be reflected in more money being provided for male competitions. The sports media is composed of a triangle of male sport leaders, male editors and male sponsors, who are together the central agents of power and dominate the industry (Lippe, 2002). Male sport is often considered more important, attracts more public interest and generates higher incomes (Pfister, 1994).

According to a report from a European project funded by the community framework strategy on gender equality, entitled "Sports, Media and Stereotypes: Women and Men in Sports and Media" (Ólafsson, 2006), which took place between 2001 and 2005, men and women are portrayed differently by the media. The former are reported much more, and the media has a tendency to idolize and promote the leading men in sport as celebrities and sportsmen. Besides being less reported than men, when women in sport are reported by the media, the focus also often diverges from their role as sportswomen. The author of the report called attention to the need to raise the media status of sportswomen, but consider that this should be done by multiplying some exemplary reporting that already exists, rather than by presenting female athletes as sex objects, or reinforcing traditional gender stereotypes.

This report was published over a decade ago, and female athletes are now receiving more attention from the media. However, sports settings are still dominated by men. Recently, the Portuguese pilot Elisabete Jacinto was the first woman to win the Africa Eco Race (in 2019). She complained about having less attention from the media than men generally, and also about the comments made by some opponents about how a woman shouldn't be there, in such an inappropriate environment for them; this was even when she had good sporting results in the competitions and was ranked ahead of them.

Other recent examples may be illustrative of the inequalities between media coverage of male and female sports. In tennis, the prize money of the Grand Slam tournaments is equal for both men and women. However, other tournaments often have different prize monies (men receive higher rewards). Novak Djokovic is one of the most important tennis players ever; he won the most important ATP competitions several times, and has been ranked number 1 in the world several times. Djokovic commented on the differences between the prize money for men and women, claiming prize monies were fairly distributed, based on who attracts more spectators, the attention of the media and who sells more tickets (www.bbc.com/news/world-us-canada-35859791). The USA competitors Venus and Serena Williams stood up against these statements, which they considered a type of gender discrimination.

Another example comes from football. Marta Vieira da Silva is one of the most talented football players ever; she won the FIFA Women's World Player of the Year award six times. She refused many sport sponsors because they refused to pay her the same as they do to some of the most influential male football players they support. She was also one of the leaders of the campaign #GoEqual, which aims to promote equality in football. However, there are some important exceptions to the higher popularity of male sport; for example, in some volleyball competitions, female teams receive higher attention from both media and spectators than male teams.

The discussion around the equality of women and men in sport is generally divided into two main positions: (1) those who consider that media coverage and public interest should dictate prize money. Here women generally receive less attention than men because the public who consume sports are generally more focused on men in sports. And (2) those who consider both sexes should have the same privileges, because if not, it constitutes discrimination based on gender. The discussion is far from reaching an end, but reflects that times are changing greatly.

Homophobia in sport

Sport still represents a cultural idealization of traditional masculinity; a culture that demands conformity with a masculine gender, privileges heterosexuality and often stigmatizes homosexuality (Baiocco et al., 2018; Brackenridge, Rivers, Gough & Llewellyn, 2007; Roberts, 2008). Homosexual athletes often feel like outsiders in sport. Denison and Kitchen (2015) conducted an international study on homophobia in sport, with 9,494 participants from 6 countries. The majority of these said that they did not believe that sports were a safe environment for homosexuals. Another survey was conducted with a sample of 1,249 sports fans across the UK (Stonewall, 2016); the football fans were the most likely to hear homophobic abuse. Most of the football fans had already seen homophobic behaviours in a sports setting, and considered that homophobia remained a problem, at all levels of competition.

In sports contexts, athletes often need to behave according to a heterosexual standard in order to preserve group relations, guarantee sponsorship and obtain financial support. These factors contribute to why those elite athletes who are homosexual often only decide to openly talk about their sexual orientation at the end of their career (Cunti, Bellantonio & Priore, 2016). Gareth Thomas, a former Welsh rugby player, one of the most influential players of his country, said publically that he was homosexual only in the final years of his career. He described in interviews how he struggled with being a homosexual in sport, how worried he was about the reaction of teammates, fans and other sports stakeholders. In the end, he felt accepted by most of the sports stakeholders and was considered an example by many. In football, the Germany team captain Philipp Lahm in his autobiography said he wasn't gay (there was rumours spreading), but gave controversial advice: he said gay players should keep their sexuality secret, or else they would be verbally abused (www.telegraph.co.uk/sport/football/news/8523864/Germany-football-captain-gays-should-keep-quiet.html).

Homosexuality, especially among men, is still rejected in the sports environment. However, things have been changing considerably in the last decades. Examples of successful athletes such as Tom Daley (swimming) or Gareth Thomas (rugby) who have openly spoken about being homosexual, reflect a more inclusive climate in sport. If homosexuality was a taboo in sport environments, it's now being discussed much more openly, and sexual minorities are less excluded. Anderson (2011) examined the evolution of homophobia in sport for three decades, since the 1980s, and described important progress made during this time period. Fortunately, things are now different and have kept changing in the last decade as well.

Disabled athletes and the influence of the Paralympics

A wider perspective of sport competition includes those who have physical limitations within elite sport.

Considering the physical disadvantages of many disabled people, the sports organizations created a new and separate format of competition to promote sport practice among disabled people. The Paralympics are divided into different levels of competition, based on the degree of disability, in order to group athletes based on their similar physical functionality. This allowed these athletes to compete on an equal basis, and brought a whole new approach to disabled people regarding sport practice and their social acceptance and recognition. The Paralympic movement showed that these athletes, despite their physical disabilities, could compete in a sports setting, and this strongly enhanced their wider participation.

These have been some important achievements in creating a more inclusive environment. The sport participation scope is becoming wider, and different populations who were left aside for a long time from sport practice are now much more integrated. However, the media coverage, public participation and prize monies are still much lower for disabled people.

Racism in sport

Sport has been used in the past to bring people together and tackle racism. The role played by the South African national rugby team after the Apartheid era is a good example of the power of sports to tackle racism. Many international entities in the last decades have developed important campaigns against racism, with good results. In football, the Union of European Football Associations (UEFA) promoted a video campaign with the participation of some of the most popular athletes in the world (www.uefa.com/insideuefa/social-responsibility/respect/no-to-racism/). However, racism is still very prevalent in sport.

It has been an issue, for example, in English football, where at the time of writing it appears to have been growing in recent years (www.iol.co.za/sport/soccer/reports-of-racism-in-english-football-rise-for-seventh-straight-year-29783261). There are numerous and severe cases of racism in the Premier League, which have recently been the focus of attention by the media and governmental institutions (www.theguardian.com/football/2019/apr/12/racism-english-football-parks-premier-league-special-investigation).
Obviously, racism is not confined to English football. All over the world there are cases reported in the media, and a huge amount of work is being and still needs to be done. Nowadays, racism is widely rejected by most sports stakeholders, due to these efforts being made internationally.

Aggressiveness, sexuality and sexual stereotypes and the understanding of violence and discrimination in sports settings

The roles of men and women in society have changed considerably, and many activities or power positions within organizations, which were exclusive for male individuals in the past, are now more equally shared with women. This is a result of long and hard work undertaken internationally. However, much remains to be done. Although progressively challenged, especially in the last decades, the traditional male and female stereotypes have remained relatively stable and still influence attitudes and behaviours.

Sports provide a very specific social setting. Sporting activities are underpinned by masculine values and (re)construct masculine hegemony (Kidd, 2013; MacDonald, 2014); they were created by men, for men. Chalabaev et al. (2013) refer to sport as a domain where inequalities between men and women are still ubiquitous, and often legitimized by athletes and coaches. Research by Plaza, Boiché, Brunel and Ruchaud (2017) suggests that sports activities are still gendered, both at the explicit and implicit levels, resulting in individuals adjusting their behaviour even outside their awareness. McClung and Blinde (2002) suggest that when analysing sport interactions among athletes, sexual stereotypes should be considered, due to their prevalence and influence on the attitudes and behaviours of athletes, coaches and other stakeholders. The fact that these sexual stereotypes are learned means that they can be changed, reflecting on athletes' attitudes, behaviours and the participation of women.

Men and women globally differ in their styles of interaction with others, and gender differences influence the expression of aggressive behaviours. By traditional gender stereotypes we refer to an overgeneralized belief about masculinity and femininity, both perceived as opposite and separate poles. The stereotypes are, by definition, generalizations which may be erroneous when focusing on particular situations, and therefore result in prejudice. Here we focus on some traditional features associated with male and female genders, aiming to better understand their influence on the behaviour of many of those engaged in sports activities.

A general perceived idea of masculinity is commonly associated with a range of qualities and skills such as physical strength, power, dominance, independence, competitiveness, leadership, capacity to deal with pressure efficiently, as well as resistance and tenacity. Aggressiveness and activity are also considered important (Blaya & Debarbieux, 2003; Lomas, 2007). The idea of being tough may result in a propensity to heterosexual ostentation along with homophobia. When referring to sports settings and the influence of sexual stereotypes on the behaviour of the athletes, García Ferrando (1990) states that the more these qualities are exacerbated, the more masculine one can be perceived to be (and vice versa). Femininity is associated with another range of characteristics opposite to masculinity, namely passivity, non-aggressiveness and fragility (Chalabaev et al., 2013). Women are thought of as less physically active than men.

By splitting masculinity and femininity, those men who do not fit the masculine stereotype are frequently considered as "less masculine" and therefore became more prone to be perceived as different. The same way of thinking can be observed regarding femininity. Women are often dissuaded from lifting weights and being aggressive due to traditional sexual stereotypes, behaviours commonly present in sports activities (Griffin, 1998; United Nations,

2007). Those women who behave in ways not based on traditional gender roles are more prone to be questioned regarding their gender identity, sexual orientation and social role (López-Albalá, 2016).

Sport is an important domain for men in general, and tends to benefit those who engage in it, especially when they have some success. Champion male athletes tend to achieve high social status (Golden, 2008), and women generally find these individuals more sexually attractive (Buss, 2017). The high status obtained by sport champions is not a recent phenomenon. There are historical records from ancient Greece and the Roman Empire that corroborate this hypothesis, especially among gladiators. Considering that athletes who reach high competitive standards represent a very small minority of male athletes, approximately 1% (Leonard, 1996), the evolutionary perspective considers that athletic success may be an aspect of sexual selection (Lombardo, 2012).

Although the participation of females in sports activities has greatly increased in Western societies, some activities including sport are still considered less appropriate for females. This assumption is based on biological ideas, but also on female stereotypes (Ross & Shinew, 2008). Girls are usually channelled into specific sports that are often culturally less valued than those typically played by males (United Nations, 2007).

Examples are the work developed by the English organization Women in Sport, which has developed several campaigns aiming to change sport culture they describe as based on sexism and gender discrimination. Important action has also been taken by Sports England which has launched a campaign entitled This Girl Can, aiming to promote sport among women. This action took place after analysing the results of a survey, which found that many women did not practise sport due to the fear of judgement by others, based on assumptions such as their supposed lower ability to perform sports, and that sport is mainly a male endeavour and women should spend more time doing other activities. UEFA promoted the campaign named Together #WePlayStrong to tackle prejudice against women in football.

In Portugal, the *Federação Portuguesa de Futebol* (Portuguese Football Federation) followed a similar path, and promoted a campaign entitled *Responde em campo* (Answer Back on the Pitch), in order to counteract the stereotyped ideas about football being exclusively for men, and women being less capable of playing it. Recently, a video campaign was financed by the Portuguese Government within the project *Desporto sem Bullying* (Sports without Bullying), composed of six storytelling videos, made by athletes who witnessed and/or suffered different types of discrimination in sport. One of the topics considered was discrimination against women in sport. A Portuguese female athlete, who has been competing internationally for the last 20 years, shared her experience of some of the difficulties in being a woman within the "male environment" of sport, and how sport is still perceived by many as a male territory. These are only a few examples. Many other campaigns and actions have taken place in many different countries all over the world. The results of these actions, along with the great sporting performances of many female athletes, have contributed to challenging the general perception of sport as a male activity.

Traditional gender stereotypes have been progressively challenged in sport and other social settings, especially in the last decades. The power imbalance between men and women in several domains of Western societies has greatly decreased, and women are now much more easily recognized as capable and independent.

Type of sport

The traditional gender stereotypes are also reflected in the taxonomy of sports. Based on their characteristics, different sports are perceived as mostly masculine, feminine or neutral, and sport choice among adolescents is influenced by traditional stereotypes. Boys are more resistant to change the classic patterns than girls, and consequently are more prone to engage in sports which are perceived as according to their gender (Alvariñas-Villaverde, López-Villar, Fernández-Villarino & Alvarez-Esteban, 2017); the participation of girls in traditionally masculine sports is typically considered more acceptable (Boyle, Marshall & Robeson, 2003).

Sports with a higher prevalence of physical contact and use of strength are often associated with male gender (e.g. rugby, football, weightlifting), sports which seek to project the body in space with elegance and harmony are often associated with female gender (e.g. dance, gymnastics, synchronized swimming), and some sports, usually those with no physical contact between opponents, are perceived as more neutral (e.g. swimming, volleyball, tennis). Men are encouraged to engage in strenuous, aggressive, competitive team sports, while women are more often encouraged to embrace aesthetically pleasing activities (Lentillon, 2009; Schmalz & Kerstetter, 2006). Freischlag and Schmidke (1980) suggested that the higher prevalence of violent episodes in male team sports may be partially explained by the high prevalence of the masculine stereotype and militarism in the teams. Tagg (2015) conducted research with male heterosexual athletes of a sport, netball, connoted as feminine, and found that there is stigma surrounding the athletes who practise that sport, because participation goes against the hegemonic idea of masculinity. The author comments that there were no hazing rituals in this sport, unlike other sports where hegemonic masculinity was much more prevalent.

A table with sport characterization, including the type of sport and gender acceptance, may be found in Table 3.3.

Research on bullying in youth sport

Research on bullying has been carried out mainly in schools, but also in other social settings, during childhood, adolescence and adulthood (Monks & Coyne, 2011; Monks et al., 2009). The characteristics of those involved and situational factors have been examined using a variety of methodological approaches and theoretical frameworks (Smith, 2014). However, although research on violence in different sports has been carried out, there has been relatively little on bullying in sport specifically (Brackenridge, Rivers, Gough & Llewellyn, 2007; Evans et al., 2016). The limited research on bullying in sport has shown that its competitive nature may promote and increase peer aggression (Escury & Dudink, 2010) and has yielded some important insights. The moral atmosphere within the sports club has shown to be a good predictor of bullying among young athletes (Steinfeldt, Vaughan, LaFollete & Steinfeldt, 2012). The research developed has also raised some particular methodological and conceptual difficulties, because the sport setting has some important differences compared to the school setting.

Conceptual issues in research on bullying in sport

Although youth sport and school interplay with each other, and there is frequent overlap of the roles enacted by victims and bullies in these two settings, there are also some important differences between them, reflected in the conduct allowed or disapproved of. These differences may include what is perceived as aggressive behaviour. If shouting and name calling can easily be perceived as negative and unacceptable by teachers in school, in many sport situations these acts are considered normal and are frequently enacted and encouraged by coaches. Some coaches at the sports club are also teachers at school, and their conduct changes from one setting to another.

A practical example may illustrate this. When collecting data for this research, the lead author (MN) went to a sports club and saw a coach shouting and saying bad words to their young athletes, while training and playing with them. Later, when being interviewed, the coach told him he was also the physical education teacher of those athletes at school, and his behaviour was totally different from one setting to the other. What he had done at the sports club was part of the game and it was OK; it was a normal and even approved way to communicate and establish a bond with the youngsters. But if done at school, these behaviours would be perceived as misconduct by the teacher.

Previous research on bullying in sport (Brackenridge, Rivers, Gough & Llewellyn, 2007) suggests that victimization may be considered a subjective experience, and describes difficulties in defining a clear threshold between aggression (bullying) and play (banter). This may reflect on bullying research. Volk and Lagzdins (2009) consider that the prevalence of victimization in sport may be under-reported, because it may be perceived as regular sports aggression rather than bullying. If some aggressive behaviours may be more easily identified as such in other social settings (for example, in school), the aggressive and competitive nature of sports, along with the particular "tough mentality" in sport (Stirling, Bridges, Cruz & Mountjoy, 2011), may combine to blur the differences between what are unacceptable aggressive behaviours, and behaviours which are tolerated and considered "part of the game".

Another concept that deserves some attention is hazing, which is also strongly influenced by the interpretation given to victimization. Kirby and Wintrump (2002) split the concepts of *initiation* and *hazing*: *initiation* they consider as a unique pre-existing event for the rookies (new entrants) to be considered definitive members, while *hazing* consists in numerous harmful activities imposed on the rookies that cause negative feelings and can even imperil their physical and mental health. Fisher and Dzikus (2010) described hazing in sport as a rite of passage wherein young athletes, neophytes or rookies are taken through traditional practices (frequently aggressive) by more senior members, in order to initiate them into the next stage of their athletic lives. Hazing rituals are seen as a way for rookies to show their socially approved masculinity. If their behaviour does not follow the accepted social standards, their reputation and social status can be in danger.

According to Kirby and Wintrump (2002), hazing rituals can be considered a form of group bullying due to their abusive nature, with short- and long-term negative consequences. The authors describe hazing as coercive, and consider the rookies to have the dilemma of accepting it or being excluded from the peer group. The power (social status) of the older athletes contributes to the abuse perpetration, especially if combined with institutional support of these practices. This suggests the need to reflect on the role of the coach and other stakeholders within a sports club as regards these hazing rituals. These authors describe some conceptual difficulties in hazing research, for example the fact of it being a taboo topic: the sensitive nature of the research allowed the existence of very different interpretations of the same behaviours, varying from feeling proud of being part of the ritual (banter) to the feeling of being humiliated, and even post-traumatic stress situations (bullying). The authors also highlighted the lack of an agreement in defining hazing, making comparative research between different cultures and countries virtually impossible.

Such conceptual issues have a strong impact on research. Brackenridge, Rivers, Gough and Llewellyn (2007) considered that harassment can be classified based on the criteria of repetition and intention to hurt or cause discomfort to the "victim". The definition of hazing given by Kirby and

Wintrump (2002) also emphasizes the importance of repetition; however, an isolated bullying episode can have a very strong impact, even chronic, and the victim may suffer the same consequences and with the same degree of damage associated with repeated victimization (Escury & Dudink, 2010).

Although the definition of bullying concerns systematic peer abuse, can we also consider an abusive coach–athlete relationship as a type of bullying? Such a relationship includes the criteria of power imbalance, repetition and intentionality. Despite being performed by sports agents, it is not between peers (the definition initially adopted in Chapter 1, called the "standard definition", includes the criterion of being among peers), which raises conceptual questions on this topic. Some research has been developed on emotionally abusive coach–athlete relationships (Stirling, 2009; Stirling & Kerr, 2007, 2009). We return to this topic in our final discussion chapter, in which bullying and abusive coach relationships are included under the same general concept of interpersonal violence in youth sport.

Methodological issues in sport bullying research

Besides the conceptual issues described, research on sport bullying also deals with some particular methodological issues which must be considered, due to their considerable impact on the findings. Escury and Dudink (2010) found that bullying behaviours in sport have some particular features different from school bullying, especially the negative selection processes already existing in youth sports training, which can push lower performing athletes into early withdrawal. The organizational structure of sports clubs is also different from school settings; the latter are more prescribed and organized and make it easier to carry out research and intervention.

Since the prevalence of bullying is measured by the number of times athletes get involved in bullying episodes, and considering that athletes spend much less of their time in sports clubs than in school, it is to be expected that there is a lower prevalence of bullying in sports settings when compared to school settings, as indeed tends to be found (Escury & Dudink, 2010; Evans, Adler, MacDonald & Cote, 2016). In Portugal, youngsters tend to spend many hours at school, and only some of the remaining free time is dedicated to sports. Furthermore, the victimization level in sport may be under-reported because it may be perceived as regular sports aggression rather than bullying (Volk & Lagzdins, 2009); this could mean that some athletes do not report some bullying episodes when surveys are carried out, pushing down the prevalence findings.

A further consideration is that victims in sports training tend to withdraw early because of their experiences (Evans, Adler, MacDonald & Cote, 2016). Athletes who were victimized, especially those who are frequently targeted, tend to abandon sports, which results in these individuals being excluded from statistics when surveys are done. This is an important difference from the school setting, in which students must stay until finishing high school; so, even if they do not feel secure and happy at school, they cannot quit and are forced to cope with bullying. There are a few exceptions like home schooling; although this can be an option in some special cases, and avoids students having to attend school as normal, only a small minority of youngsters are in this situation, and the great majority of them have to spend most of their time in school.

When comparing school to sports bullying, one should also consider that almost all youngsters must go to school, while only the ones who choose sports as their hobby become part of it. Generally, the youngsters who choose to engage in sports activities have some degree of intrinsic motivation to do so, and are more prone to be skilful and athletic. This pre-selection already means that youngsters who are not so skilled will not be part of the survey. All these factors need to be considered if comparing the prevalence of bullying in sports and school settings.

Bullying involvement in sport and its overlap with other social settings

When bullying victims and perpetrators in sport tend to repeatedly enact the same roles in other social settings, it is tempting to infer that individual traits must be responsible. We saw that the individual traits approach considers that the likelihood of involvement in bullying is heavily influenced by personality traits (such as being aggressive or inhibited) and also by family relations (Olweus, 1978; Schott & Sondergaard, 2014). Some research on aggressive behaviours in sports settings supports this approach; athletes victimized in sports clubs are usually victimized in school (Escury & Dudink, 2010; Volk & Lagzdins, 2009). According to Escury and Dudink (2010), 65% of bullying victims in sport are also victimized in other social contexts. Ventura et al. (2019) found a much lower overlap; they reported that 5.4% of the football players victimized at the sports club were also targeted at school. Courtney and Wann (2010) found that individuals who were bullies during childhood, tend to become dysfunctional sports fans as adults. This data suggests that perpetrators in sports settings maintain their social functioning pattern in other contexts and areas of their lives, including personal relations and work environments.

Although the individual traits approach provides important insights into the nature of bullying behaviours, other perspectives must also be considered. The social environment also strongly influences individuals' behaviour, including aggressive behaviours (Brackenridge, Rivers, Gough & Llewellyn, 2007; Jachyna, 2013; Vertommen et al., 2016). Group dynamics and peer pressure also influence individuals' behaviours, and we have seen how these provide important insights into school bullying (Pellegrini & Bartini, 2000; Pellegrini & Long, 2002; Salmivalli, 2010). The conjugation of all these approaches to the understanding of bullying resulted in the multi-level approach, as was described in Chapter 1.

Theoretical framework for bullying in youth sport: Ecological Systems Theory

Urie Bronfenbrenner, a developmental psychologist, was especially known for the development of *Ecological Systems Theory*, which calls attention to a range of environmental influences on child development, operating at different levels (Brofenbrenner, 1979, 1996). These levels were labelled as systems, are complementary and interplay with each other. Ecological Systems Theory has been adapted to different research topics, aiming to provide a wider comprehension of the variables that have an influence on child behaviour. Here we apply it to bullying in youth sports settings. The four systems are briefly described, including examples of each one, as well as the theoretical and practical approaches considered. This model can help us to better understand the multiple factors that influence the prevalence of bullying in youth sport, and the relation between theory and practice.

Micro-system

The micro-system is a setting or location in which the individual may establish face-to-face interactions. The elements exerting influence in psychological development here are leisure activities, social roles played and interpersonal relationships (see Table 2.1).

Table 2.1 Description of the micro-system in relation to sports clubs

Examples	Includes	Approaches considered
Family (parent–youth relationships, inter-parental violence)	Attitudes Poor athletic performance	Individual traits
School (school connectedness, school environment)	Anti-social behaviours Poor anger management skills Occurrence of stressful life events	Group dynamics
Sports club (relations with peers, sports club climate)	Peer group norms	
Individual characteristics	Social competency Sex Age	

Meso-system

The meso-system includes the interrelations between the social settings in which the individual actively participates. The meso-system forces originate from the interrelation of at least two of these social settings. Examples are provided in Table 2.2.

Exo-system

Table 2.3 refers to the exo-system, which concerns one or more social settings in which the individual does not actively participate, but which influence him or her more indirectly; for example, how national policies affect settings such as families, schools or sports clubs, and hence the individual within these settings.

Macro-system

The macro-system refers to the consistency observed within a certain culture or subculture, concerning the shape and content of its micro-, meso- and exo-systems. It refers to the belief systems or ideology underlying these consistencies. The macro-system differs from the exo-system, as it refers to general prototypes existing in the different cultures rather than a specific setting. These general prototypes influence the structures and activities that occur at the more concrete levels. Examples of the macro-system are given in Table 2.4.

A summary of the Ecological Systems approach is shown in Figure 2.1.

Table 2.2 Description of the meso-system in relation to sports clubs

Examples	Includes	Approaches considered
Interrelation of family (parents) with sports club (coach)	Family attitudes about bullying	Family (parent–coach relationship)

Table 2.3 Description of the exo-system in relation to sports clubs

Examples	Includes	Approaches considered
Parents' work place	National sport policies	Governmental sport entities (law)
Exposure to media violence		
Neighbourhood environment		
Sport agencies' policies		

Table 2.4 Description of the macro-system in relation to sports clubs

Examples	Includes	Approaches considered
Cultural norms and beliefs	Community norms	Social environment
Religious affiliation	Community policies	
Social values	Community disorganization	
Habits	Culturally accepted violence and aggression	
Sport mentality		
Sexual stereotypes		

Figure 2.1 Ecological Systems Theory applied to bullying in youth sport.

Characteristics of bullying episodes in youth sport

Having considered theoretical aspects, here we provide a brief description and analysis of the characteristics of bullying episodes based on previous research findings. We consider the types of bullying, the location where episodes occur, the ways in which victims react, and finally the coach–athlete relationship and its implications for bullying occurrence. We finish with a description of some of the consequences of victimization in youth sport.

Although bullying in youth sport is a relatively new research topic, previous research on violence, harassment and bullying in sport has been carried out in various countries including Australia, Canada, Denmark, Israel, the Netherlands, Norway, Turkey, the USA. and the UK (Stirling, Bridges, Cruz & Mountjoy, 2011). The scientific and sporting communities are gradually focusing their attention more consistently on the power dynamics and the quality of peer interactions in youth sport.

Types of bullying

Research by Evans, Adler, MacDonald and Cote (2016) in Canada surveyed 359 adolescent athletes and found that 14% of athletes reported having been bullied in the months prior to data collection. This result is significantly lower than the prevalence of being victimized at school in the same country, estimated as 1 in every 3 adolescent students (Canadian Institute of Health Research Bullying Statistics, 2012) Volk and Lagzdins (2009) also found bullying to be less prevalent in sport than in school. Both studies alert us to the fact that bullying behaviours in sport may involve different type of behaviours than in the school setting. A research study on bullying among young football players was conducted in Cataluña by Ventura et al. (2019), and surveyed 1,972 young athletes (age range 10–14 years old) from both genders (223 female and 1,739 male). From the total sample, 9% of the athletes reported having been victimized.

Different types of bullying behaviours may be observed in youth sport. Those who are perceived as different are often targeted by put downs and jokes, social exclusion or even physical aggression. The results from Ventura et al. (2019) showed that bullying is mostly multidimensional (60.8%), and when a single type of bullying is performed (39.2%), it is mostly verbal (33.2%). Although much less frequent, physical (4.6%), social (0.8%) and cyberbullying (0.6%) were also reported. When bullying episodes are performed by athletes, it appears that their behaviour is influenced by gender norms and significant others, such as peers and coaches (Fisher & Dzikus, 2017).

Homophobic abuse

Some researchers have focused attention on verbal bullying, especially of the homophobic type (Brackenridge, Rivers, Gough & Llewellyn, 2007; Jachyna, 2013; Rivers, 2010). Sports settings provide a framework for homophobic abuse, since sport is considered by many as an arena of masculine power; this perception may contribute to people perceived as homosexual having some difficulties in participating (Hemphill & Symons, 2009). Many insults, jokes or put downs of young athletes are homophobic, focusing on personal attacks related to the sexual orientation of the athletes, or their femininity or masculinity (Fisher & Dzikus, 2010). The homophobic and hypermasculine speech frequently observed in sport is similar to what can often be observed in a school playground among young students. Those who are called gay are labelled as less masculine, not desirable, non-normative, abnormal or as "not belonging to our group" (Brackenridge, Rivers, Gough & Llewellyn, 2007; Roberts, 2008).

Location

Although bullying episodes may occur in different locations, previous research suggests that inside sports clubs the changing room is the "hot spot" for bullying episodes to occur, because it is less supervised by adults (Escury & Dudink, 2010; Evans, Adler, MacDonald & Cote, 2016; Roberts, 2008; Ventura et al., 2019). Jachyna (2013) provides a comprehensive approach to changing rooms in sport, and considers that in these areas heteronormative speeches are frequently made by those who have higher social capital, and those who do not accord to masculine expectations are more prone to be targeted. Victimization in changing rooms can be traumatic to some athletes (Roberts, 2008).

Reactions of the victims

Research on the reactions and coping strategies of the victims of bullying in sports activities has highlighted silence as the most prevalent response (Ventura et al., 2019). There is a silent culture existing in sport, based on a tough mentality, which makes it difficult for victims to break silence and talk about bullying episodes. Asking for help is seen as a sign of weakness (Stirling, Bridges, Cruz & Mountjoy, 2011). Regarding hazing rituals, Kirby and Wintrump (2002) consider that accepting them is equivalent to accepting a secret code, which means that the athletes who do that agree to be part of the "game". This means submitting to aggressive behaviours and keeping silent about them (often by using intellectualized justifications for these). Brackenridge, Rivers, Gough and Llewellyn (2007) focus on homophobic bullying, and discuss the need to break the silence of victims in order to reduce bullying in youth sport. In research on bullying during physical education sessions in school, O'Connor and Graber (2014) argue that the fear felt by victims not only promotes their silence about the bullying episodes, but also increases the probability that bystanders stay quiet and do not act in order to defend the victims, instils feelings of non-safety among students in physical education places, and decreases the will of students to participate in sports activities.

Coach–athlete relationship

The coach–athlete relationship is an important topic, relevant to the understanding of bullying in youth sport. The gender of the coach and athletes may have some influence on the prevalence of bullying. Some data suggests that verbal aggression may be more prevalent in male team sports (Brackenridge, Rivers, Gough & Llewellyn, 2007), due to the tendency for coaches to devalue such bullying behaviours and not to intervene in order to stop them. Women tend to consider bullying behaviours as more severe than men do, and to act more pro-actively (Evans, Adler, MacDonald & Cote, 2016). Homophobic bullying is often perceived by teachers as a normal reaction by youngsters (Roberts, 2008), and some coaches tend to provide tacit approval to such bullying or to take no action due to misinterpretation of the behaviours, perceiving some bullying as normal and desirable banter (Kirby & Wintrump, 2002). Calling someone gay is common between peers but also done by some coaches to their athletes, used as a way to correct and punish undesirable behaviours (Brackenridge, Rivers, Gough & Llewellyn, 2007). When adults ignore verbal forms of aggression, they contribute to the acculturation of bullying by the athletes (O'Connor & Graber, 2014).

Some research has provided information about the educational programmes of coaches and physical education teachers. The contents of some curricula of physical education and pedagogy may promote the idea of dominance by those who are more skilful and athletic in youth sports. It seems important to reflect about the quality of the educational programmes of those who are going to work with children in youth sport, in order to avoid the adoption of myths and beliefs which may promote the expression of coercive behaviour among young athletes (by promoting or simply ignoring them). Youth sport is an educational setting, and should promote positive relations between peers.

One aspect here is the importance given by youngsters to body image. Hill (2015) stated that physical capital is developed (especially among boys) through investment in body shape and physical activity, as a way to increase status inside the peer group (social capital). This suggests that more athletic boys, with a more positive body image are more prone to become popular, while the ones who do not fit this standard are more prone to be rejected.

Consequences of bullying in youth sport

Being bullied in youth sport can have severe personal and social consequences for those involved (Brackenridge, Rivers, Gough & Llewellyn, 2007), similar to some of those often described for school bullying. These include increasing anxiety and suffering from social exclusion, as well as lower self-esteem and motivation to engage in social interactions and the proposed activities. These consequences and symptoms reflect a continued discomfort and worry, which are negative for the development of young athletes.

Regarding the setting of youth sport, there are specific consequences to be mentioned. Victims tend to drop out of sport practice earlier than average (Escury & Dudink, 2010; Evans et al., 2016; Ventura et al., 2019). Usually this is preceded by avoiding areas more prone to the occurrence of bullying, namely the changing rooms, due to the fear of being at the club among some peers who are perceived as threatening. However, other systematic research specifically on the consequences of victimization in sports settings is sadly lacking.

Sport as a social good and promoter of physical and emotional development

The Council of Europe has defined sports as "all forms of physical activity which through casual or organized participation, aim at expressing or improving physical fitness and mental wellbeing, forming social relationships or obtaining results in competitions at all levels" (Council of Europe, 2001). This definition covers a wide range from high performance and professional sports activities to amateur youth sport and their physical and social benefits for athletes. In this book, we mainly focus on youth sports activities, carried out within the scope of sports clubs.

Sports clubs are, besides school, places where many adolescents spend most of their free time and interact with peers, and sports practice is considered by many as a way to promote the physical and social development of young people. Not surprisingly, parents, teachers, physicians, psychologists and other professionals who work with children and adolescents frequently advise them to engage in sports activities.

Since the Lisbon Treaty in 2009, the European Union has made some efforts to promote sport and physical activity at a policy level. Adherence to sport by adolescents constitutes a short- and long-term health issue; sport practice in adolescence is a good predictor of higher levels of sport and physical activity in adulthood, and can help prevent many illnesses.

However, some data suggests that levels of participation in sport and physical activity among adolescents have declined in recent years, regardless of sex and socioeconomic status (Luiggi, Travert & Griffet, 2018).

Evidence for the benefits of sport is easily found in the scientific literature. Many research studies have shown how sports can be positive for the development of youngsters. For example, Twemlow and Sacco (1998) provided evidence that martial arts training helps to strengthen some ego functions, especially the control of aggressive impulses, and that it can be useful to help the development of juveniles with limited verbal capacities. Twemlow et al. (2008) describe an intervention based on this assumption, with positive results: the boys who participated most in the programme (higher number of sessions) showed a lower frequency of aggressive behaviours, and an increase of positive behaviours as bystanders (helping victims) in bullying episodes. Harwood and Lavidor (2017) also argue that participation in martial arts reduces externalizing behaviours and the probability that the juvenile will become an aggressor. Many other studies portray sport as a natural developmental tool, highlighting the positive outcomes derived from its practice.

Limitations of sports activity

Sports may indeed have an important role in promoting the positive development of children and adolescents in different domains of their lives, by teaching important social skills, promoting cooperation, and offering other advantages of being part of a peer group. However, sports are not good *per se*; the quality of the sport experience is influenced by a number of factors well known to scholars and sports professionals.

Andrews and Andrews (2003) argue that sport is an important factor in juvenile rehabilitation, but only if the activities used are selectively chosen, because if the programmes are not adequate, participation in sports activities may have a negative outcome. Continually being the last to be chosen for a team, overtraining or abusive parental practices are some other examples that can make the experience of practising sports very difficult for youngsters.

The limited research on bullying in sport has shown that the competitive nature of sport may promote and increase peer aggression. Escury and Dudink (2010) argue that the engagement of youngsters in sport in general, and team sports in particular, can result in positive personal outcomes for youngsters, because sports may play an important role in the development of social skills and belonging to a group of peers. Sport might foster pro-active behaviours, but also increase aggressiveness. Sport also stimulates competition and induces aggression, which may contribute to an increase in bullying. This train of thought is supported by longitudinal research by Endresen and Olweus (2005). These authors examined what they called Power Sports (boxing, wrestling, weightlifting, oriental martial arts), and concluded that participation in these kinds of activities promoted an increase in anti-social behaviour. These results are contradictory to the research of Twemlow and Sacco (1998) previously described, and suggest that sport practice among adolescents may result in different outcomes depending on culture and context.

Other factors besides involvement in sport further influence violent behaviours and aggressiveness, and a study by Mutz and Baur (2009) in Germany provided an example of this. They examined the relationship between involvement in club-organized sports activities and violent behaviour among adolescents, finding that other factors such as gender, education, social background, immigrant background, family violence and media violence all had a significant effect on violent behaviour, while sports club membership and participation in volunteer organizations had non-significant effects.

Concerning the relation between sport practice and school bullying, Melim and Oliveira (2013) in Portugal examined if participation in sports clubs would decrease the prevalence of victimization in the school setting, and found no relation between these variables. However, Volk and Lagzdins (2009) in Canada found that adolescent girls who were athletes reported higher levels of school bullying than average. In the Netherlands, Escury and Dudink (2010) also reported an overlap between school and sport victimization, and children who were bullies in sports settings were more frequently also bullies in other social settings.

In summary, engagement in sports activities by itself does not necessarily result in positive outcomes for youngsters. Although sports have a strong potential to promote the development of social skills, the quality of sport experience depends on many factors.

Summary and main conclusions

We started this chapter by providing a general framework for the understanding of aggressive behaviours in sport. A brief description of the history of sport, combined with the analysis of the influence of sexual stereotypes on the conduct of athletes was done. This general framework concerning aggressive behaviours in sport was followed by a theoretical framework specifically on bullying in youth sports training.

Bullying in youth sport is clearly a complex topic, with some important differences from school bullying due to the special features of this social setting. Although there is a considerable overlap regarding involvement in bullying as a victim and perpetrator in both social settings, youth sport has some special features which result in research and methodological difficulties in the study of bullying. Three different approaches were combined to provide a deeper understanding of bullying: social environment, individual traits and group dynamics. All of them should be considered when analysing bullying episodes. The Ecological Systems Theory provides a wider perspective about bullying in youth sport, by describing the different social settings which athletes belong to, as well as exploring their relations with each other. We then described what is known about bullying episodes, based on the fairly limited existing literature, and the negative consequences it can have. All this theoretical exposure on violence and bullying in sport preceded a discussion about the benefits of sport. We concluded that sport may be a promoter of development or, on the contrary, it may also promote maladjustment, depending mostly on the quality of the relationships within the sports settings.

Throughout the present book, the concept of bullying is used to refer to a systematic abuse of power, based on the criteria of power imbalance, repetition and intentionality. Both peer-to-peer bullying among young athletes (adolescent) and coach-to-athlete bullying will be considered. The bullying by coaches will be labelled as coach abuse. Both peer bullying and coach abuse are included under the general concept of interpersonal violence, which also includes parental abuse in relation to youth sports settings.

Chapter 3

The Portuguese context

To give readers a deeper understanding of the research described in this book, it is helpful to provide the context of Portugal as a country. In this chapter, we describe the first researches carried out on bullying in Portugal (in school settings), and then provide information about the demography and geography of Portugal; by describing the distribution of the population in Portugal, we justify sampling procedures and other methodological issues. Sports systems vary according to different countries and the organizations which govern them. A description of the Portuguese sports system is provided, including the major bodies responsible for youth sports development and policies, as well as how these interplay and cooperate with each other. We also provide a brief description of the national educational sporting plan for coach certification, developed by the Portuguese Government in recent years. The chapter ends with information about the sports studied, categorized according to the criteria of type (individual, team or combat), gender acceptance and number of federated athletes, as well as information about the number of sports clubs that we studied, and their geographical distribution.

The first researches on bullying in Portugal: the school setting

Research on bullying in Portugal started in the 1990s (Sebastião, 2009), and was mostly focused on the school setting (Pereira et al., 2004). The main objectives were to observe children's behaviour in school yards, to characterize bullies and victims, to report the frequency of bullying behaviours, and to develop a national monitoring and the first national anti-bullying programmes. The instrument mostly used was the adapted version of Olweus's questionnaire for school bullying. Findings from this research showed that there was considerable incidence of bullying in Portuguese schools, that boys were more likely to get involved in bullying episodes than girls (Carvalhosa, 2008; Pereira et al., 2004), and that the hot spot for bullying in schools was the school yard, as already found in research in other Western countries (Carvalhosa, Moleiro & Sales, 2009).

A Portuguese team of researchers participated in an EU-funded project for studying bullying at school, between 1998 and 2002. This was the Nature and Prevention of Bullying: The Causes and Nature of Bullying and Social Exclusion in Schools and the Way of Preventing Them project, funded by the European Training and Mobility of Researchers (TMR) programme, coordinated by Peter K. Smith from Goldsmiths College, University of London. Other EU State Members involved were Germany, Spain, Italy and Portugal. Portugal was represented by researchers from the Faculty of Human Kinetics, University of Lisbon (coordinated by Carlos Neto) and from the Institute of Child Studies, University of Minho (coordinated by Ana Tomás de Ameida).

The main questionnaire used for data collection in this project was developed and adapted by members of the TMR project (Ortega et al., 1999). The main objectives were to define bullying with consideration of the cultural differences between the countries involved, to evaluate and develop research on school bullying, as well as design intervention programmes. Several international meetings and scientific publications resulted from this network.

Research on sports bullying in Portugal: a general framework

Most of the research on bullying has focused on specific and restricted areas of the country. Here, we present a nationwide research on youth sports bullying. In order to deal with the large area covered, the Portuguese territory was divided into four major geographical areas.

Information about Portugal

The geographical area of Portugal is approximately 92,090 km^2. Lisbon (Lisboa in Portuguese) is the capital of Portugal, and the largest city, followed by Oporto. These are the most industrialized cities and have a high population density.

Portuguese cities with a high population density are:

- **Lisbon (Centre)**
- **Oporto (North)**
- Aveiro
- Braga
- Chaves
- **Coimbra (Centre North)**
- Guimarães
- Évora
- Setúbal
- Portimão
- Faro (South).

(Instituto Nacional de Estatística, 2015, *Estatísticas oficiais*)

Although being a relatively small country with a population of around ten million people, a considerable number of Portuguese athletes have achieved important sporting results internationally. Sport in Portugal is an important topic. In recent years, many new sports clubs have been created, and major efforts have been made by some of the major sports bodies and educational centres to improve the quality of youth sport. Most of the sports entities and federations are located in Lisbon.

Portugal is divided into 18 districts; each one has its own capital, and these local authorities play an important role in sports development. Examples of their support are the construction of sports facilities, financing educational programmes for coaches and sports leaders, and/or promoting the development of sporting events. Many sports clubs depend heavily on local governmental support to develop their activities. Although related, school sport and federated sport in clubs are separated and have different purposes. Here, we only consider the sports activities which take place in sports clubs.

The geographical areas of Portugal that we studied covered all the mainland, but not the archipelagos of Azores and Madeira. We divided the mainland into four geographical areas, with one main city in each. Table 3.1 lists which districts are within each geographical area. We sought to achieve a balance between the number of active sports clubs available in each geographical area. North and Centre are the geographical areas with a higher density of sports clubs. Lisbon and Porto are the major cities in Portugal, and

Table 3.1 Description of the geographical areas

Geographical areas	Main city	Districts included
North	Porto	Viana do Castelo
		Braga
		Vila Real
		Bragança
		Porto
		Viseu
		Guarda
Centre North	Coimbra	Aveiro
		Coimbra
		Castelo Branco
		Leiria
Centre	Lisboa	Lisboa
		Santarém
		Portalegre
		Setúbal
South	Faro	Évora
		Beja
		Faro

concentrate the majority of sports clubs. Although the Coimbra, Leiria and Faro districts also have a considerable number of sports clubs, these are surrounded by other less populated districts, with fewer sports clubs.

Portuguese youth sports organizations

The national policies developed in youth sport in Portugal and the promotion of good practices among stakeholders involve the participation of different organizations, ranked according to their functions. Although the Ministry of Sport already existed, nowadays youth sport is included in the Ministry of Education, which has a specific department responsible for it. The Portuguese Government has created an institute to develop and rule on policies in sport, which finances and coordinates the activities of the sports federations. Finally, the sports clubs must be affiliated to these. Figure 3.2 illustrates how these organizations are ranked, and specifies their main functions. Considering the aim and purpose of the research conducted, only federated sports developed within sports clubs were included; specific school sports organizations were not considered in this chart. Figure 3.1 shows the Portuguese area divided into its districts.

Figure 3.1 Map of Portuguese national territory divided into districts.
Source: author.

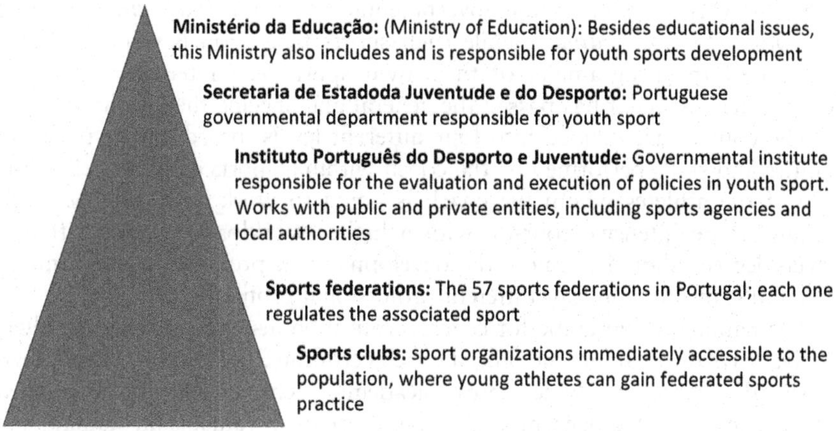

Ministério da Educação: (Ministry of Education): Besides educational issues, this Ministry also includes and is responsible for youth sports development

Secretaria de Estadoda Juventude e do Desporto: Portuguese governmental department responsible for youth sport

Instituto Português do Desporto e Juventude: Governmental institute responsible for the evaluation and execution of policies in youth sport. Works with public and private entities, including sports agencies and local authorities

Sports federations: The 57 sports federations in Portugal; each one regulates the associated sport

Sports clubs: sport organizations immediately accessible to the population, where young athletes can gain federated sports practice

Figure 3.2 Portuguese youth sports organizational chart.
Sources: (Portuguese Law): Decreto-Lei n.° 132/2014; Lei n.° 5/2007; Decreto-Lei n.° 251-A/2015.

The national educational sporting plan: certification for coaches in Portugal

In recent years, an official government policy has been developed, based on increasing concern about the welfare of athletes and the need to enhance good practices among coaches in Portugal (www.idesporto.pt/conteudo.aspx?id=94&idMenu=53). A major effort has been made regarding the creation and reformulation of educational programmes for coaches, their professional certification and the obligation for coaches to attend regular sports courses or seminars in order to obtain the credits needed to renew their certification licence.

Today, in Portugal, it is no longer possible to work as a coach based only on one's previous experience as an athlete. Since 1999, the profession of being a sports coach required professional certification. This new framework led to the publication of a new law in 2008 (Decreto-Lei n.° 248-A/2008, de 31 de dezembro), which stated that it is legally required for a coach to have a certificate to work with athletes within any age range, from amateur to professional levels. This law was complemented with another legal demand, which establishes the norms to obtain the coach certification (Despacho n.° 5061/2010, de 22 de março). These measures are embodied within the national programme for coach certification, which aims to educate and professionalize coaches. This programme is operated by the government and the sports federations.

To achieve the coach certification, it is necessary to attend and be approved through the programme for coach certification, whose contents are divided into three parts: general theory (part I); specific theory (the student's specialist sport) (part II); and finally the practical approach, which consists of an internship at a sports club for one season (part III). The general part was designed by the governmental institution (*Instituto Português do Desporto e Juventude*), while each sports federation is responsible for part II of the programme, of their own sport. The internship can only begin after a student has passed the general and specific theory phases.

The courses are divided into four different levels, based on the responsibilities and skills performed by the coach within a sports club, as well as the age of the athletes whom the coach is going to work with. Higher levels require more intensive courses, with a higher workload, because different levels/degrees should promote the development of progressive and cumulative skills, resulting in four different professional profiles.

The national programme for coach certification also aims to provide alternative ways of obtaining the official coach certificate. Besides the course previously described, in some cases, academic achievements or continued professional development may also be considered valuable in gaining the coach certificate. Regarding academic education, individuals who have a higher education degree in sport sciences may already have the equivalent of the coach certificate (article 10 of the Despacho n.º 5061/2010, de 22 de março), as well as those who have attended courses abroad, or have considerable professional experience which justifies this entry path. In both situations, cases have to be analysed and approved on an individual basis.

The national programme for coach certification includes requirements for coaches to attend seminars and courses certified by the *Instituto Português do Desporto e Juventude* in order to keep themselves updated. Coaches are required to attend educational sessions (courses, seminars, etc.) over a five-year period, corresponding to the validity of the coach certificate. Coaches need to accumulate a certain amount of credits to renew their coach certificate. By the end of this five-year period, if the coach doesn't have enough accumulated credits, the certification cannot be renewed. Those who manage the internships of new coaches within sports clubs need fewer credits to renew the coach certificate because this task also counts as credit accumulation.

The contents of the general part of the educational programme for coaches

In the general part of the programme, designed by the governmental institution responsible for managing sports activity in Portugal, coaches are presented with topics and a corresponding workload, which overlap all sports activities and should be considered in the development of every coach. These contents are described in Table 3.2 (the table does not include level 4; it was directly adapted from the official government website, in which level 4 contents are missing).

Table 3.2 Contents of the coach courses (levels 1, 2 and 3) and workload per topic

Topic	Level		
	I	II	III
Sports didactic	8h		
Sport psychology	4h	8h	10h
Sport pedagogic	6h	10h	10h
Learning and motor behaviour	4h		
Observation and analysis of sports skills	4h		
Body functioning, nutrition and first aid	8h		
Theory and methodology of sports training (individual sports)	6h	16h	20h
Theory and methodology of sports training (team sports)	6h	16h	20h
Ethics and deontology		2h	
Sport physiology		8h	10h
Sport biomechanics		6h	
Nutrition, training and competition		4h	
Sport traumatology (injuries)		4h	
Adapted sport (disabled)	1h	2h	
Preventing doping	2h	2h	2h
Evaluation of sports movement			10h
Sport management			10h
Different specialists co-work within the technical team and undertake sports training (seminar)			12h

Source: Adapted from www.idesporto.pt/conteudo.aspx?id=94&idMenu=53. h = hours of formation (direct contact).

The topics into which consideration of bullying and other types of interpersonal violence could be incorporated are Sport Psychology, and Ethics and Deontology. However, despite many coaches considering bullying and coach abuse to be very important topics, the approach to these is still missing in the programme for coach certification. Although the quality of interpersonal relations, and athlete welfare and ethics, are considered in coach certification, most of the programme contents focus on training skills to enhance sports performance. Although training children to behave properly and show respect for others is a demanding and specialized task, it seems to be perceived as less valuable because its main purposes are not based on winning competitions.

Description of sports studied in our project

The estimated total number of federated athletes in Portugal, in 2015, was 566,366. Table 3.3 provides information about each of the sports studied. It gives a brief description of the main characteristics of each sport, the gender acceptance (sports considered more masculine or feminine) and the number of federated athletes in 2015. Each sport was categorized as an individual, team or combat sport.

Information about the sports clubs

When defining sampling criteria, we aimed to cover a wide area, with all four regions to be approximately equally represented as regards the number of

Table 3.3 Description of the sports studied

Sport	Category	Description/setting	Gender mostly associated	Number (total number of federated athletes in 2015)
Athletics	Individual	No physical contact between opponents. Speed race, long jump	Masculine	15,284
Football	Team	Face-to-face opposition with physical contact. Football field	Masculine	161,167
Gymnastics	Individual	No physical contact between opponents. Projection of body in space (aesthetics)	Feminine	14,004
Handball	Team	Face-to-face opposition with physical contact. Handball field	Masculine	50,224
Judo	Combat	Face-to-face opposition with physical contact. Ring	Masculine	12,208
Rugby	Team	Face-to-face opposition with physical contact. Rugby field	Masculine	6,324
Swimming	Individual	No physical contact between opponents. Swimming pool	Masculine & feminine	43,083
Volleyball	Team	No physical contact between opponents. Volleyball field	Masculine & feminine	43,120
Wrestling	Combat	Opponent's subjugation by using the body. Ring	Masculine	721

Sources: Cashmore (1996), García Ferrando (1990).

sports clubs and participants. We specified that each sport should be represented by at least two sports clubs per region. However, when approaching sports clubs, we realized that there were some logistical issues that we could not control, such as the lack of representativeness of sports clubs that fulfilled the inclusion criteria (age and gender of the athletes) in some geographical areas. This resulted in a few exceptions to the sampling criteria we aimed for. No wrestling clubs were found in the Centre North geographical area, and only one club was found in the North geographical area. Only one volleyball sports club was found in the South geographical area. In these cases, more sports clubs were considered in other geographical areas to compensate for those in which sports clubs were under-represented. In the end, data was collected from a total of 97 sports clubs, representing the 9 sports studied: athletics (12), football (9), gymnastics (11), handball (12), judo (12), rugby (12), swimming (12), volleyball (8) and wrestling (9).

The number of clubs we worked with is divided by category of sport and by geographical area. The majority (41) of the sports clubs were from team sports, with nearly half of these (21) from combat sports. The

Figure 3.3 Geographical distribution of sports clubs.
Source: author.

remaining (35) sports clubs represented individual sports. Regarding the geographical areas, Centre was the most represented (31) followed by North (26) and South (18). The geographical area labelled as Centre North was the least represented, with a total of 18 sports clubs. The geographical distribution of the sports clubs is shown in Figure 3.3.

Summary

The first researches on bullying carried out in Portugal were focused on school settings. The Olweus questionnaire was largely used, which was originally used to describe the prevalence and nature of bullying (mostly) in school yards, and to establish a baseline for this kind of behaviour.

The general organization of youth sport in Portugal is influenced by several governmental bodies with different functions. These interplay with each other, but are responsible for the design and development of youth sports policies, to be applied in schools and sports clubs. In Portugal, it is necessary to undertake an educational programme in order to become a certified coach who can work with youngsters. However, these courses lack bullying and interpersonal violence in their contents, and are mostly focused on seeking to enhance the performance of the athletes and help them achieve victory.

Portugal is divided into 18 districts, which we divided into four geographical areas for research purposes. The sports that we studied were individually described and grouped into three different clusters, based on their common features.

Part II

Research on bullying in youth sports training

Chapter 4
Methods

Introduction

The methods chosen in a research project depend heavily on its objectives. The general aim of this research was to describe the nature and prevalence of bullying episodes in youth sports training, and several specific objectives were also considered. The methods chosen were based on the specific objectives of each study and the concept of bullying considered as systematic peer abuse, influenced by the individual traits of the victims and perpetrators, but also by other variables like group dynamics (role of the bystanders, peer pressure), and the social environment (sports mentality) (see Table 2.1).

Regarding the individual traits approach, Schott and Sondergaard (2014) argue that this approach may contribute to the exclusion of labelled children. If other approaches to the understanding of bullying behaviours are considered beside individual traits, such as the analysis of group dynamics and/or sports culture, then other methods must also be considered. Some researchers using a qualitative approach are influenced by Michel Foucault's understanding of power, which considers that the power imbalance in bullying is a result of social relations (Foucault, 1966, 1985). The individuals who are not in line with social and moral orders (e.g. gender, ethnicity, sexuality) are attacked by those who try to guard the normative moral order (Jachyna, 2013; Schott & Sondergaard, 2014).

Different approaches and perspectives can provide deeper insights. In this research, we compared the perspectives of different participants, namely athletes, coaches and ex-elite athletes. We also used triangulation of methods: both quantitative and qualitative approaches.

The quantitative approach aimed to provide a general perspective and a framework for the development of more in-depth qualitative research. In this quantitative approach a nationwide sample was used to calculate the prevalence of athletes who engaged in bullying episodes as victims, bullies and/or bystanders. The instrument used for data collection was a questionnaire with closed questions, and the information provided was analysed statistically. The qualitative approach aimed to provide complementary information by exploring the symbolic meanings ascribed by stakeholders to bullying behaviours. Here we used smaller samples and interviews, allowing us to explore what participants think about certain topics. Although qualitative data can be quantified and statistically analysed, we opted for a less structured and more in-depth thematic data analysis.

Study 1: quantitative analysis of bullying in youth sports training

Here, we describe the objectives, sample and reasons for using a self-report questionnaire, as well as the procedures followed for designing and validating the instrument. We finish with a description of the procedures used for data collection and analysis.

Objectives

The main objectives of this study were to describe and analyse bullying behaviours in different sports, in male gender youth sports training athletes, across Portugal, and to establish a baseline of its prevalence. Considering the lack of research on this topic, we thought it crucial to have a general overview of its nature and prevalence.

Sample

To achieve this aim, a large and nationwide sample was needed. The participants consisted of 1,458 male youth sports training athletes recruited from 97 sports clubs, spread all over Portugal (see Figure 3.3). A list of all existing clubs was compiled, based on the databases of sports federations, and we contacted a sample of clubs and invited them to participate in the research. The sports clubs were chosen based on having representation across all areas of the country. All the sports clubs approached agreed to participate. The participants were federated athletes from all nine sports being studied, spread across the four geographical areas (clusters), and the age range focused on adolescence.

The Long-Term Athlete Development (LTAD) model (Balyi, Way & Higgs, 2013) was used to categorize athletes according to their age and developmental stage. Due to the fact that age categories of various sports differ, we standardized the age of the athletes according to a common criterion, so comparisons between different sports could be made. The LTAD model was designed considering the psychosocial and biological development of young athletes, and describes the things athletes need to be doing at specific ages and stages. In the *Fundamental* stage (6–10 years), athletes are participating in basic playing. In the *Training to Train* stage (10–14 years) athletes learn how to train more seriously. In the *Training to Compete* stage (14–18 years) athletes are already training with competition in their minds. Finally, in the *Training to Win* stage (>18 years), athletes are training in order to win competitions. The majority of the participants belonged to the Training to Compete stage (77.2%), followed by the Training to Train stage (17.4%), Training to Win stage (5.1%) and Fundamental stage (0.2%). The sports practice length mean value was 6.01 years (SD = 3.6). Thus, the majority of the athletes were adolescents and the sports practice length was generally high.

Type of questions

In this first study, we used a questionnaire with closed questions, which enables us to analyse the prevalence and nature of bullying roles in youth sports training. We can also assess the types of bullying, and feelings reported, by victims, bystanders and bullies; the frequency of bullying episodes, who victims speak with and who approaches perpetrators when bullying occurs (if someone does), and the number of participants involved according to both victims and bullies; the coping strategies of victims; the reasons ascribed by the bystanders for bullying occurrence, and their reactions to bullying episodes; and, finally, the duration and location of victimization episodes and the activities during which they occurred, and the support sources for victims.

Instrument chosen

The methods mostly used to study peer aggression and bullying are self-report questionnaires from peers and adults (Pepler & Craig, 1995; Pellegrini, 1998a; Smith, 2014). Anonymous questionnaires are generally recommended in order to avoid socially desirable answers. When data is collected in a group situation, participants have a higher perception of anonymity, resulting in a higher probability of being honest when asked about sensitive topics (Hoyle, 2002). The setting of the data collection should also be considered; according to Bordens (2002), it has an influence on the sense of anonymity of participants. To enhance this sense of anonymity, participants should be able to fill in their questionnaire in privacy. A researcher should be present to avoid comments between participants and provide support for the task if necessary.

In our study, after questionnaires were filled in, each participant was asked to insert their own questionnaire on top of the pile of those already completed. They were told that the last person to complete their questionnaire should shuffle all the questionnaires on the pile before handing them over to the researcher. This procedure enhanced the sense of anonymity of the last participants, because their questionnaires were now mixed with the others, rather than being the ones on the top of the pile. This procedure was especially important in smaller groups, and we believe it helped participants to be more genuine in their answers.

Questionnaires have considerable advantages compared with other instruments. They are low cost, easy to administer, avoid interviewer bias, and can collect a large amount of data in a short period of time (Bordens, 2002; Trochim, 2001). When anonymous, they may facilitate genuine answers and avoid socially desirable answers of targeted participants when approaching sensitive subjects such as sexuality or anti-social behaviour. Personal delivery of questionnaires helps in explaining the objective of the research to participants. One study found only about 1% of questionnaires were not valid for data analysis (Whitney & Smith, 1993).

A possible weakness of self-report data collection in bullying research is the differences in understanding and interpretation of the questions, such as what is meant by "bullying". This issue can be dealt with effectively if the conceptual definition of bullying is clearly written at the start of the questionnaire, and includes criteria such as power imbalance, intentionality and repetition (Juvonen, Graham & Schuster, 2003). Besides providing this written definition, the researcher should discuss the concept of bullying and victimization orally with the participants before collecting the data, and should also be available to provide support during data collection. In the questionnaire itself, in order to properly estimate victimization and to avoid idiosyncratic interpretations of bullying (Barrio et al., 2008), it is helpful to ask clearly specified questions about specific behaviours (e.g. In what way have you been victimized in the sports club since last season? "They punched, kicked and pushed me", "I was threatened", etc.), quantified data of episodes (e.g. How frequently have you been victimized in the sports club since last season? "1 or 2 times", "3 to 6 times", "Once a week", etc.), and time length of bullying (e.g. For how long did victimization last in the sports club? "One week", "Several weeks", "All this season", etc.), rather than general and subjective information.

The information collected (especially for multiple choice and closed questions) is limited to the items provided for participants to choose from. Questionnaires are not so suitable for collecting in-depth information or finding out about unexplored or new topics. This is why we also chose to have the qualitative dimension in our research programme.

Development of the questionnaire

The Olweus questionnaire, developed in the 1980s and 1990s, is widely used in Europe (Smith, 2014). However, questionnaires for bullying have evolved considerably in the last decade or so (Gutiérrez et al., 2008), leading to reformulations and the creation of new instruments based on scientific developments on this topic. The development of instruments based on psychometric standardized procedures for content validation should be followed (Haynes, 2001), and the research objectives should be clearly specified. The validity and reliability of an instrument are essential to ensure high standards of methodological quality (Vichery, 1998), achieve more elucidating conclusions and provide credibility to the research findings (Hoyle, 2002).

Procedure for validation

The Sport Violence Study and Prevention Questionnaire: Bullying in Sport, which we used, was adapted from a questionnaire used in an EU-funded project for studying bullying at school (Ortega et al., 1999). This first version proved to be a reliable and consistent instrument when used to collect data on school bullying in Portugal. An expert panel composed of four experts in sport psychology and/or psychometrics, and with fluent English skills, oversaw the content validity of the questionnaire and its translation into Portuguese. The reverse translation method (Brislin, 1970) was used, with two of the experts translating the original instrument into Portuguese, and the other two doing the reverse translation. The final version of the instrument was reached when all four experts reached consensus about the accuracy of the translation. The first draft of the newly adapted questionnaire was made, based on scientific literature and then submitted for evaluation by an expert panel.

EXPERT PANEL

To test the suitability of an existing questionnaire for collecting data from a different sample to the one for which it was originally designed, it should be evaluated by people who have a deep knowledge of the elements being studied, in order to evaluate the content validity and suggest the elimination and/or reformulation of any questions that are not appropriate (Hill & Hill, 2005). The use of an expert panel is a possible methodological option. Experts are asked to analyse the instrument, and to provide a reasoned opinion about its validity to measure the topic being studied, by providing an evaluation of the pertinence of each dimension and item of the instrument (Leedy & Ormrod, 2009).

The expert panel we used was composed of four male and female researchers, each with different theoretical backgrounds, but all familiar with research on bullying. The purpose of the research was explained, together with what was expected from them concerning the validation process. Each expert received a guidance document which contained the description of the instrument, an explanation about how to evaluate the questionnaire and a quotation grid. The experts were also asked to provide a global qualitative evaluation of the instrument, and to evaluate the content validity of each item of the questionnaire, according to a 3-point scale (1 = essential; 2 = important but not essential; 3 = unnecessary). This quantitative approach was complemented by a qualitative one. The experts were asked to provide a comment about the general capacity for the questionnaire to assess bullying in sport, about the quality of its design, to provide a general comment, and also to refer what items they considered should be deleted or added (if there were any).

An adjusted Kappa was used (Multirater Kappa Free, Randolph, 2010) to calculate the level of agreement between experts, and the value of 0.92 obtained was considered satisfactory. The four experts on bullying evaluated each of the 22 questions about bullying in sport, by expressing their agreement or disagreement. The experts also provided similar opinions about the instrument and consider it valid. The results from their evaluation were very positive and tiebreaks were not needed.

Based on the comments, a few reformulations were considered. This process led to the second version of the questionnaire, which was then submitted to a pilot test.

PILOT TEST

The pilot test is very useful for all researches and is considered an important procedure in instrument development (Litwin, 1995). It is a trial to ensure that the data collection can happen as planned, and to allow any unexpected problems to be dealt with before the full study commences (Fink, 1985). In ideal conditions, it should be done with participants with similar characteristics to those in the planned research sample, and is expected to lead to some final reformulations.

We piloted the questionnaire with 92 young male athletes, within the selected age range and covering each of the sports studied: athletics (5), football (14), gymnastics (6), handball (13), judo (12), rugby (15), swimming (10), volleyball (11) and wrestling (6). We approached one sports club for each sport studied and restricted our data collection to the Lisbon geographical area. The participants were informed about the purpose of the research and asked to make a critical analysis of the content of the questionnaire and the clarity of the questions asked. The pilot test resulted in a few minor changes proposed by the participants. This led to a pre-final version of the questionnaire, which was submitted to a test-retest reliability assessment.

TEST-RETEST

One way to assess the reliability of a questionnaire is by calculating its temporal stability. This is done by collecting data from the same sample, at two different periods of time (Leedy & Ormrod, 2009) called test-retest. This procedure is the simplest way to calculate reliability (Bordens, 2002). When the second data collection is finished, the researcher should calculate the correlation between the results of both questionnaires. The final result should be higher than 0.70 to consider the instrument to be reliable (Fink, 1985; Litwin, 1995).

The time lag between first and second data collection is critical. It should be neither too short nor too long (Hoyle, 2002). According to Bordens (2002), this time lag depends on the variables being studied and several weeks are usually enough, and Hill and Hill (2005) suggest the time gap should be at least one week.

For our purposes, to test reliability, the questionnaire was filled in by a group of four athletes with the same characteristics as the research sample. The procedure was repeated two weeks later, and the first and second versions of the questionnaire were compared for each individual.

The correlation between data collected in both test and retest procedures was 0.97 (much higher than 0.70), allowing us to conclude that the questionnaire is reliable. Once the adaptation process was finished, and following several minor reformulations and corrections, the final version of the questionnaire was reached. This is provided in Appendix 1.

Questionnaire description

The final questionnaire was composed of 23 questions, divided into four sections. Section one collected general data about

- The type of sport;
- Geographical area of the sports club;
- The age of the athletes;
- The number of years of sports practice;
- Number of friends inside the peer group.

Section two collected data about participation in bullying episodes as a victim. The variables considered were

- Frequency of bullying episodes (occasional: 1–2 times or 3–6 times since the beginning of the season two months ago; or repeated: once a week or many times a week);
- Duration (low: one week or several weeks; or high: all this season or since many seasons ago);
- Location (inside club; in competition);
- Bullying types (verbal, social, physical, cyber);

- Number of peers involved in bullying episodes (individual; group);
- Activities in which bullying occurred (training; competition);
- Feelings towards bullying (positive; negative; avoidance; neutrality);
- Coping strategies used (focused on emotion; focused on problem solving; or both);
- Who victims speak with about bullying (silence; peers; family; adults inside club);
- Support sources (coach; family; peers) (no support; support with negative results; support with positive results).

Section three collected data about participation in bullying episodes as a bystander. The variables considered were

- Types of bullying (verbal; social; physical; cyber);
- Reactions towards bullying episodes (join bullying; being victimized; observe; defend victims);
- Feelings towards bullying (positive; negative; avoidance; neutrality);
- Reasons ascribed for bullying (bullies and/or victims' accountability).

Section four collected data about

- Participation in bullying episodes as a bully, and considered frequency (occasional: 1–2 times or 3–6 times since the beginning of the season two months ago; or repeated: once a week or many times a week);
- Number of peers involved (individual; group);
- Types of bullying (verbal; social; physical; cyber);
- Feelings towards bullying (positive; negative; avoidance; neutrality);
- Who approaches perpetrators when bullying occurs (silence; peers; family; adults inside club).

The questions regarding bullying frequency, duration, number of athletes involved in bullying episodes and victims' support sources (family, coach, peers) were multiple choice and only allowed for one answer to be given. However, the questions regarding types of bullying, location, activities, feelings, communication (who victims speak with, and who approaches perpetrators about bullying), victims' coping strategies and bystanders' reactions, allowed the participant to give more than one response. For example, an athlete could report more than one type of bullying (e.g. verbal and social). In such cases of multiple answers, we made a sum of the number of responses given, referring to this as multiple types.

Procedure for data collection

Data were collected two months after the beginning of the season for each sport. Bullying episodes tend to peak in the initial formation of peer groups when status is uncertain and affiliative bonds are weaker, and then gradually decrease over time (Pellegrini, 2003). For athletics, football, gymnastics, handball, rugby, swimming and volleyball, data collection took place in October–November (2013 and 2014); since judo and wrestling sports begin the season in January, data collection took place in March–April of 2013.

All data was collected directly in the sports clubs, by the first author (MN). In the verbal briefing before distribution of the questionnaire, a bullying definition was provided, as an aggressive and anti-social behaviour between peers, based on the criteria of intentionality, repetition and power imbalance between bullies and victims; practical examples were mentioned, and the concept clarified in order to avoid any misunderstanding. Then the questionnaires were given to the participants, who were asked to situate themselves throughout the available training area in order to ensure privacy of responses. Once finished, participants were asked to put the questionnaires in a pile, face down. The last athlete to put their questionnaire in the pile should shuffle them all, and only then were the questionnaires collected by the researcher. This procedure increased the sense of anonymity, and was especially useful in smaller groups of participants.

Data analysis

Each of the 23 questions in the questionnaire had a multiple choice of answers. In some questions, the participants' could only choose one answer item, because these were mutually exclusive (e.g. number of good friends), while in others they could choose more than one possible answer (e.g. types of bullying behaviours observed).

The information collected needed to be organized into different variables, to allow comparisons and establishment of relations between them when performing statistical analysis. Although some items clearly related to certain theoretical concepts (e.g. types of bullying), others collected information about concrete topics, and were not related to any theoretical concept (e.g. location of bullying episodes). When the items did not assess specific concepts, they could be categorized based on criteria defined by the researcher. Location of victimization is a good example. Here, the researcher may opt to organize it into two categories (victimization inside the sports club vs. victimization outside the sports club), or prefer to analyse each item separately, avoiding putting them together in pre-defined categories. In some cases, there may be more than one valid way to treat data. This allows us to look at the same data from different angles, which may provide new insights. Still, to proceed with statistical analysis, data must be organized according to a logical and explicit pattern.

The items of each question were categorized according to the evaluation of the researcher, and this categorization procedure was later validated by two experts in scientific research and bullying. Each of the instrument questions was analysed, and the best way to categorize its items by grouping them under a common concept was discussed. When the experts provided overall approval, the categorization procedure of the variables was finished.

For statistical analysis of the data collected, we used frequency distributions and chi-square tests. In sections two, three and four of the questionnaire, which correspond to the victim, bystander and bully perspectives, participants were divided into victims, bullies, bystanders and respondents who did not report experiencing or witnessing any bullying episodes. In a further analysis, we only considered the athletes who got involved in bullying episodes as a victim, bystander or bully, and analysed the relations between these roles and the variables of each section. Statistical significance was set at $p < 0.05$ and the Holmes-Bonferroni correction was applied to counteract the problem of multiple comparisons. When the probability of the chi-square test was less than or equal to the alpha value, we compared the size of the standardized residuals to the critical values that correspond to an alpha of 0.05 (±1.96) and report the statistically significant results.

Studies 2, 3 and 4: qualitative analysis of bullying in youth sports training

In this section, the method used in the qualitative studies is described. The common procedures in the design and validation of all three interview scripts are described together. Some specific explanation is given for each study as regards the description of the participants, the instrument description and the procedures for data collection.

Objectives

Studies 2, 3 and 4 aimed to provide an in-depth complementary methodological approach to Study 1. Qualitative methods allow enquiry about complex processes which contribute to understanding bullying, including attention to group dynamics (Schott & Sondergaard, 2014). The objectives were to explore how different stakeholders (young athletes, coaches, ex-elite athletes) perceived and experienced bullying, and to compare their points of view in order to achieve a more complex and in-depth perspective of bullying in youth sports training.

Samples

Study 2

The participants were 127 adolescent male athletes recruited from 20 sports clubs spread across Portugal. All four geographical areas previously defined (North, Centre North, Centre and South) and all nine different sports (athletics, football, gymnastics, handball, judo, rugby, swimming, volleyball, wrestling) were represented in our sample.

Study 3

The participants were 32 coaches, of both genders, recruited from the same sports clubs in which the Study 1 interviews took place; we interviewed the coaches of the athletes who participated in Study 1, in order to obtain data about their point of view and compare it with their own athletes' perspectives.

Study 4

We interviewed one ex-elite athlete from each of the sports studied. The participants were ex-athletes who were previously involved in elite competition and had achieved national and/or international recognition (e.g. won national and international competitions, been part of the Portuguese national teams, participated in Olympic Games). All participants were male, and some also had experience as coaches. The age range was from 35 to 58 years old. The average age in years of each participant, from youngest to oldest, was: gymnastics – 35, handball – 39, swimming – 40, football – 42, rugby and wrestling – 45, judo – 48, athletics – 52 and volleyball – 58.

Type of questions

The interview is used as a means of data collection, in order to understand how individuals think and feel about certain topics. The scripts of all three interviews had common topics related to bullying circumstances, roles and practical implications; however, each group of participants also answered some specific questions.

The questions were open ended; participants were asked to describe bullying episodes in which they had participated, and to share their feelings and thoughts about it. The interviewer facilitated the participants in covering all the topics considered in the script.

Instrument chosen

Interviewing is a very common means of collecting data in qualitative research and one of the most used methods to collect data in qualitative research on bullying (Smith, 2014). Interviews can be classified according to their degree of structure: in qualitative research, they are usually open ended or semi-structured and designed to cover some critical topics. These types of interviews can be more flexible, allowing the collection of more relevant information. Some specific topics are covered, but the order in which the questions are asked need not be precisely specified or followed (Trochim, 2001).

Interviews are a good way to collect data in narrative and autobiographical research (Clandinin & Caine, 2008; Freeman, 2008). The topic of bullying has been studied using this type of methodology. Cooper and Nickerson (2012) analysed the personal histories of parents who had been victimized during childhood, and its relation with the coping strategies used and the level of concern about bullying among children. A recall study by Boulton (2012) analysed the relation between different types of victimization and actual social anxiety. Some research has focused on the relation between involvement in bullying episodes in childhood, and later consequences in adulthood: for example, involvement in bullying episodes in the school setting and the quality of life as an adult (Allison, Roegen & Reinfeld-Kirkman, 2009), or involvement in bullying episodes during childhood and adolescence and its relation with psychological problems in adulthood (Sesar, Barisic, Pandza & Dodag, 2012).

Concerning interpersonal violence in the sports setting, research using interviews for data collection has focused on abusive coach patterns (Stirling & Kerr, 2007, 2009) and homophobic bullying in sports areas inside school (Roberts, 2008).

Development of an interview script

The procedures for designing an interview script are similar to the ones used for creating a questionnaire. It starts by identifying the research topic, followed by the creation of the first draft of the script, which includes the selection of important topics to be covered, and the elaboration of the questions. The questions should be neutral, clear and individual, and based on the scientific literature existing about the subject, the interviewer's knowledge and the opinion of those who work in the area. The script should be submitted to validation processes, namely the evaluation of its content by an expert panel and finally a pilot test. During the procedures to create an interview script, some topics may be added and/or eliminated (King, 2004), and the thematic dimensions and dynamics of each question must be evaluated (Kvale, 1996).

Exploratory interviews, such as those we planned, seek depth and aim to develop new ideas and research hypotheses, and to understand how people think and feel about the topics of the script (Patton, 1990). The interviewee is an active participant in the research, and the relationship established with this person should be taken into account (King, 2004). Variability among the interviewers should be minimized (Patton, 1990) and, ideally, all participants are interviewed by the same person (Breakwell, 1995). The interview should start with a briefing, in which the aim of the interview is explained and permission asked to record the conversation; once data is collected, the researcher should give a debriefing (Kvale, 1996), in which what the person said is summarized, and the interviewee is allowed to add or modify this (Lincoln & Guba, 1985). This procedure gives more validity to the data collected.

When the script is less structured, interviews should be recorded (Leedy & Ormrod, 2009), but only if the interviewed person agrees. Recording allows the researcher to make a transcription of the content; this is a very slow process, but helps raise the quality of the data (Patton, 1990). Transcription should be followed by content analysis.

Procedures for validation

To design and validate the scripts, we followed the recommendations of Daniels, Gabel and Hughes (2012). We designed an interview script based on scientific literature on the topic, which was first validated by an expert panel and then submitted to a pilot test.

EXPERT PANEL

The first draft of each script was analysed and validated by three experts on scientific research and bullying, who received a document with tables to be filled in with information about the questions of the script, and another document with instructions about how to perform their task. Once the evaluation process was performed by filling in the tables, the documents were collected and the data provided analysed, resulting in some minor changes. The second draft of the scripts resulted from this procedure, and this was then submitted to a pilot test.

PILOT TEST

A pilot test aims to correct possible ambiguities or misunderstandings (Bordens, 2002) and to ensure the instructions given by the interviewer are clearly understood. It is also important to verify if any important topic has been left out of the script, and to estimate how long the interview takes (Kvale, 1996). The pilot testing should be carried out with participants with similar characteristics to the ones of the final sample (Breakwell, 1995).

The pilot tests of the scripts for both athletes and ex-elite athletes were undertaken with three participants each, and the pilot test of scripts for coaches had two participants. In all cases, the participants in the pilot tests had similar characteristics to the research participants who took part in the main studies. Based on the information collected, some reformulations were made. From this last validation procedure the third and final versions of the interview scripts resulted, which were used for data collection.

Interview description: Study 2

The athletes were interviewed based on the previously designed script, which started by asking participants to express their thoughts about bullying prevalence in youth sport, and then report on their own involvement as perpetrators, victims and/or bystanders. The script was divided into three sections, which corresponded to these three roles, and some specific questions were asked according to the role played by the participant in bullying episodes. There was a thematic overlap across all three sections of the script, concerning bullying types, location of bullying episodes, number of peers involved, profiles of victims and perpetrators, social setting overlap and the role of the coach. Both victims' and bystanders' scripts also asked about coping strategies used to deal with bullying, and perpetrators' scripts included questions about behavioural inhibiting mechanisms. The interview script is given in full in Appendix 2.

Interview description: Study 3

The perspective of the coaches were important to complement the information of the athletes' narratives, and also to provide some new information. Although coaches may get involved in bullying episodes (implicitly or explicitly), their perspective is more like an outsider who observes peer relations from a different angle from them. Besides topics related to bullying circumstances, roles and practical implications (also described in the athletes' script), in section one the coaches' script also included questions about conceptual issues. In section two, about bullying circumstances and types of bullying, the reasons for its occurrence and social setting overlap were explored, but some new topics were also added like the crucial moments for bullying occurrence, the existence of hazing rituals, and the perception of changes in bullying behaviours over time. In section three, roles and information about the profiles and social status of victims and bullies was collected. Finally, in section four practical implications, prevention and intervention strategies were discussed. The interview script is given in full in Appendix 3.

Interview description: Study 4

The script designed for ex-elite athletes had a similar structure to the one designed for adolescent athletes, because these participants were also asked to report their direct involvement in bullying, although from a retrospective perspective. The participants were asked to express their thoughts about bullying prevalence in youth sport, reporting on their own involvement as perpetrators, victims and/or bystanders. When athletes reported not having been involved in bullying episodes, their opinion was asked about the importance of the topic, and the possible relationship between victimization and early drop out of sport. The remaining script was divided into three sections, which corresponded to involvement as victim, bystander and perpetrator. There was a thematic overlap to the three sections of the script, concerning frequency and location of the episodes, bullying types, number of peers involved, reasons for bullying, profiles of victims and perpetrators, feelings towards bullying and social setting overlap. Both victims' and bystanders' scripts also considered coping strategies used to deal with bullying, and the perpetrators' script included questions about empathy. The interview script is given in full in Appendix 4.

Procedures for data collection (Studies 2, 3 and 4)

Study 2

All the sports clubs approached agreed to participate. Each one was sent a letter by post which contained a protocol with a research description, an ethical concerns statement and informed consent forms for athletes. On the day agreed with the sports club for data collection, the researcher collected the informed consent forms signed by athletes' parents or legal tutors authorizing them to participate in the research, before collecting any data. All data was collected directly in the sports clubs, and interviews were conducted in spaces inside the sports clubs which allowed participants to have privacy. The same researcher (MN) gathered all the data.

In the briefing before starting the interview, participants were asked if they agreed to the use of an audio recorder in order to facilitate the transcription of the interview and data analysis; they were assured that the audio records would be deleted after being transcribed. All participants agreed to this. Participants were told that any verbal content which could possibly identify people, locals or institutions would be codified during transcription, ensuring participants' anonymity. They were also told that their involvement was voluntary and that they could quit whenever they wanted to. The researcher also mentioned that after finishing the interview, the participants could choose some contents to be off the record, and that access to the interview contents would not be shared with other people. After these procedures, a definition of bullying was provided, as an aggressive and anti-social behaviour between peers, based on the criteria of intentionality, repetition and power imbalance between bullies and victims; practical examples were mentioned, and the concept clarified in order to avoid any misunderstanding.

The interviews started by questioning athletes about their possible involvement in bullying episodes in sports settings. Participants who answered that they had not been involved in bullying episodes were asked about the reasons for this not happening. Participants who had been involved in bullying episodes were asked to describe them spontaneously. Questions were asked when certain topics of the script were not covered by the athletes' answers, or when a deeper explanation or clarification was needed. The questions varied according to the role of the participant in bullying episodes as victim, bystander and/or perpetrator. Frequently, athletes reported different roles in their involvement in bullying episodes. In the end, a debriefing was made: participants were asked if they wanted to share some extra information, and if some contents should be deleted and not transcribed. Verbal contents recorded were transcribed and analysed.

Study 3

Coaches were approached once the interviews of their group of athletes were finished, and invited to participate in the research. All interviews were undertaken in a location with privacy, by the same researcher and were recorded. Both briefing and debriefing provided were similar to the ones given to athletes. Verbal contents recorded were transcribed and analysed.

Study 4

The ex-elite athletes were approached personally or by telephone. Information regarding the purpose of the research, procedures and ethical precautions was provided. Once the invitation to participate was accepted, data collection was scheduled. All interviews were undertaken in a location with privacy, by the same researcher and were recorded. A briefing and a debriefing were also considered, as described before for athletes' and coaches' interviews. Verbal contents recorded were transcribed and analysed.

General information

The order in which the questions were asked was not standardized; the objective was to collect as much information as possible about each topic. The language was adapted to the participants, and special care was taken to avoid suggestive or leading questions. This procedural flexibility aimed to increase the validity of the data collected by making the participants' speech more spontaneous and by following up interesting aspects of the responses, when they occurred.

When making the transcriptions, some notes were written (e.g. non-verbal behaviours, voice tone) in order to provide extra information considered important in data analysis. When this task was finished, the audio records were destroyed.

Regarding the examples of text quotes given in Chapters 7, 8 and 9, special attention was taken to avoid decontextualized citations, which could express different ideas from those actually intended by the interviewee.

Data analysis

To analyse the data collected, we used content analysis. This is characterized by well-defined procedures and objectives, and aims to examine systematically and in detail the content of the interviews. Content analysis identifies patterns, topics and concepts, in which raw data become organized into categories or themes (Krippendorff, 1980). The technique is characterized by objectivity and systematization (Bordens, 2002). The process of analysis should be described in detail and be explicit, in order to be replicable (Krippendorff, 1980; Leedy & Ormrod, 2009). This detailed description of the coding process of the categories gives fidelity to the whole process. Fidelity is ensured by the methodological process, which decreases ambiguity and, consequently, increases fidelity.

The analysis of the data should be exhaustive, representative and pertinent (Krippendorff, 1980). The categorization process must be precise, and the categories created must be clearly defined (Bordens, 2002). Categories may be created *posteriori*. In these cases, the data analysis consists of open procedures, which means that categories are generated during the process of data analysis, depending on the data being analysed and also on the criteria adopted by the researcher to define it (Krippendorff, 1980). This procedure allows for exploratory analysis of the data.

The coding process is crucial in content analysis and needs to be explicitly described. When analysing data, each unit should be inserted in a table, which allows for later use of statistical analysis, although such quantitative analysis is optional as a further approach (Leedy & Ormrod, 2009). Content analysis is purely descriptive, which means no establishment of causal relations between the variables is aimed for (Bordens, 2002).

The interviews started with open-ended questions, asking the participants to share their thoughts about bullying in youth sports training, based on episodes reported by them. When some of topics in the script were not covered by the narratives of the participants, they were directly asked about. Some of the topics analysed were not initially part of the script; however, if they occurred repeatedly and were important for the understanding of bullying, they were included in the analysis.

Considering the exploratory nature of the three studies, *a posteriori* categorization was undertaken, which led to the creation of 133 categories, each having an operational definition. During the categorization process, some categories were deleted, or merged (creating a wider one), according to the research need. The content analysis was carried out by hand; although the use of software may facilitate content analysis, it does not ensure any extra quality to the analysis, because it depends on how the researcher performs the task (Patton, 2002).

There is no single definitive and objective perspective of social reality, which means that different researchers can interpret the same data differently. Peer revision aims to give validity to the process, help the solitary researcher, and promote insights on the developing theory (Burnard et al., 2008). Here, the categorization procedure was validated by two experts on scientific research and bullying. Overall, approximately 10% of the total content of all data collected was analysed, which corresponded to 15 interviews. Concerning the high amount of data, and the high level of agreement between codifiers (experts), this procedure gave validity to the categorization process previously performed by the researcher. The sample analysed included interviews from all nine sports studied. For each analysis unit (n = 940) an independent evaluation was made by each of the experts, who expressed agreement or disagreement with the categorization process. The experts were also asked to comment on the validity of the categories defined, and the level of accuracy of the operational definitions provided for each. Cohen's Kappa was calculated as a measure of the inter-rater agreement for the qualitative items. A value of 0.80 or higher would be considered as very good; here the result obtained was 0.825.

The data collected was organized into tables in order to efficiently deal with the considerable amount of information. Although categories have been quantified, for methodological and epistemological reasons the results presented in Chapters 7, 8 and 9 correspond to the data most important to the understanding of bullying in youth sport, which does not necessarily mean the most prevalent categories. Every single part of the speech of the participants needed to be considered and categorized for content analysis purposes; however, some data collected was not relevant. By most important data, we mean data that provides useful information to describe and analyse bullying in sport.

Ethical issues

Athletes

When agreeing to participate, sports clubs signed an informed consent form in which the research design, objectives and procedures were described, as well as ethical precautions. Before data collection, athletes' own informed consents were collected. The first author (MN) met with the athletes to clarify the objectives and procedures, making it clear that participation was voluntary. They were assured that the data would be confidential and not used beyond the scope of the investigation. Additionally, for athletes under 18 years old, the parents' or tutors' informed consent was obtained.

Coaches

Coaches were approached after interviews were undertaken with their group of athletes. Information regarding the purpose of the research, procedures and ethical precautions were provided and an informed consent form was signed. Permission was asked to record the interview (it was always given).

Ex-elite athletes

When agreeing to participate, the ex-elite athletes were informed about the purpose of the research, procedures and ethical precautions. Before starting the interview, an informed consent form was signed and the researcher asked for permission to record the interview (always given). The participants were told that they could review their interview once transcribed, and ask to delete some contents which they might consider inappropriate.

All the stakeholders approached agreed to participate in the research, and all procedures were conducted in accordance with the Code of Ethics for Research of the Faculty of Human Kinetics at the University of Lisbon, Portugal.

Summary

To better address bullying, when studying it, different methods should be employed. A quantitative approach was best to establish a baseline for the prevalence and nature of bullying behaviours. To achieve this, a questionnaire was used for data collection, with a large and nationwide sample. Statistical analysis was used to analyse this quantitative data.

The later qualitative approach aimed to seek the symbolic meanings of bullying behaviours, to describe and explain peer interactions, their motivations and perceptions. Different stakeholders (athletes, coaches and ex-elite athletes) were interviewed, providing complementary perspectives on bullying. Content analysis was used for the data obtained.

The description of the questionnaire, and of the interview scripts used, was provided, together with details of their construction and validation.

Chapter 5

Frequency of bullying behaviours

Introduction

Most previous studies of bullying in sport have been on relatively small samples. Here, we aimed to study a range of issues in a substantial and national sample. The main objectives were to describe and analyse bullying behaviours in different sports, in male gender youth sports training athletes, across Portugal. To collect this data in order to establish a baseline for bullying prevalence, we used a quantitative approach based on the questionnaire previously described (see Chapter 4).

In this chapter, we analyse the prevalence of bullying roles in youth sports training considering the frequency of bullying episodes reported by victims, bystanders and bullies, as well as the influence of general variables like differences between sports and geographical areas, and the number of good friends in the sports club. Although the age of the athletes is an important variable, we will only focus on it in the next chapter when analysing victims and perpetrators separately. All participants reported the types of bullying and feelings towards bullying episodes, which led to the analysis of the prevalence of these common variables.

Prevalence of bullying behaviours

In total, 44% of the athletes did not report any involvement in bullying episodes, even as a bystander; while the remaining 56% reported being involved as either a victim, bystander and/or bully. Altogether 10.0% reported being a victim (defined as victimization frequency of at least 1–2 times since the beginning of the season), 11.3% as bullies (defined as involved in episodes as a bully at least 1–2 times since the beginning of the season) and 34.7% as bystanders (defined as having seen peers being victimized by some type of bullying behaviour since the beginning of the season). In some cases, there was an overlap of roles with 2.7% being bully-victims (defined as victimization frequency and involvement in bullying episodes as a bully, at least 1–2 times since the beginning of the season), 6.1% as victim-bystanders (defined as victimization frequency at least 1–2 times and as having seen peers being victimized by some type of bullying behaviour since the beginning of the season), 9.2% as bully-bystanders (defined as involvement in bullying episodes as a bully at least 1–2 times, and as having seen peers being victimized by some type of bullying behaviour since the beginning of the season) and 2.4% reported involvement in bullying episodes as victims, bullies and bystanders. These percentages of involvement in bullying episodes as victim, bully, bystander and mixed roles are shown in Figure 5.1.

This data was important to establish a baseline for bullying in sports training (Nery, Neto, Rosado & Smith, 2018). When compared with the frequency reported for bullying at school in Portugal (Pereira, 2008; Rebolo Marques & Neto, 2001), the frequency of bullying episodes in sports clubs appears to be lower. Some factors should be considered when considering these results. Escury and Dudink (2010) suggested that victimization frequency in sport could be lower when compared to school bullying because victims have a tendency to abandon sports practice early due to victimization. Unlike school attendance, sports practice is not obligatory, which means that the athletes who have been victimized and have quit sports practice would not be part of the sample. In addition, Volk and Lagzdins (2009) suggest that lower percentages found in bullying in sport may be due to victimization in sport being considered as part of the normal aggression existing in this social context, rather than being considered as bullying.

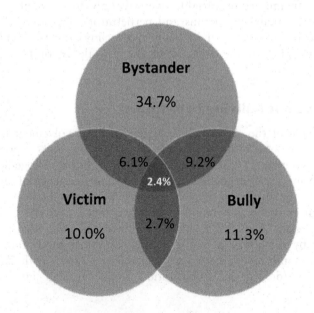

Figure 5.1 Percentages of different roles of athletes involved in bullying episodes.

Involvement in bullying episodes

Research hypotheses about the involvement in bullying episodes and the influence of general variables

The prevalence of bullying behaviours may vary according to sports differences (type of sport and female gender acceptance), geographical area, and number of good friends in the sports club. The possible influence of these variables in the prevalence of victimization is analysed next. For this, we considered all athletes, including those who have not reported being victimized. We aimed to examine if these variables had some influence on overall reports regarding possible victimization.

Hypothesis 1: frequency of victimization and type of sport (individual, team, combat)

Different sports have different properties and particular cultures, and these may exert some influence on the prevalence of bullying behaviours. Many coaches discuss which is the best sport for promoting the development of youngsters. In the interviews conducted with coaches, it was possible to observe a clear tendency of coaches to consider his/her type of sport as the best to promote social improvement of youngsters, which according to their perspective resulted in a lower prevalence of bullying. Many arguments were used but no definitive answer was reached as to whether there were some sports that promoted more positive interactions between teammates than others. If team sports were labelled as ideal to promote interaction between teammates, combat sports were frequently thought of as a way to promote the sublimation of aggressive impulses, and other individual sports were perceived as ideal for promoting discipline within a close relationship with the coach. Previous research has analysed the prevalence of bullying behaviours in different sports. Escury and Dudink (2010) focused on comparing bullying prevalence between a team sport (football) and a combat sport (judo), but found no significant differences. Evans et al. (2016) considered bullying prevalence to be higher in male team sports than in individual ones. There is a lack of consensus regarding this topic.

Here we analysed the differences in bullying prevalence in individual, team and combat sports. Football, handball, rugby and volleyball were categorized as team sports; athletics, gymnastics and swimming as individual sports; and judo and wrestling as combat sports.

Hypothesis 2: frequency of victimization and type of sport (female gender acceptance)

There is a range of taxonomy that can be used to divide sports based on different criteria. As shown in Table 3.3, sports can be divided based on the acceptance of female athletes' engagement. Great efforts have been made in recent decades to increase the participation of women in sport, and this has resulted in a considerable increase of high competition female athletes and lower discrimination of women in this setting. However, organized and competitive sports are still usually considered a mostly masculine activity (Messner, 2002).

Different sports have different characteristics, which has led some authors to distinguish them based on female acceptance (Chalabaev et al., 2013). Some research suggests there may be differences concerning the prevalence of aggressive behaviours in sports, based on it (Browitt, King & Martinez-Expósito, 2006; Jachyna, 2013; Tagg, 2015). All taxonomy can be considered questionable. However, for research purposes, here we divide the sports studied, considering gymnastics, swimming and volleyball as sports with high female acceptance, and athletics, football, handball, judo, rugby, and wrestling as sports with low female acceptance. This division was based on the works of Cashmore (1996) and García Ferrando (1990). These classifications based on gender were corroborated by a statistical analysis of the prevalence of male and female participation in different sports (French Department of Sport, 2000). We wondered if the type of sport (more "masculine" or "feminine" oriented) would influence the prevalence of victimization.

Hypothesis 3: frequency of victimization and geographical area

In our sample collection, Portugal was divided into four geographical areas (see Chapter 3). We wanted to test if cultural differences within a country could have some influence on bullying prevalence. Previous research by Pereira (2008) tested this hypothesis on school bullying, and no significant differences were found between schools in Lisbon and Porto.

Although Portugal is a relatively small country, there is considerable cultural diversity. We wondered if the prevalence of victimization would be influenced by geographical area.

Hypothesis 4: frequency of victimization and number of good friends within the sports club

Bullying victims are often described as socially inept (Trautmann, 2008), which can be reflected in being more isolated (Olweus, 2010) and more frequently suffering from peer social exclusion (Losel & Bender, 2011). However, peer support has been shown to be a very important factor in dealing with victimization. Cowie and Smith (2010) argue that in the right circumstances a well-organized peer support system can contribute to victims breaking their silence and seeking help.

Here we analyse the relation between victimization and number of good friends in the peer group. The friends considered belong to the peer group within the sports club, and were teammates. We predicted that athletes with a lower number of friends would be more prone to suffer from victimization.

Testing the hypotheses about the involvement in bullying episodes and the influence of general variables

Hypothesis 1: frequency of victimization and type of sport (individual, team, combat)

No significant differences were found, $\chi^2(4, N = 1454) = 2.70$, $p < 0.05$. Although individual, team and combat sports have some particular features, the prevalence of victimization does not significantly vary between them.

Hypothesis 2: frequency of victimization and type of sport (female gender acceptance)

The relation between type of sport (female gender acceptance) and victimization was not significant, $\chi^2(2, N = 1454) = 2.37$, $p < 0.05$. Although sports in which female gender participation is more easily accepted would be expected to have lower levels of victimization, this did not appear to be the case in our sample.

Hypothesis 3: frequency of victimization and geographical area

No significant differences were found, $\chi^2(6, N = 1454) = 3.40$, $V = .034$, $p < 0.05$. The prevalence of bullying in sports training did not vary by the four geographical areas into which we divided Portugal.

Hypothesis 4: frequency of victimization and number of good friends within the sports club

We found that the relationship between victimization and number of good friends in the peer group within the sports club was significant, $\chi^2(8, N = 1451) = 51.59$, $V = .133$, $p < 0.05$. Further inspection showed that athletes who reported having one good friend often tended to be victimized, while those who reported having two or three good friends were less often victimized, those who reported having four or five good friends were only occasionally victimized, and those athletes who reported having more than five good friends tended not to be victimized. The data clearly shows that having more friends means less victimization (and vice versa), as shown in Table 5.1.

Summary

Although previous research has suggested that the type of sport could exert some influence on the prevalence of bullying behaviours, the data analyses showed that in our sample only the relation between number of good friends in the peer group in the sports club and bullying prevalence should be considered. Type of sport, and geographical area, were not significant so far as bullying prevalence was concerned, while the social network and capacity to develop friendships inside the peer group should be considered in the development of intervention programmes. This topic will be further developed in Chapter 12.

Analysis of the common variables: bullying types and feelings

Bullying types, and feelings about bullying episodes, were the only two variables answered in common by victims, bullies and bystanders. Our findings comparing these three roles are shown in Table 5.2.

Verbal bullying was the type most often reported, followed by social bullying, then physical, and least often cyberbullying. This was a consistent finding for victims, bullies and bystanders. However, these three roles differed in terms of feelings about bullying. Victims and bystanders more often reported negative feelings about bullying and hardly ever reported positive feelings; whereas nearly one-third of bullies reported positive feelings about it.

In summary, there is some consensus that verbal bullying is the most prevalent type among young athletes. Most of them disapprove of bullying behaviours; however, bullies reported more positive feelings towards bullying than victims and bystanders. The results may suggest that bullying is performed mostly by using "trash talk", and bullies may consider it normal banter rather than an aggressive form of communication. Some light will be shed on this hypothesis in Chapters 7, 8 and 9, dedicated to qualitative research and in-depth data about the meanings of bullying behaviours.

Summary and main conclusions

Our findings show that bullying in youth sport is not infrequent and is a reason for concern. Sports bullying prevalence does seem to be lower

Table 5.1 Analysis of victimization frequency by number of good friends

Variable	Number of good friends											P value
	None		1 friend		2 or 3 friends		4 or 5 friends		More than 5 friends		Total group	
	N	%	N	%	N	%	N	%	N	%	N	
Frequency												
Non-existent	19	1.5	31	2.4	187	14.3	229	17.5	841	64.4	1307	<0.001
Occasional	0	0.0	4	3.1	29	22.3	39	30.0	58	44.6	130	
Repeated	1	7.1	2	14.3	7	50.0	0	0.0	4	28.6	14	

Table 5.2 Frequency of bullying types and feelings towards bullying for victims, bystanders and bullies

	Victims (%)	Bystanders (%)	Bullies (%)
Type of bullying			
Verbal	45.9	44.8	59.6
Social	23.0	17.6	11.6
Physical	8.2	7.1	9.6
Cyber	1.6	2.6	4.1
Multiple types	21.3	27.9	15.1
Feelings towards bullying			
Negative	45.2	62.0	22.4
Neutrality	14.1	11.9	18.6
Avoidance	0	2.7	0
Positive	0	1.0	32.9
Multiple feelings	40.7	22.5	26.1

than school bullying. But nevertheless, a significant minority of young athletes reported involvement in one or more bullying roles. The type of sport practised and the geographical area did not influence the prevalence of bullying behaviours. However, the number of good friends in the sports club did influence the frequency of victimization; victims tend to have fewer good friends, and conversely having more good friends results in less victimization. These findings alert us to the need of creating and developing a solid peer support system to help victims.

Verbal bullying is the most common. Social type is also frequent, and physical bullying was much less reported. These findings are consistent among perpetrators, victims and bystanders. However, when it comes to feelings towards bullying, these differ according to the roles. Victims and bystanders are more likely to experience negative feelings towards bullying, while perpetrators more frequently expressed positive feelings.

Chapter 6
Circumstances of bullying episodes

Introduction

In this chapter, we focus on the circumstances of bullying episodes. We considered those athletes who reported their involvement as victims, bullies or bystanders. The results of their participation in bullying for each role are analysed separately.

For the **victims**, we examine:

- The age of the victims;
- The frequency and duration of the bullying episodes;
- Their location;
- The activities in which they occurred;
- The number of athletes involved;
- Who they speak with (if they do) about bullying episodes;
- The support sources of the victims: peers, coach and family;
- The coping styles used by victims when targeted.

For the **perpetrators of bullying**, we examine:

- The frequency of bullying episodes;
- The age of the perpetrators;
- The number of athletes involved;
- The types of bullying;
- Feelings of the perpetrators;
- Who spoke with the perpetrators (if someone did) about their bullying behaviours.

For **bystanders**, we examine:

- The feelings towards bullying;
- The reasons ascribed for episodes to occur;
- Their reactions.

We start by giving a descriptive analysis, and then describing some hypotheses. We finally analyse the relations between the variables studied. For these analyses, we use chi-square tests; we only report in detail the statistically significant differences. Although the frequency distribution of bullying types has already been analysed in the previous chapter (and consequently is not described here), this variable is also taken into account here when performing chi-square analysis for both victims and bullies. As mentioned in Chapter 5, victims and bullies tend to have opposite feelings about bullying behaviours; this variable will be considered here, when analysing the results of the bystanders.

Descriptive analysis about the circumstances of victimization

A summary of the percentages of the main variables is given in Table 6.1. Most of the victims report occasional bullying episodes. These usually occur inside the sports club, less often in multiple places, and occasionally in competition. Training is the main activity during which it occurs, followed by competition, and multiple activities (both training and competition activities). Victimization is mainly reported as of low duration.

Table 6.1 Frequency, duration, location, activities and number of athletes involved in victimization episodes

Variable	%
Frequency	
Occasional	90.4
Repeated	9.6
Location	
Club	71.8
Multiple places (club and competition)	21.8
Competition	4.5
Activities	
Training	76.5
Competition	12.2
Multiple places (training and competition)	10.4
Duration	
Low	73.5
High	26.5
Participants (number of athletes)	
Group	55.0
Individual	45.0

Involvement in bullying episodes as victims

Research hypotheses about victimization

The hypotheses described here are about victimization, and some possible significant relationships between the variables considered to analyse the circumstances of bullying episodes, as well as the coping styles, who victims speak with (if they do) about bullying, and support sources of the victims.

Hypotheses about the circumstances of victimization

Hypothesis 1: frequency of victimization and age of the athletes

The quality and frequency of involvement in bullying episodes tend to vary based on age: younger children are more often victimized and bullying becomes less frequent as they get older (Barrio et al., 2008; Smith et al., 2004). So, we examine if the prevalence of victimization varies with age in our sample. To do so, we divided the athletes into different categories based on their age and developmental stage, according to the Long-Term Athlete Development (LTAD) model (see Chapter 4).

Hypothesis 2: frequency of victimization and its duration

Firstly, we examine if a higher frequency of bullying episodes is related to a longer duration of the episodes. These were expected to be related, because bullying episodes tend to reach their peak in the initial phase of peer group formation, when the social status of members is uncertain and affiliative bonds are weaker, and then to gradually decrease over time (Pellegrini, 2003). Isolated or low frequency episodes could have occurred only in the initial period of the peer group's formation based on this aim for social status, while high frequency episodes could have extended over time and targeted repeated victims.

Hypothesis 3: frequency of victimization and activities in which it occurred

Although bullying episodes may occur in every social setting and activity, we wondered if the frequency of victimization would be higher in specific types of activities, due to their nature and location. The activities described in the questionnaire were divided into training and competition, which differ in their characteristics; namely, that the former is performed mostly inside the sports club, while competition takes place mostly outside the club.

Hypothesis 4: duration of victimization and its location

The changing room has previously been found as the hot spot for bullying to occur (Evans et al., 2016). We examine if the duration of victimization is related to the location of the episodes.

Hypothesis 5: duration of victimization and activities in which it occurred

Bullying tends to be less prevalent in activities which involve the presence and supervision of adults. In school settings, although bullying may occur inside the classroom, it mostly takes place in less structured activities in the school yard (Rebolo Marques & Neto, 2001). We examine if the duration of victimization is related to the activities in which it occurred.

Hypotheses about the coping styles, communication and support sources of the victims

Hypothesis 6: communication of victimization and coping

The coping style adopted is important to understand how individuals deal with stressful situations (Lazarus, 1991). Youngsters who use coping focused on problem-solving strategies employ more pro-active strategies in order to deal with victimization. These individuals are expected to be more prone to break silence and talk about bullying, while those who use coping focused on emotion strategies are expected to be more prone to ignore victimization and try to deal with their feelings. We examine the relationship between who victims speak with about bullying, and the coping styles used.

Hypothesis 7: communication and frequency of victimization

Victims often remain silent about victimization (Mora-Merchán, 2006). Frequency of victimization has been related to who athletes speak with or whether they keep silent about bullying. A higher frequency of victimization contributes to silence about bullying. We examine if who victims speak with and frequency of victimization are related.

Hypothesis 8: frequency of victimization and support from peers

Victims tend to become silent and to cope with bullying alone. However, when victims talk about bullying, they feel more able to cope with it (Naylor, Cowie & Del Rey, 2001). Peers are an important support source for the victims, and often sought by those who want to talk to someone. We examine if the frequency of victimization is related to the extent of peer support.

Hypothesis 9: frequency of victimization and support from the coach

Research on school bullying suggests that teachers are an important support source for the victims (Francisco & Libório, 2008). The coach has the main responsibility for the safety of young athletes inside the sports club. We examine if the frequency of victimization is related to the support provided by the coach to the victims.

Hypothesis 10: frequency of victimization and support from the family

Research on bullying in school settings suggests parents are an important support source for the victims (Barrio et al., 2008). We examine if the frequency of victimization is related to support from the family.

Testing the hypotheses about the circumstances of victimization

Hypothesis 1: frequency of victimization and age of the athletes

No significant differences were found, $\chi^2(2, N = 132) = 2.67$, $p < 0.05$. The frequency of victimization does not significantly vary with age.

Hypothesis 2: frequency of victimization and its duration

The relation between frequency and duration was significant, $\chi^2(2, N = 78) = 14.79$, $p < 0.001$. Table 6.2 compares experiences of occasional and repeated victims regarding the duration of bullying.

Table 6.2 Victimization frequency by victimization duration and activities in which victimization occurred

Variable	Victimization frequency					P value
	Occasional		Repeated		Total group	
	N	%	N	%	N	
Duration						
Low	56	96.6	2	3.5	58	< 0.001
High	12	60.0	8	40.0	20	
Activities						
Training	77	95.1	4	4.9	81	< 0.001
Competition	10	90.9	1	9.1	11	
Multiple[1]	5	50.0	5	50.0	10	

1 Training (50%) + Competition (50%).

Hypothesis 3: frequency of victimization and activities in which it occurred

The relation between frequency and activities was significant, $\chi^2(3, N = 103) = 20.73$, $p < 0.001$. Table 6.2 compares experiences of occasional and repeated victims regarding the activities in which victimization occurred.

Table 6.2 shows that significantly more victims get involved in occasional bullying episodes and these tended to occur during training activity and to be of low duration. Although relatively few participants reported repeated episodes, many of those who did so reported it happening over a long duration and in multiple activities (training and competition).

Hypothesis 4: duration of victimization and its location

The relation between duration of the victimization and location was significant, $\chi^2(6, N = 73) = 12.81$, $p < 0.05$. Table 6.3 compares the experiences of low and high duration by location.

Hypothesis 5: duration of victimization and activities in which it occurred

The relation between duration and location was significant, $\chi^2(6, N = 75) = 26.72$, $p < 0.001$. Table 6.3 compares the experiences of low and high duration by activities.

Table 6.3 shows that victims were more likely to get involved in low duration episodes, and these episodes tended to occur mainly during training activity and inside the sports club. The high duration victims reported being

Table 6.3 Victimization duration by activities and location

Variable	Victimization duration					P value
	Low		High		Total group	
	N	%	N	%	N	
Activities						
Training	43	76.8	13	23.2	56	< 0.001
Competition	5	71.4	2	28.6	7	
Multiple[1]	2	22.2	7	77.8	9	
Location						
Club	45	86.5	7	13.5	52	< 0.05
Competition	1	33.3	2	66.7	3	
Cyberbullying	2	100.0	0	0.0	2	
Multiple[2]	6	33.3	12	66.7	18	

1 Training (50%) + Competition (50%).
2 Club (84%) + Competition (16%).

bullied in multiple activities (training and competition) and also in multiple places (mainly inside the sports club but also in competition).

Descriptive analysis about the coping styles, communication and support sources of the victims

Table 6.4 describes the coping styles used by victims, who they talk with about bullying and their support sources. Victims tended to use coping strategies focused on emotion to deal with bullying, and often remained silent about it. Victims did not often seek support from family or the coach, although when they asked the coach for help, victimization tended to decrease or stop. The findings regarding peer support suggest that this may play an important role in helping the victims, because peers are the victims' major support source, which is mostly perceived as having positive outcomes (bullying decreases or stops). This is in contrast to families,

Table 6.4 Victims' employed communication and coping strategies

Variable	%
Coping	
Coping focused on emotion	53.4
Coping focused on emotion + coping focused on problem	24.1
Coping focused on problem	22.6
Communication	
Silence	49.1
Peers	26.7
Multiple communication (parents and peers)	13.8
Family	8.6
Adults inside sports club (besides coach)	1.7
Coach support	
No support	77.8
Positive results (victimization decreased or stopped)	15.7
Negative results (victimization maintained or increased)	6.5
Family support	
No support	90.3
Negative results (victimization maintained or increased)	5.8
Positive results (victimization decreased or stopped)	3.9
Peer support	
Positive results (victimization decreased or stopped)	45.5
No support	40.0
Negative results (victimization maintained or increased)	14.5

from whom support is seldom sought, and when it is results are often negative.

Testing the hypotheses about the coping styles, communication and support sources of the victims

Hypothesis 6: communication of victimization and coping

Who the athletes speak with, if they were victimized, is shown in Table 6.5. The relationship between them was significant, $\chi^2(8, N = 109) = 22.59, p < 0.05$.

Hypothesis 7: communication and frequency of victimization

Table 6.5 also shows the relationship between frequency of victimization and who athletes speak with about bullying, which was significant, $\chi^2(4, N = 102) = 13.65, p < 0.05$.

Table 6.5 shows that the athletes who used coping focused on emotion (CFE) strategies tended to maintain silence about victimization, while the athletes who used coping focused on problem (CFP) strategies more often talked with peers about bullying episodes. Occasional victims are more prone to remain silent, while repeated victims more often talk with peers about victimization.

Hypothesis 8: frequency of victimization and support from peers

No significant differences were observed, $\chi^2(2, N = 99) = 1.41, p < 0.05$.

Hypothesis 9: frequency of victimization and support from the coach

No significant differences were observed, $\chi^2(2, N = 100) = 6.94, p < 0.05$.

Hypothesis 10: frequency of victimization and support from the family

Victims tend not to share the experience of victimization or seek support, and become more and more silent and alone as bullying gets more severe. However, when analysing the support sources, we found a significant relation between family support and frequency of victimization, $\chi^2(2, N = 95) = 17.59, p < 0.05$. The breakdown is shown in Table 6.6. Occasional victims tend to keep silent, while repeated victims more often seek the support of family, although they feel it has negative outcomes: bullying maintains or increases its frequency. Thus, although repeated victims seek support from their families, they perceive it as non-effective or even negative.

Table 6.5 Victims' communication by coping styles and frequency of victimization

Variable	Communication											P value
	Silence		Peers		Adults		Family		Multiple[1]		Total group	
	N		%	N	%	N	%	N	%	N	%	N
	N	%	N	%	N	%	N	%	N	%	N	
Coping styles												
CFE	34	58.6	14	24.1	1	1.7	6	10.3	3	5.2	58	< 0.05
CFP	9	40.9	10	45.5	0	0.0	0	0.0	3	13.6	22	
Multiple[2]	10	34.5	4	13.8	1	3.4	4	13.8	10	34.5	29	
Frequency												
Occasional	48	52.2	25	27.2	2	2.2	8	8.7	9	9.8	92	< 0.05
Repeated	2	20.0	3	30.0	0	0.0	0	0.0	5	50.0	10	

1 Peers (44%) + Family (35%) + Adults (15%) + Silence (4%).
2 CFE (50%) + CFP (50%).

Table 6.6 Victims' family support by frequency of victimization

Variable	Victimization frequency				Total group	P value
	Occasional		Repeated			
	N	%	N	%	N	
Support of the family						
Silence	82	93.2	6	6.8	88	< 0.05
Positive support	1	50	1	50	2	
Negative support	2	40	3	60	5	

Summary and main conclusions for victims

In our sample, the age of the victims was not related to the likelihood of their involvement in bullying episodes. These findings are contradictory to many previous researches on school bullying, which suggested that age is one of the most significant variables related to bullying victimization (Smith, Madsen & Moody, 1999). We found that victimization was mainly occasional, tended to occur inside the sports club, and in training sessions. Moreover, the frequency and the duration of bullying episodes were significantly related, and when victimization was more frequent and the duration was higher, episodes tended to occur in a wider context which also included competition activity and areas outside the sports club.

Victims who used emotion-based strategies talked significantly less about victimization with other people, compared to peers who used problem-focused strategies, who were more prone to seek social support. Occasional victims tended to keep silent about bullying, while repeated victims were more likely to share their experience with other teammates, and to seek support from their families. However, if peers are those victims who often speak about bullying and their support is usually perceived as positive, on the other hand, athletes tended to avoid talking with their relatives and family support was perceived as negative.

The results highlight the importance of communication and the coping strategies used by the victims to deal with bullying. Problem-solving strategies are more pro-active and more efficient in dealing with bullying because they act directly on problem resolution, and facilitate seeking help and breaking silence. Efforts to regulate the internal emotional state (emotion-based strategies) often contribute to maintaining silence.

Communication is a key factor in tackling bullying. Although victims tend to keep silent and cope alone with victimization, the ones who seek support among their peers or others often perceive it as resulting positively for them. Improving the communication of the victims and building solid support sources inside the sports club may result in very positive outcomes. Peers are the major support source and their actions are perceived as positive by the teammates who are being victimized. It seems important to create a solid peer support system in order to help victims to deal with bullying.

Involvement in bullying episodes as bullies

Descriptive analysis about the circumstances of the involvement in bullying episodes

A summary of the main percentages related to frequency and number of athletes involved in bullying episodes is given in Table 6.7. Bullying behaviours were mainly occasional, although a minority reported repeated participation. Bullying was mostly performed by a group, more rarely by an individual.

When bullying occurred, usually nobody approached the bully about his/her behaviour (62.9%), and when somebody did it was usually peers (17.1%), adults inside the sports club (8.6%) or multiple sources (7.1%), and least often the family (4.3%).

Research hypotheses about involvement in bullying as perpetrators

Hypothesis 1: frequency of the episodes and age of the athletes

Research suggests that the frequency of involvement in bullying behaviours tends to vary with age (Barrio et al., 2008). We examine if the prevalence of involvement in bullying episodes as bullies varies based on age. Once again, we categorized age according to the LTAD model.

Table 6.7 Summary of main results for bullies

Variable	%
Frequency	
Occasional	87.8
Repeated	12.2
Participants (number of athletes)	
Group	82.8
Individual	17.2

Hypothesis 2: frequency of the episodes and types of bullying

Verbal provocations are common among athletes, especially targeting new incoming members at the beginning of the season. Some of these are perceived by these individuals as banter, while others may be bullying (Kirby & Wintrump, 2002). However, those who are targeted often experience multiple types of bullying rather than one isolated type of behaviour (Gutiérrez et al., 2008). Bullying may start as "merely" verbal (e.g. jokes and provocations), and when aggravated by becoming more frequent, it can become a combination of several types, including exclusion of the victims. We examine if the frequency of bullying is related to the types of bullying.

Hypothesis 3: communication and feelings of the bullies

Bullies more often express positive feelings about bullying than bystanders and victims. Some intervention on bullying is based on confronting the bullies with their behaviour, and trying to make them understand what victims feel, seeking to enhance empathy (Smith, 2016). We examine if who approaches bullies about their behaviour is related to their feelings towards bullying. Communication of the bullies refers to those who have eventually approached the bullies about their behaviour.

Hypothesis 4: communication and frequency of episodes

Victims and bystanders often remain silent about bullying episodes, while coaches and families tend not to be aware of what is going on among youngsters. However, some individuals do talk with bullies, and/or act on the behalf of the victims. We examine if approaching bullies about their involvement in bullying episodes is related to the prevalence of these behaviours.

Hypothesis 5: communication and number of athletes involved in bullying episodes

Bystanders often remain silent about bullying and observe without interfering. Among other reasons, their behaviour is based on conformity and fear of also being targeted. The influence of the peer group in adolescence is considerable, and many youngsters fear peer group rejection (Blakemore & Mills, 2014). We examine if the number of athletes involved in bullying is related to whether anyone approaches the bullies about their behaviour.

Testing the hypotheses about the circumstances of the involvement in bullying episodes

Hypothesis 1: frequency of the episodes and age of the athletes

No significant differences were found, $\chi^2(2, N = 149) = 5.40, p < 0.05$.

Hypothesis 2: frequency of the episodes and types of bullying

The types of bullying and frequency of bullies' behaviour are shown in Table 6.8. These variables were significantly related, $\chi^2(4, N = 118) = 12.88, p < 0.05$. Occasional bullies reported mainly verbal bullying, while repeated bullies more often reported multiple types of bullying.

Hypothesis 3: communication and feelings of the bullies

No significant differences were found, $\chi^2(12, N = 126) = 12.01, p < 0.05$.

Hypothesis 4: communication and frequency of episodes

No significant differences were found, $\chi^2(4, N = 114) = 7.77, p < 0.05$.

Hypothesis 5: Communication and number of athletes involved in bullying episodes

Who approaches bullies when these individuals are involved in bullying episodes is shown in Table 6.9. The relationship between these variables was significant $\chi^2(4, N = 114) = 12.80, p < 0.05$. The athletes who participate in group bullying tend not to be approached by their peers, while the athletes who perform individual bullying are more often verbally approached by their peers about bullying episodes.

Summary and main conclusions for bullies

The findings on behaviours of those who bullied show that their age was not related to the likelihood of their involvement in bullying episodes. Occasional bullying was mostly verbal (mainly mocking and insults), and repeated bullying was mostly a combination of verbal bullying and exclusion (social bullying). These findings suggest that a higher frequency of bullying leads to more severe consequences for the victims who, besides being the butt of jokes, are also excluded and become more and more isolated. Bullying, especially in sports settings, tends to be a taboo. Although it happens frequently and has severe consequences, victims tend to keep

Table 6.8 Type of bullying by frequency of bullying episodes

Variable	Physical		Verbal		Social		Cyberbullying		Multiple[1]		Total group		P value
	N	%	N	%	N	%	N	%	N	%	N		
Frequency													
Occasional	9	8.9	69	68.3	9	8.9	3	3.0	11	10.9	101		<0.05
Repeated	2	11.8	5	29.4	2	11.8	1	5.9	7	41.2	17		

1 Verbal (46%) + Social (30%) + Physical (15%) + Cyber (7%).

Table 6.9 Bullies' communication per number of athletes involved in bullying episodes

Variable			Communication										
	Silence		Peers		Adults inside sports club		Family		Multiple[1]		Total group		P value
	N	%	N	%	N	%	N	%	N	%	N	%	
	N	%		%	N		%	N		%	N		%	

Variable	Silence N	Silence %	Peers N	Peers %	Adults inside sports club N	Adults inside sports club %	Family N	Family %	Multiple[1] N	Multiple[1] %	Total group N	Total group %	P value
Number of athletes													
Individual	7	36.8	7	36.8	2	10.5	2	10.5	1	5.3	19	100	< 0.05
Group	68	71.6	11	11.6	7	7.4	2	2.1	7	7.4	95	100	

1 Adults inside sports club (40%) + Peers (36%) + Family (18%) + Silence (4%).

silent and bullies are often not approached by peers, or by the coach, who is often not aware of what is going on.

Involvement in bullying episodes as bystanders

As reported in Table 5.2, victims mostly reported negative feelings towards bullying, while bullies reported a higher rate of positive feelings. Bystanders, on the other hand, were most likely to report a range of opposite feelings about bullying episodes. We examine how the way these athletes feel about bullying episodes influences their cognitive evaluation and reaction towards bullying. The feelings of the bystanders are included in data analysis, because different bystanders reported opposite feelings towards bullying, and these may influence the reasons ascribed and their reactions.

Descriptive analysis about the feelings, reasons and coping of the bystanders

The bystanders' perceived reasons for bullying occurrence and their reactions are described in Table 6.10. When bullying episodes occurred, bystanders usually defended the victims or observed without interfering, and many reported multiple reactions. Only a few bystanders reported joining the bully, or said that they also became a victim. When asked about the reasons for why the bullying occurred, nearly half considered that the bully was responsible for what happened. Nearly as many referred to multiple reasons, mainly holding the bullies' responsible, but with one fifth also

Table 6.10 Summary of main results for bystanders

Variable	%
Reasons	
Responsibility of bullies	47.2
Multiple	46.1
Responsibility of victims	6.7
Reaction	
Defence of victim	34.4
Multiple reactions	33.3
Observation	27.0
Join bullying	4.4
Victimization	1.0

considering the victim responsible. Only a small minority of bystanders considered the victim exclusively responsible.

Research hypotheses about involvement in bullying as bystanders

Hypothesis 1: feeling towards bullying and reasons ascribed

Attitudes are composed of emotional, cognitive and behavioural components (Ajzen & Fishbein, 2005), which interplay with and influence one another. We examine if the way bystanders feel about bullying is related to the reasons perceived for this behaviour to occur.

Hypothesis 2: feeling towards bullying and reactions (coping)

Many interventions for bullying target the bystanders, due to the strong influence that their attitudes may have in normalizing these behaviours, or rejecting them, influencing their prevalence and acceptance (Salmivalli, 2010). Considering the close relation between emotions, cognition and behaviour, we examine if the feelings of the bystanders towards bullying are related to their reactions when involved in these episodes.

Testing the hypotheses about the feelings, reasons and coping of the bystanders

Hypothesis 1: feeling towards bullying and reasons ascribed

The relation between these variables was significant, $\chi^2(8, N = 415) = 42.15$, $p < 0.05$. Table 6.11 shows the breakdown of findings for these variables.

Hypothesis 2: feeling towards bullying and reactions (coping)

The relation between these variables was significant, $\chi^2(16, N = 455) = 101.34$, $p < 0.05$. Table 6.11 shows the breakdown of findings for these variables.

Table 6.11 shows the feelings of the bystanders by reasons and reactions. Both hypotheses were confirmed. Bystanders who considered the bully responsible for what happened also reported negative feelings towards bullying episodes, while bystanders who considered the victims responsible tended to report avoidance of bullying. Those who reported negative feelings for what happened tended to defend the victims, while those who expressed neutrality or avoidance tended to observe without interfering. A minority of bystanders also reported neutrality and tended to join the bully.

Table 6.11 Bystanders' feelings by bullying reasons and reactions towards bullying

Variable	Feelings										Total group		P value
	Negative		Avoidance		Neutrality		Positive		Multiple[1]				
	N	%	N	%	N	%	N	%	N	%	N	%	
Reasons													
Responsibility of bullies	139	70.2	5	2.5	20	10.1	3	1.5	31	15.7	198		< 0.05
Responsibility of victims	18	66.7	3	11.1	1	3.7	1	3.7	4	14.8	27		
Multiple[2]	98	51.6	3	1.6	14	7.4	0	0.0	75	39.5	190		
Reactions													
Join bullying	11	55.0	1	5.0	7	35.0	0	0.0	1	5.0	20		< 0.05
Victimization	4	66.7	0	0.0	0	0.0	0	0.0	2	33.3	6		
Observation	95	63.8	10	6.7	26	17.4	1	0.7	17	11.4	149		
Defence of victims	125	77.6	0	0.0	12	7.4	2	1.2	22	13.7	161		
Multiple[3]	50	42.0	1	0.8	9	7.6	2	1.7	57	47.9	119		

1 Negative (88%) + Avoidance (7%) + Neutrality (3%) + Positive (1%).
2 Bullies' accountability (80.8%) + Victims' accountability (19.2%).
3 Victims' defence (39%) + Observation (21%) + Join bullying (9%) + Victimization (3%).

Summary and main conclusions for bystanders

Most of the bystanders do not like bullying, consider the behaviours to be wrong, and criticize the bullies. Very few bystanders expressed positive feelings about bullying, but there is a small group characterized by an avoiding attitude, who considered bullying to be the responsibility of the victims. The bystanders who reported negative feelings about bullying tended to consider bullying to be the responsibility of the bullies, while the bystanders who reported avoidance considered that bullying is both the victims' and bullies' responsibility. The bystanders' interpretation of the reasons for bullying to occur was strongly related to their feelings and attitudes towards bullying behaviours.

Negative feelings tended to lead to defence of the victims, while avoiding and neutral feelings were related to just observing the bullying without interfering (and feeling neutral was also related to joining in the bullying). The data suggests that athletes who have negative feelings about bullying tended to defend the victim and, on the other hand, athletes who reported an avoidance attitude and neutrality tended not to act and just watch. It's important to state that some athletes who reported feeling neutral about bullying have also joined the bully and attacked the victim. The attitudes of the athletes towards bullying strongly shape, but do not completely determine, their behaviours.

General conclusions

The analysis of the results of the victims shows victimization is mainly occasional, and victims often become silent about the bullying. It seems important to improve the communication of the victims and their coping strategies, in order to tackle bullying more efficiently. The more pro-active coping strategies allow victims to beak silence and share their experience of victimization, which is often perceived as positive by them, especially when victims talk with peers. The development of peer support systems should be considered.

Bullies tend to mock and exclude victims, and are not usually approached by others when they target the victims, especially if bullying is performed in a group (which happens in most of the cases).

How bullying is perceived by the bystanders is related to their reactions towards it: the ones who disapprove of bullying are more prone to act on behalf of the victim, while those who approve of bullying more often join the bully. The majority of the bystanders dislike bullying; however, a considerable proportion of them merely watch and do not interfere when bullying occurs. Attitudinal change should be considered when developing anti-bullying programmes, in order to enhance the likelihood of bystanders defending the victim, and approaching the bullies.

Chapter 7

Narratives of the athletes

In this chapter, we move to a qualitative approach by presenting the results of a study in which 127 athletes from all 9 sports previously surveyed were interviewed. These participants were asked to share their thoughts about bullying in youth sports training. Here we provide the major results concerning the athletes' point of view on this topic. The perspectives of victims, perpetrators and bystanders are compared: the groups of athletes who participated in this study included young athletes who had performed each of these roles when involved in bullying episodes (and on some occasions overlapped roles). Sometimes the same episodes were reported by different participants, but with different points of view about what had happened. This provided important information, and allowed us to contrast these different perspectives and achieve a deeper understanding of bullying episodes.

Analysis of the narratives of the athletes

Following the completion and transcription of the interviews (see Chapter 4), we organized the data according to content themes.

A major division was between (1) those athletes who did not think that bullying existed in sport at all; (2) those athletes who never got involved, but still thought that it can happen; and (3) those athletes who got involved in bullying episodes as victims, bystanders and/or perpetrators.

For group 1, we explored how these athletes thought about or defined bullying, and their perceptions regarding the reasons for bullying not happening in sports settings, under the category "bullying or banter?". Nearly one-third of the athletes belong to this category (n = 35).

For group 2, we explored the reasons for why bullying might occur in sports settings, and some risk factors that facilitated its possible occurrence (n = 23).

For group 3, in order to better understand the nature and prevalence of bullying behaviours, we formed three main content categories; namely, the circumstances of bullying episodes, the roles enacted and practical implications. Each one of these was further divided into the following sub-categories:

- **Bullying circumstances** has six sub-categories: types of bullying; location; number of athletes involved in bullying episodes (individual or group); reasons for bullying occurrence; factors which facilitate or make difficult the integration of new members into the peer group; and the possible overlap of bullying behaviours in different social settings;
- **Roles enacted** has three sub-categories: profiles (victims and perpetrators); social status; and the role played by the coach in peer group management;
- **Practical implications** has two sub-categories: bullying consequences and prevention/intervention coping strategies adopted by victims and bystanders.

Nearly half the athletes reported being involved in bullying episodes (n = 69).

When presenting the data, we often give some illustrative quotes. There are some comments within [brackets], that we have provided to enable better understanding of the idea being expressed. These comments are not part of the speech of the athletes.

(1) Narratives of athletes who did not think that bullying happened in sport

Bullying or banter?

These participants referred to verbal attacks as mere banter rather than bullying, and considered them to be normal and to have no negative or major consequences for the victims. Some of the participants described these kinds of interaction as healthy and desirable due to their playful nature.

HANDBALL ATHLETE: I don't know if it can be called bullying; I mean, some teammates are sometimes targeted more than others when it comes to mocking. They suffer more from mockery ... it's not physical; it's more verbal or related to relationship. But it's ... it's not repeated and it's not serious; sometimes it's just mocking a bit.

WRESTLING ATHLETE: There is no bullying because ... it's a combat sport so ... there's no bullying. "If you have a problem, let's solve it in the ring" following the rules! (laugh).

These athletes justified their opinions with several reasons, highlighting positive bonds between peers and the role of the coach in monitoring these kinds of behaviours. Both reasons are common to all the sports studied.

The positive bonds between athletes may also be seen as a consequence of bullying not happening, rather than a reason for it not happening. The role played by the coach in monitoring the aggressive and abusive behaviours of the athletes seems important, and may contribute to decrease or even eliminate bullying behaviours.

The interpretation of the behaviours varied according to the role played by an athlete when involved in bullying episodes. Perpetrators tended to devalue the impact of bullying behaviours on others and to label these as mere banter, while victims, and in many cases also the bystanders, reported the same episodes, expressing negative feelings about them. When carrying out the interviews with several athletes from the same peer group, it was common to find different interpretations of the same occurrences: a group of athletes referring to the same peers (identified as victims) and regarding the same episodes, expressing very distinct perspectives about the victims' behaviours, based on their feelings about bullying episodes. Many participants described bullying episodes as banter, while others recognized its aggressive component, but justified it by saying the victim deserved to be treated that way, because he was somehow perceived as different, having some particular characteristic or behaviour that did not accord to peer group norms.

RESEARCHER: How do you think he feels when you make fun of him?
HANDBALL ATHLETE: His face turns mad. I don't know what is wrong with him; I don't know what goes on in his brain because he starts getting furious or, instead, shuts up, and then starts saying "Stop it!" (enacting an angry scream) (laugh).
RESEARCHER: Do you feel bad when you do that?
HANDBALL ATHLETE: No!!! (astonished) he has always been like that.

Many participants started their narratives by saying bullying was not part of sport and that they never saw any episodes, but while speaking and reflecting on the topic, they started to describe bullying episodes in which they had participated. Initially, many interactions described were considered normal and funny, but their speech gradually changed and became more empathetic with the victims.

(2) **Narratives of athletes who never got involved, but still thought that it can happen**

Although some athletes never got involved in bullying episodes in their sports club, they reported it could happen and highlighted some general factors to justify their perspective. These athletes frequently reported the occurrence of bullying episodes at school, where every type of adolescents were mixed and must co-exist. They referred to their sports clubs as friendly environments and to their teammates as having positive relationships. Common goals and/or interests among athletes, the moral atmosphere or the organization within their sports club were frequently evoked as possible reasons for bullying not to occur. However, they considered bullying could happen in youth sport, especially targeting those who were perceived as different and less athletic. By different, they referred to those who have different interests and behaviours from the majority of the members of the peer group, and by being less athletic they referred to those with lower physical ability and body issues, such as being overweight and/or having a lack of coordination. These individuals were considered different from the image of a typical athlete.

In these cases, the athletes haven't experienced (even as bystanders) bullying in their own sports club. However, unlike athletes in group 1, these athletes differ in that they don't describe and label possible bullying episodes as banter and don't refer to sport as being free from bullying; they acknowledge that it can occur, and point to some risk factors based on their own analysis of sports culture and peer dynamics.

(3) Narratives of athletes who participated in bullying episodes

Here it is important to note that the participants frequently varied between different roles, enacted on different occasions, performing more than one role in bullying episodes (as is also found in bullying in other contexts, including school, see Chapters 1 and 2).

Circumstances

Types of bullying

The athletes who got involved in bullying episodes reported verbal bullying (e.g. mocking) as the most prevalent type of bullying, followed by social (e.g. social exclusion). Although injury was frequent, verbal bullying was mostly composed of mocking, and the main reasons identified were low sports performance, body issues (e.g. being overweight, having particular characteristics) and sexual jokes, especially calling others gay or making jokes about others' mother, sisters, cousins or girlfriends.

> FOOTBALL ATHLETE: (...) They used to have a close circle of friends, which is OK but, sometimes, some players were low quality ... usually they are technically weaker or just the worst players, so they were a target of mocking. Not that kind of healthy mocking [banter], but one with malevolent intentions.

The exclusion previously referred to was made by ignoring a teammate or not letting him become part of the peer group, excluding him from conversations and social interactions. It could be done more subtly, by not passing the ball, not saying hello (only to that peer member) when a peer group gathered, excluding an athlete in training situations, or making it harder for the victim to access resources (e.g. pressure to be the last one to drink water from a common source or to have access to a shower).

RUGBY ATHLETE: Yes, older athletes tend to pass the ball only between them.
FOOTBALL ATHLETE: Here is the deal: some new guys got here, some of them were black. The peer groups were already made because people already knew each other from school or their neighbourhood where they live ... So, the new guys had more difficulty in integrating, and sometimes it was obvious there was a bad social environment in the changing room, due to the exclusion of some players.
RESEARCHER: How was that exclusion made?
FOOTBALL ATHLETE: It's like ... sometimes in the shower for example: one athlete lends the shampoo to other teammates except for one particular athlete because he is the new guy or ... everybody is in line to drink water and the teammates all pass ahead of him because he is the new guy and hasn't got enough time to consolidate his social position in the peer group. Those kind of things ... .

Openly physical bullying was rarely reported. However, there were a few cases in which physical aggression took place, usually along with other types of bullying.

Besides these three types of bullying, bystanders frequently described what we called "disguised aggression", which is a type of banter between peers, based on an implicit aggressive component, such that aggressive behaviours (especially verbal ones) are dissimulated and the perpetrator pretends to just be bantering rather than bullying the victim. In these cases, the focus is on how aggression occurs, rather than its contents: it has more to do with the way it is performed (e.g. tone, intensity) than observable content. Irony and sarcasm are frequently used to disguise aggression. "Disguised aggression" also applied to physical contact situations. Some athletes, especially in sports which involved physical contact, tended to be more aggressive in normal training situations with the victims than with other athletes. This was often perceived by the victims and the bystanders as a way to frighten the victims and to show dominance. If observed from the outside, the perpetrator could excuse himself by saying he was just training harder rather than intimidating his teammate.

RUGBY ATHLETE: I'll give you an example: once, we went on a trip to X and a teammate of ours ... he is a bit different from others, but is a funny person, and he started saying jokes and we were all also saying jokes but, at some point, my teammates weren't laughing at his jokes anymore; instead, they were laughing at him and he felt bad about it, and excluded by others. So, it's one of these episodes ... .

The athletes described another type of social interaction that we labelled "cross fire". This consists of play behaviours between peers, similar to banter: peers provoke each other with verbal attacks. This kind of behaviour frequently has the purpose of seeing how athletes react to provocations and, based on their reactions, to establish the role of each and their hierarchical position in the peer group. This social interaction occurs in group settings and is considered as a bantering activity. However, on some occasions, there is an implicit aggressive component in some of the comments made, or aggressive behaviour can be observed in how some athletes make fun of the over-reaction of teammates when provoked. This over-reaction is considered funny by the perpetrators, and as a sign of weakness and lack of emotional control in the victim. If an athlete does not react, it can also be perceived as submission and result in them being more prone to be targeted. Although "cross fire" isn't necessarily a type of bullying by itself, sometimes it can be the basis of future bullying behaviours.

Location

Athletes reported that bullying episodes occurred mainly in the changing room, because it is a less structured setting and less supervised by the coach or other adults. The "cross fire" interaction previously described tends to occur mostly in the changing room, which is also perceived as an area with a high degree of freedom, not being dedicated to any specific sports activity, and a place in which athletes are more likely to behave informally in their interactions with each other.

SWIMMING ATHLETE: I've seen some situations in the changing room, both verbal and physical.
RESEARCHER: Why the changing room?
SWIMMING ATHLETE: Because only the athletes are there. There are no parents or coaches.

Training areas were also mentioned as places where bullying episodes occur, but here it is usually disguised, due to the presence of the coach. A handball athlete who was a perpetrator, reported an episode in his interview about it. He used to bully a teammate in the changing room, and also provoke him in the training areas by using disguised aggression.

On one occasion, he along with three other teammates started repeatedly provoking the victim during a training session, until the victim reacted by shooting a ball in their direction. The coach, who only saw this last part of the whole episode, ended up punishing the victim for his behaviour. The perpetrators laughed at the victim behind the coach's back. This is a good example of the use of disguised aggression in training areas.

Number of athletes

All participants referred to bullying episodes as involving several athletes, mentioning the need of perpetrators to have others watching their actions. In some cases, bullying can start between only a perpetrator and a victim, but it promptly becomes a group interaction, which includes several types of bystanders. Bullying is described as a type of interaction which only makes sense when performed in a group situation with bystanders, serving as a framework within which the abusive relation between victim and perpetrator can develop.

JUDO ATHLETE: I think usually people don't mock alone; they only do it when they are in a group situation, because mocking alone to attack another person doesn't make any sense.
RESEARCHER: Need an audience?
JUDO ATHLETE: Yes, exactly (…) sometimes it's not to attack; it's more like to be funny for others [bystanders], but the targeted person may not feel it's funny … I think that's it, basically.

Reasons

The athletes reported several reasons and explanations for the occurrence of bullying episodes, which were categorized as fundamental reasons, peer pressure and individual characteristics (Table 7.1).

Fundamental reasons concern individual factors, while **peer pressure** includes behaviours which result from pressure suffered by peers in order to act according to standards. Finally, **individual characteristics** relate to the profile of the victims, which are considered to increase the probability of being victimized. These theoretical categories and the reasons described are interconnected and interplay with each other.

Abuse of perceived power describes a coercive interaction with the intent to obtain social status in the peer group, by attacking and devaluing the more vulnerable athletes. This mechanism of power and systematic abuse of colleagues has a considerable overlap with the concept of bullying itself. It can be considered a reason, but also, at least partially, a definition of bullying. The purpose of the abuse of power is frequently to increase social status and popularity in the peer group.

Table 7.1 Reasons for bullying occurrence

Category	Reason	Definition
Fundamental reasons	Abuse of perceived power	Attitudes and behaviours with the aim to diminish a colleague in order to raise the social status of the perpetrator in the peer group.
	Hierarchy	Older and higher social status athletes exert power over new incomers and low status athletes, and justify their behaviour as being older and/or being in the sports club for a longer period.
	Envy	The envy of other peers, or jealousy felt towards the relationship between another athlete and the coach, which may reflect similar behaviours (e.g. wanting coach's full attention, devaluing others).
	Rivalry	Peer sportive rivalry.
Peer pressure	Divergence from standard	The athlete is perceived as different from the accepted standards of the peer group.
	Imitation	Athletes who imitate aggressive behaviours and engage in bullying, in order to be accepted and valued by others (especially the bullies).
	Victims' responsibility	Athletes consider victims to contribute to their involvement in bullying behaviours by the way they interact with peers.
Individual characteristics	Low sports performance	Athletes with low sports performance, low skills and less ability, usually considered the worst athletes.
	Body issues	Reference to physical issues which are considered negative and/or not according to an athletic body.
	Personality	Behaviours (ways of thinking or acting) such that the athlete is considered a misfit by other peer members.

JUDO ATHLETE: I'm going to give you an example; I always … Actually I don't mock that much, but when I did it, it was to devalue or make fun about some characteristic of another, which resulted in feeling more confident myself. Makes me feel better!

RESEARCHER: It's like somehow … .

JUDO ATHLETE: … I think it's not right! But yes, it inflates the ego. I think it really inflates the ego!

Hierarchy refers to the coercion of victims, due to perpetrators being older or belonging to a sports club for a longer period, which gives them a higher social status in the peer group. The concept of hierarchy has a considerable overlap with the concept of power, but there is a particular aspect related to coercion being exerted by older athletes. These athletes target the younger ones in order to consolidate their social status in the peer group.

ATHLETICS ATHLETE: When we were doing some exercises during training sessions, older guys use to mock, criticize or insult us repeatedly, just because they think they are superior and want to show us that the way they do exercises is more accurate; so, they annoyed us until we did it their way.

Another fundamental reason very often given to justify bullying episodes was *envy*; the wish of an athlete to have another athlete's qualities and skills, or feeling jealous because the coach is thought to have more attachment to one of his teammates (more prevalent in individual sports), paying him more attention. Envy implies a dyadic relationship, while jealousy is characterized by a triadic relationship. In both cases, an athlete may repeatedly attack other(s), in order to cope with a feeling of personal inadequacy, which can be partially and temporarily disguised by devaluing the positive features of others.

The last fundamental reason referred to was *rivalry*. This is closely related to envy: athletes used rivalry to explain bullying by saying that peer aggression is due to sportive competition between colleagues. This means that bullying behaviours were based on the idea of attacking other peer members who were perceived as a threat (real or imaginary) inside the peer group, due to their athletic and sportive skills.

These fundamental reasons considered here are related to one another and there is a high conceptual overlap. Participants frequently combined more than one of these reasons to explain bullying episodes, and also with peer pressure, in order to explain actions as being according to certain standards and values accepted by the peer group.

The following three **peer pressure** reasons were also described.

Divergence from standard consists of athletes being victimized for not fitting the accepted standards of the peer group. The standards are attitudes and/or behaviours which define how athletes should behave. Being different is considered negative, and a reason to be attacked.

Imitation is a mechanism used by some athletes who act according to the accepted and valued behaviours of the peer group – mostly done by higher social status members – in order to get/feel closer to these peer members and, consequently, to obtain higher social status. The athlete changes his behaviour according to what he thinks is expected by significant others. The new behavioural standards are convergent with what is expected by peers, and can even be antagonistic to the social values of the individual who adopts them.

HANDBALL ATHLETE: He was the king [referring to a bully]! We were a group of more or less 14 people, and there were two guys who used to mock others, so we used to feel an obligation to laugh at what they did, so they could appreciate our presence and, consequently, we could feel better [more integrated among high status athletes].

Victims' responsibility was used mostly by bystanders to explain bullying episodes, considering that the way victims interact with peers actively contributes to their victimization. It is important to make a distinction between victims' responsibility and blaming, the latter being frequently used by perpetrators. Victims' responsibility is a rational, clear and objective argumentation about how the behaviour of the victims influences others and may eventually contribute to involvement in bullying episodes, while blaming consists of arguing that the victims deserve to be targeted, and may be perceived as an attack by itself.

VOLLEYBALL ATHLETE: It's like if I was being mocked but, at the same time, that's the moment when everybody is listening to me. If I'm alone, then there is nobody listening but as long as I am being mocked, I have plenty of people listening to me and I'm popular. Attention is focused on that person.

The third and last category is **individual characteristics**, and these are the personal issues of some athletes which may increase the probability of being victimized. The three main types we found are *low sports performance*, *body issues* (peculiar physical aspects or defects, especially lack of coordination, clumsiness, being overweight) and the *personality* of victims, which goes against the accepted standards. Concerning personality, we should highlight "passivity" and "over-reaction": the first is a non-confrontational attitude towards provocations and attacks, and the second consists in having some difficulty in relativizing banter from peers (especially when "cross fire" occurs). In these cases, the targeted person over-reacts when feeling attacked, and this situation may even promote bullying because perpetrators consider it funny and keep doing it. The lack of assertiveness and losing one's temper are considered a sign of weakness.

Integration

In many narratives, athletes focused on a particular period during the season in which bullying episodes tend to occur. This is when new incomers are integrated into an already existing peer group. The introduction of new athletes may be done without any constraints or, on the contrary, it may generate a strong rejection from former members. Athletes mentioned some factors which may facilitate the integration of new members into the peer group; namely, the existence of previous friendships with a former member and an extra effort to improve their sports performance, which is especially used by low performance athletes in order to fit in with the accepted standards and which tends to be valued by teammates. As individual characteristics, high sports performance and being active, a confrontational attitude towards provocations and mastering social skills in this social setting, may also facilitate integration of new teammates. On the other hand, factors mentioned as increasing the risk of being rejected are low sports performance, passivity towards provocations and conflict avoidance.

Social settings

The majority of participants mentioned that their involvement in bullying episodes overlapped across different social settings. Athletes who got involved in bullying episodes inside the sports club tended to enact the same roles in other social contexts; this was especially true of victims and perpetrators. This observation of a stable behavioural pattern of victims and perpetrators focuses attention on individual characteristics, rather than social setting particularities. However, this does not necessarily mean that contextual factors should not be considered to better understand bullying episodes.

VOLLEYBALL ATHLETE: Yes, sometimes he gets home upset and ... because it happens in school and also here. It could be just in school, but sometimes it is here too.

Roles

Profiles

Bullies were described as usually more active and better athletes. Being more active consists of a pattern of behaviour associated with being more physically active, dominant and extrovert (among other characteristics). Perpetrators tended to present a more confrontational attitude and to be exhibitionist. Impulsivity was also associated with bullies; they were described as having difficulties in reflecting on others' emotional experience and on the consequences of their actions for others. They also had a tendency to blame others for both personal and team failures, focusing their attacks mostly on more vulnerable members, usually low performance athletes. Many participants also described bullies as trouble makers, and considered the origin of their problems as due to their having been raised in dysfunctional families.

GYMNASTICS ATHLETE: (...) they have that look of someone who wants to be the leader of the group. They want ... They want to control the others to ... so they can insult others, to devalue them and say: "This is who I am; I'm cooler than all the others".

Victims tended to be considered as not fitting the accepted standards, for having different personal interests, different ways of thinking and usually not behaving according to what peers expect. Basically, being perceived as different makes athletes more prone to be victimized. Other factors are passivity and body issues, mostly peculiar characteristics, clumsiness, being overweight and a lack of skills for sports practice in general.

JUDO ATHLETE: The ones who are usually victimized are physically weaker, or shorter, or plump. One doesn't feel ... They are the ones who are not able to intimidate others and show respect. This makes us intimidate and target them. It can also be some guys who are not that intelligent or can't give the right answer in the right moment and let things go ... they listen and listen, and don't fight back.

Although victims tended to be more passive than other athletes, participants mentioned that in some situations, some victims over-reacted to banter and lost control. This happened because they showed some rigidity and had difficulties in dealing with provocations, which caused perpetrators to increase these provocations (especially in "cross fire" as previously described) because they considered the over-reaction of the victim to be a source of amusement.

HANDBALL ATHLETE: (...) As an example: we have a teammate here (...) he has a hot sister and everybody provokes him. If he doesn't pay attention, others get bored and stop provoking because it's not funny. But when he gets pissed off, they keep provoking him and he gets even more [fun to provoke] ... so he gets really upset.

Victims are usually low performance athletes and many of them try hard to improve their skills in training sessions. This extra effort is an attitude of sacrifice to cope with marked difficulties in sports practice due to lack of ability; it has the purpose of increasing sports performance and, consequently, being valued by peers and feeling part of the group.

Social status

Victims and perpetrators also differed regarding their social status and popularity in the peer group. Bullies usually had a central position in the peer network, a high social status and popularity. Although some athletes criticized perpetrators and disliked their behaviours, bullies tended to have a high social status. On the other hand, victims tended to have a low social status, low popularity and to be less socially recognized by peers, which resulted in their exclusion and isolation.

FOOTBALL ATHLETE: They are (...) the changing room bosses. They are the team and changing room leaders. The ones who like to exhibit ... They somehow have ... they are those who are respected in the sports club. The ones who are respected in the team. Well, that's it: the ones who are more respected.

Coach

The coach can play an important role in bullying episodes between athletes, because of the way he/she manages peer relations. When asked about how the coach perceived both bullies and victims, a considerable number of athletes provided new information by describing three main types of coach management, which we label as involvement, artificial selection and equal opportunities.

Involvement refers to the coach actually taking part in bullying episodes, either implicitly or explicitly. Implicit involvement includes ignoring the bullying; one possible explanation for this may be that some coaches consider some aggressive behaviours, especially between boys, as part of the game and normal in sports culture. Explicit involvement includes episodes in which a coach joins the perpetrators and directly contributes to bullying episodes by mocking the victims and supporting the bullies.

RESEARCHER: What do you think your coach thought about those two isolated colleagues of yours?
FOOTBALL ATHLETE: That they were weak (laugh).
RESEARCHER: How weak? Explain to me.
FOOTBALL ATHLETE: He was worried about our football; concerning football performance they were ... very weak.
RESEARCHER: So what he wanted was the team to improve, is that right?
FOOTBALL ATHLETE: The mister didn't ... he used to speak more with us; in the speeches he wasn't much ... In X sports club, mister only used to speak to us [the high performance athletes].

Artificial selection consists of a progressive selection of the best athletes, to whom privileges are given. By using artificial selection, coaches focus their attention mostly on sports performance, and gradually exclude lower performance athletes by devaluing them.

Equal opportunities is based on giving equal opportunities for sports participation to all athletes, without taking account of their sports performance level. Here, a coach focuses attention on the psychosocial development of athletes instead of on sports performance and winning at all costs. This type of management is more inclusive and promotes participation of all youngsters.

Our findings suggest that *artificial selection* is generally the most used type of management in youth sports training. Although youth sports training should be focused on skill development and inclusion of all, artificial selection is considered normal and expected by many stakeholders, in light of the competitive nature of sport.

Practical implications

Consequences

The victims and bystanders in our research tended to consider bullying episodes as negative, and alluded to the consequences of victimization. Many different consequences were reported, which makes it difficult to put them in specific categories. However, there was a considerable convergence of narratives considering victimization as strongly contributing to early drop out of sports practice; this brought about a gradual exclusion of bullying victims from sports practice. Victimization could also lead victims to search for another social setting, perhaps another sports club, or to engage in a different sport, in order to fit in, rather than drop out of sport altogether.

> FOOTBALL ATHLETE: *They are weaker! The players who perform really bad and don't withstand ... they kind of die: don't endure and quit. Usually they are the ones who quit; they are mentally weak! I wouldn't say physically, but they are mentally weak.*

Prevention and intervention strategies

When being victimized, or observing bullying episodes as a bystander, athletes used coping strategies to deal with the situation. Both victims and bystanders reported and described several strategies they considered helpful to deal with bullying, as well as the ones they actually used when involved in bullying episodes (Table 7.2).

Both victims and bystanders considered that crucial strategies to effectively tackle bullying were the intervention of the coach, sensitizing actions and talking to bullies about their behaviours. The coach is considered an authority figure who should intervene to manage and regulate disruptive behaviours, and deal with bullying episodes. By sensitizing, we mean educating sports agents (athletes, coaches, sports leaders) about bullying. This is mainly a prophylactic measure, and has the aim of raising awareness about the topic, identifying behaviours and providing guidelines to deal with peer aggression. Finally, dialogue with the bullies means talking to perpetrators about their aggressive behaviours in order to stop them getting involved in bullying episodes.

Table 7.2 Coping strategies used by victims and bystanders

Role	Strategy	Coping style
Victims	**Proposed**	
	Revenge	CFP
	Avoidance	CFE
	Used	
	Seek support	CFE
	Avoidance	CFE
Bystanders	**Proposed**	
	Punishment	CFP
	Monitoring	CFP
	Peer resolution	CFE
	Victims' responsibility	CFE
	Used	
	Avoidance	CFE
	Awareness	CFE
	Defence of victim	CFP
	Active integration	CFP
	Support to victim	CFP
	Dialogue with bullies	CFP

CFP = coping focused on problem; CFE = coping focused on emotion.

However, many victims and bystanders stated that bullying cannot be tackled and has no solution. This viewpoint considers bullying and its consequences to be inevitable.

Victims also mentioned ignoring and *avoidance* as strategies commonly used to deal with bullying. However, on many occasions, victims also expressed a will to adopt a more assertive attitude and to confront perpetrators, based on *revenge* (an eye for an eye). Although victims did not usually react in this way, they often described a wish for justice to be done, to be able to counter-attack the bullies and do to them the same as they had suffered.

Victims tended to report more strategies based on coping focused on emotion, while bystanders proposed more pro-active strategies to deal with bullying. Examples of some of these coping focused on problem resolutions are *punishment* of bullies, and more substantial and accurate *monitoring* of less supervised areas (hot spots for bullying occurrence). However, these strategies can be complemented by less pro-active ones like the ones we labelled as *peer resolution*, without adult intervention and *victims' responsibility*. Peer resolution suggests that bullying episodes are dealt with more successfully among peers because adult intervention is perceived as negative, while victims' responsibility suggests the need to consider how victims contribute to the beginning and maintenance of the bullying cycle, and to promote some insight about it in victims in order to help them to change their behaviour.

When asked about the strategies actually used, victims reported *seeking support* among other adults besides the coach, or avoiding getting involved in bullying episodes by searching for other areas where it was less likely to occur.

The bystanders also reported strategies used when involved in bullying episodes. Besides avoidance (like the victims), bystanders also mentioned a more pro-active range of strategies like *defence of the victim*, combined with *talking with perpetrators* and the *emotional support of the victims*. Defence of the victim means actively protecting the targeted athlete from bullying, while talking with perpetrators has the aim of changing their behaviour and stopping abusive behaviours. Finally, support of the victim means affective support of more vulnerable and targeted athletes. Another strategy commonly used by bystanders was to actively contribute to the *positive integration* of isolated and excluded athletes, especially the new incomers who lack social references in the new peer group, by inviting them to engage in group activities and to interact with others. This inclusive attitude contributes to help excluded and/or more introverted athletes to feel (and eventually become) part of the peer group. Finally, bystanders mentioned the need of reflection and *awareness* about the impact of bullies' behaviour on the victims, which may lead to the decrease of victimization by developing empathy. This strategy was reported to be used mostly in the cases in which bullies had also been victimized in the past.

Regarding perceptions of the effectiveness of strategies used to deal with bullying, victims tended to consider that their efforts produced little change. Bystanders were divided their opinions: some of them considered their interventions ineffective, while others considered their strategies to have been effective in tackling bullying, bringing about a decrease or total cessation of bullying episodes.

Discussion

Bullying or banter?

Although a clear operational definition of bullying exists, the interpretation given to aggressive behaviours may vary considerably. One of the major difficulties in developing research on bullying in sport is the subjective nature of the concept, which allows quite distinct interpretations of the same episodes. It's important to discuss the definition and nature of bullying behaviours in sport in order to acknowledge them, and to understand the differences between bullying and other misunderstand concepts.

In our data analysis, we divided the athletes' narratives according to their involvement in bullying episodes as victims, bullies and/or bystanders. These different roles are clearly defined and we think of them as separate, but in practice these boundaries tend to blur because athletes often reported their involvement in different roles in various circumstances; indeed, as in school bullying, only a minority of children are exclusively victims or bullies.

Circumstances

Types of bullying

The most prevalent type of bullying is verbal (e.g. mocking, insults), followed by social (e.g. social exclusion, ignoring). Physical bullying was also reported (e.g. bullying episodes involving physical contact), but was less prevalent. Athletes tended to use mostly verbal aggression and then if the bullying became more aggravated – if its frequency and duration increased – they tended to also exclude the victims.

The contents of the narratives suggest the existence of sports culture based on the traditional male stereotype, which defines acceptable and desirable behavioural standards, and the perfect body image. This increases the probability that those who do not fit these standards will be victimized, in line with research previously conducted (Brackenridge, Rivers, Gough & Llewellyn, 2007; Hill, 2015; Roberts, 2008). Often more important than the content of verbal abuse, is the way things are said. Disguised aggression allows the perpetrator to defend himself if the victim breaks silence and talks with an adult about having been verbally victimized, because he can say it was just banter and that the victim is the one who should have the capacity to engage in it, rather than over-reacting to simple provocations.

Location

The changing room is the location in which bullying episodes tend to occur, because it is a less supervised area, and allows perpetrators to target their victims without being approached by adults.

In training areas, the activities are supervised by the coach, which can explain why the prevalence of bullying is lower. Although the presence and intervention of the coach are crucial to decreasing bullying prevalence, the way the coach manages the group of athletes and the peer interactions among the young athletes themselves, influences the expression of bullying behaviours; it can even increase bullying prevalence and the acceptance of aggressive behaviours among athletes (Evans et al., 2016; Kirby & Wintrump, 2002; O'Connor & Graber, 2014).

Number of athletes involved

Bullying episodes are mostly performed by a group of athletes rather than just one to one; this result is in line with previous research on school bullying (Smith, 2014). The need for bystanders for bullying to occur was described as a way of enabling bullies to show their dominance towards the victims to other athletes within the peer group.

Reasons

Fundamental reasons

Abuse of perceived power, hierarchy and rivalry are strongly related, in so far as bullying behaviours serve to obtain social status among peers. Envy consists of the desire to possess things another has. This feeling may be at the root of some of the attacks made by the perpetrator in order to feel powerful by devaluing the other. The concepts of abuse of perceived power and hierarchy have a considerable overlap, and both have the aim of attacking the victims by subjugation, devaluation, intimidation and blaming.

Concerning the bullying behaviours based on rivalry, these consist in struggling to have a privileged status within the peer group, or a privileged relationship with the coach. Envy and jealousy can also sustain some of these aggressive behaviours.

Peer pressure

To understand bullying in sport it's necessary to consider group behaviours. "Divergence from standard" and "imitation" are two different group mechanisms, but they have two things in common: the target of the attacks are athletes who diverge from established norms and do not fit the accepted standards, and the attacks have the purpose of obtaining social status in the peer group. Some of the young athletes interviewed expressed a considerable need for peer acceptance, which may lead them on some occasions to engage in aggressive behaviours, seeking external approval from peers, even if these behaviours are not in accordance with their own social values and moral standards. This is corroborated by several narratives of athletes who criticized their own past behaviours, and showed regret for getting involved in bullying episodes as perpetrators. Their involvement in those episodes was justified by their incapacity at that time to think about the consequences of their actions for the victims, and the need to feel accepted by other high status peer members who valued aggression.

The category *victims' responsibility* seems to fit in this domain. Here the purpose is to get attention from peers, even in a negative way, considering that it's better to be the centre of attention by being mocked rather than feeling indifferent to others. We found that victims put some effort into fitting the peer group expectations and being accepted, but sometimes these athletes felt incapable of doing it properly, and thought that nobody understood them.

Individual characteristics

The individual characteristics describe some of the characteristics associated with the victims' profile, and also help to partially explain bullying episodes. Victims are described as not fitting the accepted standards concerning personality, body image and general ability for sports activities. Being perceived as different makes them more prone to being targeted; however, the capacity of the athletes to establish positive relations with their peers, to develop playful interactions and to cope with provocations seems to be most important to avoid bullying.

Integration

The integration process of new incomers into the peer group is a time of higher risk for them. New members may be perceived as valuable, and their integration usually proceeds without difficulty. On the other hand, the new incomer may be rejected and excluded based on many of the reasons described above. The athletes who fit in the accepted standards are more easily accepted and vice versa. A lack of physical ability and clumsiness (Escury & Dudink, 2010), low sports performance, and being perceived as different (Roberts, 2008) increase the probability of an athlete being verbally attacked.

The extra effort previously described can frequently be perceived as intent to be accepted in the peer group, by improving one's sports performance, which is strongly valued in sports groups and may contribute to gaining acceptance from higher status athletes. This strategy was frequently adopted by athletes who initially felt excluded but wanted to be part of the group, so they coped with their difficulty in this way.

Social settings

The majority of athletes consider bullying to overlap across different social settings. Volk and Lagzdins (2009) also found that bullying involvement tends to co-occur across the sports club and school. These findings suggest the existence of stable behavioural patterns of victims and perpetrators, although do not necessarily mean ignoring environmental factors to understand bullying episodes. These results are corroborated by other researchers, who consider that bullying involvement in sports settings tends to extend to other social settings such as school (Escury & Dudink, 2010; Ventura et al., 2019).

Roles

Profiles and social status of bullies and victims

The profiles of perpetrators clearly overlap with an exaggerated stereotype of masculinity. Activity and high sports performance were clearly highlighted by most of the athletes. Both are valued in sports settings, because masculinity is partially measured by success in sports activities (Roberts, 2008). Bullies are usually popular and have high social status. Athletes also described bullies as individuals with low empathy and who seek to criticize and blame others for their personal failures.

Victims were generally described as passive and with less ability to perform sport. Some of them were also described as over-reactive to provocations, which remits to lack of control. This profile may be considered a risk for being targeted in sport (Brackenridge, Rivers, Gough & Llewellyn, 2007; Hill, 2015; Jachyna, 2013; Roberts, 2008), and contributes to victims having a low social status in the peer group.

Coach

The athletes from all the sports studied, considered the coach to be an authority figure and a leader regarding the management of the peer group, and that he could have a strong influence on the prevalence of bullying behaviours among athletes. However, sports culture, which normalizes some types of aggressive behaviours, may contribute to the maintenance or escalation of bullying episodes, especially among boys. The adults responsible for managing the athletes' group (coach or teacher) sometimes get implicitly involved in the bullying by avoiding dealing with aggression, devaluing its significance, or for being present but doing nothing when it occurred. This can contribute to the acculturation of bullying (O'Connor & Graber, 2014). There are some coaches who directly and explicitly participate in bullying, by insulting and mocking athletes, using it as a method to correct them (Brackenridge, Rivers, Gough & Llewellyn, 2007).

Artificial selection is an attitude of the coach towards the group of athletes highly focused on sports performance and winning (instead of on the psychosocial development of the youngsters), and it contributes to a progressive elimination of low performance athletes over time. This management approach contributes to excluding the less successful athletes, and turns youth sport into a selective activity, which can only be accessed by the best athletes. Considering victims are often low performance athletes, this extreme focus on winning may contribute to justify some forms of exclusion and bullying.

Practical implications

Consequences

Athletes mentioned several consequences of bullying, in particular early drop out of sports practice due to victimization, which was suggested by previous research (Escury & Dudink, 2010; Evans et al., 2016). However, our data shows that some athletes do not quit practising but, instead, change sports club and/or the sport practised, seeking another social setting in which they feel more accepted, in order to escape victimization.

The early drop out of sport by victims contributes to the segregation and exclusion of athletes who don't fit the accepted standards. This is largely accepted in sport, and in some cases seems to be supported by both athletes and coaches.

Coping strategies

Victims reported *revenge* and *avoidance* as the most efficient strategies to deal with bullying. This may seem strange, as these coping strategies are rather opposite to each other. Many of the victimized athletes mentioned that they would have liked to react more actively, and expressed negative feelings towards being dominated by perpetrators. However, when asked about how they dealt with bullying when they were victimized, many of them mentioned searching for *support*, but mostly *avoidance*. Avoidance is associated with a coping focused on emotion style, which is less effective in the resolution of continual stressful episodes (Lazarus, 1991). This coping style is less pro-active, and when combined with the silence of the victims about their involvement in bullying episodes, it can contribute to the maintenance of victimization.

Bystanders consider the best strategies to deal with bullying are control of disruptive behaviours by using *punishment*, and *monitoring* the hot spots where bullying episodes tend to occur. These are behavioural strategies which can be implemented in sports clubs. Bystanders also mentioned other strategies such as *peer resolution* and direct intervention with victims in order to make them understand how they may contribute to bullying involvement (*victims' responsibility*). *Peer resolution* means that athletes should learn how to solve bullying without the intervention of adults. The athletes who reported this strategy argued that adult mediation was often negative, and that peers can regulate their behaviour within the peer group. The responsibility of the victims is not the same as blaming; the former points to having a positive discussion with the athletes who are victimized, but somehow promote being targeted due to their disruptive behaviour. This discussion has a positive purpose, and aims to help the victim to break the cycle of aggression.

When involved in bullying episodes, although some coping focused on emotion strategies were used (*awareness*, *avoidance*), bystanders have mostly used coping focused on problem resolution strategies, which are more pro-active and effective in changing a stressful situation. This may help explain the perception of success of their interventions to deal with bullying. Hawkins, Pepler and Craig (2001) found that when bystanders to school bullying react on behalf of the victim, they tend to be effective in solving a bullying episode.

Summary and main conclusions

Many athletes devalue the importance of bullying behaviours, considering them normal banter and part of the game.

The most frequent type of bullying is verbal. However, social bullying was also frequently reported; this was mostly being excluded and ignored (rumour spreading was much less reported). Openly physical bullying was rarely reported. Bullying episodes tended to occur in changing rooms because these are less supervised areas, and coaches are usually not aware of its occurrence. In the changing room, "cross fire" can often be observed; it may be considered a social interaction to assess relative peer social status. It may lead to bullying, but cannot be considered a type of bullying in itself.

Amongst the many factors that may help to explain bullying, athletes highlighted three: fundamental reasons, peer pressure and individual characteristics.

When a new season begins, the integration of new athletes in the peer group may be harder and some athletes tend to be rejected. There are some factors which may promote integration, while some others promote exclusion.

Bullying episodes occur in different social settings besides sport. Victims and bullies tend to enact the same roles elsewhere as they do in sports settings. This highlights the need to describe the profiles of victims and bullies, and to consider individual factors. Bullies are usually high status athletes, more physically active, with higher sports performance, characterized also by a confrontational attitude and impulsivity. On the other hand, victims are described as low status athletes, different from the accepted standards, more passive and usually with body issues (e.g. overweight).

The coach plays an important role in bullying. The way the coach manages the peer group (e.g. acceptance or disapproval of bullying) reflects on athletes' behaviours.

Both victims and bystanders use a variety of coping strategies to deal with bullying. These may be more or less efficient; the way athletes cope with bullying needs to be analysed in order to improve their skills. There is considerable convergence of opinion that many athletes may abandon sport early due to being victimized.

Chapter 8
Narratives of the coaches

Here we present the findings from the study of 32 coaches who had trained the athletes interviewed in the previous chapter. Although the coaches were not directly involved in bullying episodes between peers, they provide a complementary outsider perspective, very helpful for better understanding bullying episodes. The focus on the coach perspective led to the inclusion of new topics and brought some new information, which allowed deeper insights about bullying in youth sports training. Some topics not initially included in the interview script occurred spontaneously in the majority of the interviews; their high prevalence and importance led to their further exploration and inclusion here in the results and discussion. The findings presented here can be compared with those from the athletes in the previous chapter. On many occasions, coaches described the same episodes reported by their athletes when they were interviewed.

The narratives of the coaches

The data collected was organized according to content themes. A major division was between (1) those coaches who considered that bullying did not occur in sports settings (n = 11), and (2) those coaches who acknowledged the existence of bullying among athletes (n = 21).

For group 1, we explored some conceptual issues. How these 11 coaches perceived aggressiveness, and how they defined bullying, under the category "bullying or banter?", were issues that came up frequently for most of them.

For group 2, from the narratives of these 21 coaches we formed three main content categories: the circumstances of bullying episodes; the roles enacted; and practical implications. Each one of these was further divided into the following sub-categories:

- **Bullying circumstances** has seven sub-categories: types of bullying; reasons for bullying occurrence; different social settings overlap; crucial moments for victimization; factors which facilitate or make difficult the

integration of new members into the peer group; hazing rituals; and changes over time (prevalence and types);
- **Roles enacted** has three sub-categories: profiles (victims and perpetrators); social status; and the role played by the coach in peer group management;
- **Practical implications** has two sub-categories: bullying consequences and prevention/intervention coping strategies adopted by victims and bystanders.

When presenting the data, we often give some illustrative quotes. There are some comments within [brackets], that we have provided to enable better understanding of the idea being expressed. These comments are not part of the speech of the athletes.

(1) **Narratives of coaches who considered that bullying did not occur in sports settings**

Conceptual issues: aggressiveness

Many of these coaches considered aggressiveness to be important and useful for sports practice. It was considered to have an instrumental character, leading many coaches to encourage their athletes to be aggressive, based on their definition of the concept.

HANDBALL COACH: The role of aggressiveness is to try to improve each time, which means not to give up a ball disputed with the opponent or in any dispute at all. In these cases one has to be aggressive. I don't mean fight or punch; don't do that but be aggressive. Knowing that people are there fighting for something. And are doing things for a common cause; in this case, it's the team.

Some coaches considered the enactment of aggressiveness crucial to improve the performance of the athlete and to compete properly. Although some coaches made a clear distinction between bullying (and other forms of anti-social behaviour) and what they labelled as *positive aggressiveness* described above, others considered that bullying did not occur in sport at all, and that aggressive behaviours were part of the game and there was no reason to be worried about them.

Bullying vs. banter

Another common theme was to label bullying behaviours as normal and desirable banter among athletes rather than systematic abuse. There is a thin line between these two concepts; however, some important differences must be acknowledged. How coaches label these interactions was based on the perceived evaluation of the feelings of the athletes involved. The coaches who considered that bullying did not occur, tended to devalue the impact of competitive or aggressive peer interactions by considering them normal and even desirable. They considered that both parties also tended to express positive feelings or, in the case of a conflict, could resolve it quickly and easily. These peer interactions were labelled as banter, or teasing, because there were no perceived negative consequences for those involved.

(2) Narratives of coaches who acknowledged the existence of bullying among athletes

There were also coaches who considered that bullying did occur, criticized these behaviours and were alert to the need to tackle them. These coaches considered that at least one of the athletes involved in such aggressive interactions felt bad about them, and considered them negative and abusive. These coaches not only acknowledged the existence of bullying in youth sport, but also reported episodes and described the circumstances.

Besides the pre-defined topics of the interview scripts, some other topics such as *crucial moments*, *integration* or *coach actions*, were frequently brought up by most of the coaches. These were considered important and are also analysed here.

SWIMMING COACH: In my opinion there is bullying in swimming. I'm not talking about any case in particular, but I've seen bullying episodes among athletes, which on many occasions led to the dropping out of sport early. I think it exists; there are some more severe cases and others less severe but yes, it exists.

Types of bullying

The most prevalent type of bullying reported was verbal (especially mocking), followed by social bullying (mostly exclusion). The coaches described how athletes might mock and insult peers, and how those ones targeted in this way can end up being excluded from the rest of the peer group.

Reasons

Concerning the reasons for bullying occurring, the coaches described what we label as *hierarchy, abuse of perceived power, rivalry* and *envy*. The hierarchy was considered as strongly associated with the period of integration of a younger athlete into a group of older teammates. The new athletes are often tested and their acceptance and success in the integration process may be easier or harder, depending on the acceptance of the new incomer.

FOOTBALL COACH: Even when I was a player I was part of a relatively good team, and especially in the first training session of the season, the new players who went there to train were ostracized.

RESEARCHER: The ones who were new members and had played so far in other sports clubs? There was an already formed group of athletes; it was done to the ones who had recently arrived?

FOOTBALL COACH: Exactly. Even those ... even before being integrated into the group, in this period, the ones who tried to be part of the group used to be mocked and stuff like that.

Abuse of perceived power was described as the main mechanism to explain bullying episodes. It basically consists of an aggressive coercion towards another who is perceived as weaker, with the purpose of increasing the social status of the perpetrator. Besides this, *rivalry* and *envy* were also referred to by coaches as reasons for bullying episodes to occur. Rivalry between athletes and the competition among them to achieve better sporting results were highlighted as a possible source of peer conflict, and a reason for bullying. Envy was also described as partially explaining bullying, and it can be divided into two important but distinct mechanisms: the first is the envy felt by some athletes regarding others' qualities or sports results, which could lead to attacks on these teammates. The second is the jealousy felt by some athletes towards the relationship between one of his colleagues and the coach; in these cases, an athlete feels that more attention is given to certain athletes, and may attack them for that.

GYMNASTICS COACH: They [the perpetrators] are usually not good athletes; they are average or even low performance athletes. Very often, bullying occurs because of the envy felt by these individuals; because they want to be like others and can't do it, so, bullying is the only way to put teammates down, to prejudice, to create difficulties ... several times even ... because the best athletes are well accepted by everybody and usually everybody likes them. So, in this case, the person who feels rejected may engage in bullying with the purpose of getting others to dislike them [the best athletes] and to be noticed [by the remaining peers].

Social settings

The majority of the coaches considered that athletes also tend to engage in bullying episodes in other social settings, and to enact the same roles as they did in sport. This suggests some stability of the behaviours, based on the profiles of victims and perpetrators. It does not necessarily mean social and environmental factors should not be considered when analysing bullying behaviours, but it highlights the importance of the characteristics of both victims and perpetrators for bullying occurrence.

Crucial moments

The period of integration of younger athletes in the older group of athletes is considered a sensitive phase by many coaches, which means a greater risk to new and younger incomers of being ostracized and victimized. The main reasons reported for this were hierarchy and rivalry issues, and the differences of maturity between the older and the younger athletes. A mentality which supports hierarchy may legitimize the abuse of younger athletes, and rivalry may increase with the incoming of new athletes to the training group. Mixing athletes of different ages, especially during some periods of adolescence in which maturational differences are particularly apparent, was considered a potential source of abusive relations, because older athletes perceive younger athletes as weaker. This aspect was mostly present in team sports. In individual and combat sports, when an athlete integrates into the older athletes' group, he is inserted into a group, but not into a team. When sports are individual, the transition to the older athletes' group seems less important.

> JUDO COACH: I totally agree [that the integration of younger athletes may be difficult]! When younger athletes are integrated into the older athletes' group, considering the fact they are the younger ones, makes them a more appetizing target. This is quite clear! Those who have strong personalities are rarely victimized, but the ones who are more passive, who aren't good athletes, who aren't top, they suffer ... They really suffer! But in judo, at least in this sports club, everything is very smooth. No one gets pissed off and there is a good social environment. Sometimes bullying is not aggressive; instead, it's pedagogic.

Integration

Most of the coaches referred to a positive integration of the athletes in the peer group, which was facilitated by high sports performance, activity and extra effort. Being highly skilled in sports activities and active were two factors related with high social status among male adolescents. Although extra effort tends to be associated with low performance athletes as a way to improve their sports skills and to be accepted by peers, it's perceived as valuable by the peers. These factors are considered positive by the rest of the group members, and help new same-age athletes to be accepted, and also younger athletes. However, a considerable number of coaches also reported episodes in which athletes were excluded by peers. The reasons highlighted for this negative integration of peers were two personal characteristics: passivity and low sports performance.

ATHLETICS COACH: What usually happens in both individual and team sports is ... when a new incomer arrives, he is always tested: if peers realize he is strong enough, can handle himself and possibly counterattacks [then], he is accepted. If they see the contrary, I feel he always will be ...

Researcher: ... more vulnerable.

Athletics coach: ... more vulnerable! Now, he has two possibilities to be successful: either he is technically good – even if he doesn't have a confrontational attitude – he is physically and technically good and others respect him for that, or because he is much better than the others. If his skill level is a little bit lower and he doesn't reply properly (to provocations), he is screwed.

Hazing rituals

The participants reported hazing rituals and described both positive and negative effects. The opinions and attitudes towards hazing rituals were divided. Some coaches considered these behaviours to positively influence the integration of new incomers, justifying it by considering hazing rituals to have a playful component, which promoted a positive social environment and strengthened peer bonds, while others described hazing as nonsense and negative, and considered it abusive. There was no clear consensus on this topic. Some coaches who strongly expressed themselves against bullying, supported and in some cases even participated in hazing rituals. On the other hand, some other coaches were strongly against hazing and considered it an aggressive interaction and a type of bullying.

Changes over time

Regarding the perception of the coaches about the changes in bullying behaviours over time, most coaches considered that bullying behaviours tended to be expressed differently, at different ages. Two main positions were reported: coaches who considered bullying behaviours to be more frequent in younger athletes and to decrease over time, and coaches who considered adolescence to be the most sensitive period for the occurrence of bullying behaviours.

Many of the coaches described how in individual and combat sports, the negative sporting results of an athlete do not negatively affect the relationship of that athlete with his peers. They justified it based on the fact that in these cases, each athlete depends exclusively on himself to influence his sports performance. On the other hand, so far as team sports were concerned, several coaches described negative team results as a risk factor to increasing interpersonal conflicts among peers. When these kinds of conflicts occurred, some athletes were thought to blame others for the low performance of the team and to exclude them from the peer group. Coaches also considered that when sporting results are positive, even if there were some latent conflicts, these tended to be ignored and camouflaged and only to rise up when results started to be negative. However, some coaches also described negative moments, in which the team was having difficulties in achieving the expected sporting performance, as an opportunity for peers to unite in order to cope with adversity.

RUGBY COACH: Oh yes, clearly. (...) If the results are bad ... And also, the contrary: when a team starts winning, a winning attitude also arises, but sometimes it may happen ... a team that wins and suddenly loses one or two games may fall ... when they put their feet on the ground and realize they were competing at a higher level than their own, that may be difficult for them to accept.

Researcher: and how about blaming? What happens when results are bad?

RUGBY COACH: Blaming? They are quite comfortable to point the finger at each other. But we [coaches] are here to minimize those things, because in a team sport like rugby, it's not just one athlete's fault, isn't that right? There are 15 kids on the pitch, and none of them can enter into the team and do it by himself, especially in older teams. While in sub 8, sometimes a boy can grab the ball and play almost alone, when they reach 16 years old, they can't do it anymore, so ... but blaming? Yes, there is clearly a tendency to point the finger and say: "you didn't do this or that".

Roles

Profiles

The perpetrators were described by the majority of the coaches as high performance athletes, more active, with a confrontational attitude, impulsive and with a higher tendency to blame others for personal or team failures. Although this was the prevalent picture of the bullies, some coaches described them as low performance athletes, who attacked their peers based on the envy felt for being less skilled than them.

ATHLETICS COACH: Well the thing is ... in handball, as far as I remember, they [the perpetrators] were relatively good athletes. They were good athletes! (...) they were kids who wanted to assert themselves and didn't have much tolerance towards others, didn't have the necessary empathy to understand if the other person feels funny about what happens or not; and there is the one – besides the bully – who has a higher predisposition to suffer from bullying, which is the one who has more difficulties in reacting to provocations and banter, and then an aggressive circle is created.

There was also a high convergence concerning the profile of the victims, who were generally described as low sports performance athletes, with excessive reactivity to provocations. Particular physical characteristics such as being overweight were also often mentioned.

RUGBY COACH: As athletes, they [victims] are the ones who start ... they make impressive progress concerning technique, but they make an incredible extra effort on the pitch for that ... inside and outside; they are ... they seek to know more, they want more, but they also lack some technical skills and motor coordination. Usually they can achieve high performance later, with extra work and training; not now at this age we are talking about [adolescence], but some years later they can get there and achieve a high performance.

Social status

The perpetrators were described as having high social status, being popular among peers and enjoying getting involved in bullying episodes, while victims were considered to have a low social status and to express negative feelings towards bullying.

ATHLETICS COACH: They [bullies] are very often the group leaders, exactly because of that status; I think it's related with the sports results they can achieve. They tend to be the leaders of the group and other peers admire them, and follow them, which provides them with a social status that allows them to mock younger athletes without suffering the consequences of themselves being approached by some teammate or excluded from the peer group.

Coach action

The way coaches manage the peer group was considered an important topic to partially explain bullying episodes. Although not included in the interview script, this topic was brought up several times, with a considerable convergence of opinions. The coaches tended to make an "artificial selection", which means they tended to help the athletes with higher sports performance, focusing their attention on winning the competitions. The elimination and early dropping out of athletes with low performance over the years was considered normal, and a part of youth sports training, turning it into a social setting in which there is no room for the ones who are considered weaker, and not matching up to the standards based on extreme competitiveness.

FOOTBALL COACH: As they grow as athletes, when they are about to reach 15, 16 years old (...) we can clearly observe a radical selection, because only the strong ones can reach here [and], the weak stay behind. And the ones who were part of that group before and were susceptible to suffer from bullying, they no longer ... they don't interact with these players anymore.

JUDO COACH: (...) the judo competition is based on that selection. There is no room for weakness in judo! There is a continuous and individual selection in this setting (...) when they reach seniors age, usually the ones who are not very, very strong, can't handle it. In the end, it's like it was a natural selection!

Implications

Intervention

The coaches from all sports named several different prevention and intervention strategies. The most reported ones were the existence of a high "cohesion" in the peer group and of "coach intervention" in preventing and intervening against bullying. The coaches from combat sports also quite often mentioned the "philosophy" of these sports, described as being against violence and bullying, and consequently to act as a moderator effect in any aggressive behaviour of the athletes.

Another factor frequently pointed out by combat sports coaches was the "coach as a father figure", which means that in these sports, the coach is usually seen as someone who takes care of his athletes and functions like a father. This tight emotional bond was described as an inhibitor for getting involved in bullying episodes.

WRESTLING COACH: The only thing missing is to be their real father; it's quite true. I help them in all possible ways, sometimes with negative consequences for my own [children] ... or my personal things ... it's for the good of the wrestling and for their own good, for when they leave sport. We develop them at a personal level, and also as athletes. Later, we meet them on the street and it's a delight: we see them a few years later and they say "hey, here is my coach!", it's always a good response.

Another factor highlighted by coaches from all the sports studied was what we called the "support chain", which is a way of promoting the gradual integration of younger peers into the older athletes' group, with the cooperation of older athletes in this task, helping the coach to promote a gradual and positive integration of new incomers.

VOLLEYBALL COACH: It depends. I think it depends on what? First: usually, and in most of the sports, the training groups are divided into groups of athletes within a 2-year range, so, there are those who ... athletes from first year, and athletes from second year. What happens? If the person who is integrated in the older squad has already belonged to the peer group – because two years ago he and his teammates were part of the same training group – there is no problem at all, because he already knows how things work, including the relations with other peers of that group, each one's social position, and even each one's personality; that helps! If we are integrated in a group and don't know anything about people, they get a little suspicious with others, and the others [older athletes] think like: "you come here to take my place" and also always have the tendency to protect themselves. If they know each other, then they think: "OK, it's you". They may think: "you want my place; Oh, but that's OK; I've already played with you and you are my friend ... "

Consequences

Another important topic which was not part of the initial script, but was brought up frequently and seemed important, is the consequences for the athletes who are victimized. If the integration of new incomers into the peer group fails, this can result in early drop out of sports practice, or changing the sports club as a consequence of victimization and/or as a strategy to avoid exclusion. The majority of the coaches mentioned a high prevalence of early sports drop out by victimized athletes, which converges with the perception of the athletes previously interviewed. However, coaches also reported other reasons for early sports drop out, namely the lack of opportunities to play, the lack of ability and sports skills, and athletes who changed the focus of their attention to other ludic activities (especially in adolescence).

ATHLETICS COACH: Absolutely; no doubt about that! By the time I was playing handball, I would have dropped out of sports practice a long time ago if it wasn't for my parents, who insisted that I keep playing. I was there at the sports club where I played handball and I wasn't feeling good so, it didn't make any sense. It all changed when I started practising athletics.

Discussion

Aggressiveness in sport

The majority of the coaches interviewed considered aggressiveness crucial for a good sports performance, seeing it as part of the practice of sport. This aggressiveness is perceived as positive when channelled for the right purposes (play respecting the rules), as a way to increase sports performance.

Considering this, the coaches tended to encourage athletes to be aggressive in both training sessions and competition.

However, aggressiveness and assertiveness are two separate concepts and should not be confused. The frequent encouragement of athletes to be aggressive is in line with a perception of sport based on the traditional stereotype of masculinity, which includes – among other attributes – the ideas of strength and aggressiveness. The possible misunderstanding of the differences between these concepts may contribute to the normalization of some bullying behaviours.

Bullying vs. banter

Regarding the existence of bullying in sports settings, the opinions of the coaches diverge between those who considered that bullying clearly exists in youth sport, and those who stated that bullying behaviours in sports settings do not occur. These coaches who considered sports settings to be free of bullying, described the interactions between athletes as banter, rather than bullying. However, some of them started their narratives considering this perspective, and changed their opinion when reflecting more deeply on this topic. Some coaches initially considered the interactions between athletes to be funny and free of aggressive content, but then reported some bullying episodes and abusive relations.

Although some stakeholders consider that bullying in youth sport does not happen, the data suggests that many of these coaches acknowledge the behaviours, but label them differently from bullying, because they evaluate aggressive behaviours in sport as "part of the game", resulting in their normalization and social acceptance (Volk & Lagzdins, 2009).

However, when interviews were conducted with the athletes who were trained by some of these coaches (who considered that bullying did not occur in sport), they often described episodes of victimization. Some of these episodes could not be acknowledged by the coach because they occurred out of his/her sight (e.g. changing room), but some others were reported with the tacit or even open approval of the coach. Tacit approval of the coach regards the acceptance of abusive behaviours among athletes, while open approval of the coach regards the episodes in which the coach reinforced the behaviours (e.g. laugh) or even joined the bullies. These coaches tended to devalue the consequences for the victims and provide justifications for their behaviours. Perhaps in some cases, there might be a misunderstanding about the nature of abusive dynamics of power.

When reporting data about the *crucial moments*, there is a quote of a Judo coach who stated "*Sometimes bullying is not aggressive; instead, it's pedagogic*". This is also an interesting perspective of bullying behaviours. Here, the aggressive behaviours are given a positive connotation, by considering them as a way to modulate the conduct of the athletes who need to get "tough". This idea of bullying as punishment or something to enhance the resilience of the athletes was also presented by some other coaches.

Circumstances

Types

The two main types of bullying reported by coaches were verbal and social bullying. Verbal bullying is expressed especially by mocking, and social bullying by multiple kinds of social exclusion. These two types of aggressive behaviours are intimately related; bullying tends to start with mocking, and when victims are clearly identified and are more frequently targeted, they also start to be excluded by the peer group. This leads to a progressive isolation of those athletes not accepted by teammates.

Reasons

The reasons given by the coaches to explain bullying behaviours correspond to abuse of perceived power, envy, rivalry and hierarchy. The narratives of the coaches focused on reasons which have to do with essentially individual reasons, and mostly personality traits, to explain bullying.

Social settings

There was a strong convergence of opinion concerning the existence of an overlap between different social settings for bullying roles. Athletes tend to engage in the same roles in bullying episodes, in different social settings. Coaches described the existence of stable behavioural patterns of victims and perpetrators. This data does not necessarily mean that coaches don't consider the social environment and peer pressure to partially explain bullying episodes, but that the personal characteristics of victims and perpetrators are considered the most crucial by coaches to explain bullying.

Crucial moments

Coaches considered the transition of younger athletes to the older peer group a sensitive period, with a higher likelihood of victimization of younger athletes. This transitional period can be problematic, and older and more powerful athletes may exert some pressure and be abusive to incoming and more vulnerable members. This may happen due to the need of some athletes to bully others in order to reaffirm their status among peers (targeting the new and vulnerable members), or due to a more collective attitude of the peer group in rejecting new members because they are felt to threaten the peer group's balance. As described by

Sherif (1958) many years ago, groups tend to create a proper identity and to exclude and compete with the ones considered outsiders. However, the majority of coaches also described a way to deal with this, which we called "support chain". Here, younger athletes are gradually integrated into the older athletes' group (e.g. start participating in some training sessions of the older athletes' group in the previous season) and some older athletes help the coach in the integration of the new incomers. This helps to diminish the boundaries between the older athletes and the new members, and to decrease any rejection of them.

Integration

Regarding the integration of incomers (same age) into an already existing group, both positive and negative episodes were described by the coaches. The factors described which contribute to a positive or a negative integration are high sports performance, being more active, presenting a confrontational attitude and making the extra effort to improve sports skills. These factors contribute to a positive integration, while athletes who are more passive and have lower sports skills have a higher tendency to be rejected.

Hazing rituals

Coaches reported distinct attitudes towards hazing rituals in youth sport, which may be divided into two major positions, based on the feelings towards hazing. Some coaches have a positive attitude towards hazing rituals and consider these behaviours a playful activity, which contributes to the integration of new members and promotes companionship. These participants usually allow athletes to haze the incomers, and sometimes even participated in these rituals themselves. On the other hand, there were coaches who expressed a negative attitude towards hazing rituals, described them as abusive behaviours and said that they did not allow these kinds of behaviours among their group of athletes.

Our data did not suggest a strong overlap between the concepts of bullying and hazing rituals: several coaches who reported bullying in youth sport, also reported positive attitudes towards hazing rituals and vice versa. Although hazing rituals were considered abusive by some coaches, these are not considered bullying. This result is contrary to the findings of Kirby and Wintrump (2002), who described hazing rituals in sport as normative abusive relationships and akin to bullying.

Changes over time

The coaches were divided into two main groups concerning their perceptions about the changes in prevalence and types of bullying behaviours through childhood and adolescence. The first group considered that bullying occurred mainly among younger children and decreased over time. These coaches referred mostly to physical bullying, and consider it to be childish. The second group considered bullying prevalence to reach its peak in adolescence, justifying this view by saying that adolescence is a more emotionally unstable period of life.

Roles

Profiles and social status of bullies and victims

The profiles of both victims and perpetrators provided by coaches have a considerable overlap with the ones provided by athletes. Both groups of participants describe bullies as high status athletes who fit into the accepted social standards, based on a tough mentality and traditional male stereotype, while victims are described as not fitting in with these accepted standards. Coaches also described how perpetrators have positive feelings when they victimize other teammates, while victims suffer from being involved in bullying episodes.

School bullying research has shown that victims are usually perceived as more likeable than bullies. However, perpetrators tend to be the most popular youngsters and to have a high social status, especially in social environments which accept and promote aggressive behaviours. Reaching popularity is a major concern among male adolescents, which is much more important than being a well-adapted youngster for many.

Coach

In "artificial selection" the coach focuses attention on the sports performance of the athletes rather than on their psychosocial development, which leads to an increasing pressure to eliminate the low performance athletes. It seems this way of management of the peer group promotes the exclusion of less adapted young athletes (by justifying it) and contributes to making youth sport an elitist setting, which is against the values of inclusion and equal opportunities to participate, in which youth sport is rooted.

Practical implications

Prevention and intervention strategies

The coaches pointed out many different prevention and intervention strategies. However, the most highlighted ones, by coaches from all sports included in our sample, were group "cohesion" and the "coach intervention". The coaches from combat sports also highlighted the "philosophy" of combat sports, which is considered to modulate aggressive behaviours, with the coach having a caregiver role towards his/her athletes.

Although less often, other factors were also frequently mentioned such as the surveillance of the "hot spots" for bullying to occur, direct intervention with peers, parents and other stakeholders, and raising awareness about the consequences of bullying behaviours.

Consequences

The most highlighted consequence of bullying in youth sport was early drop out of the victims. Changing sports club was also mentioned very often, which can be considered a consequence or a coping strategy. Still, some coaches who did not consider bullying to occur in youth sport, usually associated early drop out from sport with other factors such as lack of ability, or lack of engagement in competition.

Summary and main conclusions

Many coaches labelled bullying behaviours as normal banter, and often considered the threshold between these two concepts as being hard to define. The most reported type of bullying was verbal bullying, and coaches explained bullying behaviours based mostly on the same fundamental reasons as previously described for athletes.

There are specific moments in which the risk for bullying increases. The most important is when younger athletes are being introduced into an older peer group; they run a risk of being victimized due to issues around hierarchy (among others). However, the integration of new athletes tends to be positive, and some promoting factors for this were described.

Although many coaches disapprove of hazing rituals, there is no clear overlap between their attitudes to hazing and to bullying.

Coaches often describe bullies as high performance athletes, more physically active, with a confrontational attitude, impulsive and with a tendency to blame other peers for their personal failures. However, a considerable number of coaches also considered some bullies to be low performance athletes, who attacked popular and high performance athletes based on envy. Victims were described as more passive and usually low performance athletes.

Coaches considered their intervention (both preventive and direct) to be useful and important in managing bullying episodes.

Concerning the consequences of bullying, there was considerable consensus regarding early sports drop out of many athletes due to victimization. However, coaches also mentioned other reasons for athletes to quit sports practice.

Chapter 9
Narratives of the ex-elite athletes

In this chapter, we present the results of the recall study, in which nine ex-elite athletes (one from each sport studied) were interviewed. We explore the involvement of these older and experienced athletes in bullying episodes when they were younger and in training. These participants had had long and successful sports careers as athletes, and some of them had kept working in sports settings as coaches. They had a deep knowledge of the culture and mentality in their respective sports.

This retrospective approach provides another complementary perspective about bullying in youth sport. The results presented here can be compared with those described by both athletes and coaches in the previous chapters.

Analysis of the narratives of ex-elite athletes

The data collected was organized according to content themes. A major division was between (1) those ex-elite athletes who considered that bullying did not occur in sports settings (n = 4), and (2) those ex-elite athletes who considered that bullying happened and were involved (n = 5).

For group 1, we explored some conceptual issues. How these ex-elite athletes defined bullying, under the categories *bullying or banter?* and *normalization*. These participants also mentioned the *reasons* for which they believed bullying did not occur in sport, and reported *other types of interpersonal violence* which they did acknowledge. These ex-elite athletes who had never seen or got involved in bullying episodes as young athletes mostly represented individual sports athletes: football, gymnastics, judo and swimming.

For group 2, from the narratives of these ex-elite athletes who considered that bullying happened and were involved (athletics, handball, rugby, volleyball and wrestling), we formed three main content categories: the circumstances of bullying episodes; the roles enacted; and practical implications. Each one of these was divided into the following sub-categories:

- **Bullying circumstances** has seven sub-categories: frequency; types of bullying, number of athletes involved (individual or group); location; crucial moments; feelings towards bullying episodes; reasons for bullying and the possible overlap of bullying behaviours in different social settings; and the description of other types of aggressive behaviour;
- **Roles enacted** has two sub-categories: profiles (victims and perpetrators) and social status;
- **Practical implications** has two sub-categories: bullying consequences and prevention/intervention coping strategies adopted by victims and bystanders.

When presenting the data, we often give some illustrative quotes. There are some comments within [brackets], that we have provided to enable better understanding of the idea being expressed. These comments are not part of the speech of the ex-elite athletes

(1) **Narratives of ex-elite athletes who considered that bullying did not occur in sports settings**

Bullying or banter?

The judo and swimming ex-elite athletes alluded to isolated and less frequent interpersonal conflicts, but tended to devalue the aggressive behaviours and their impact on victims, and also considered the victims' responsibility for any aggression.

JUDO: There was always that thing to "put the kid in the right place", when they were more saucy, to squeeze him a little bit more in combats, which is perfectly normal ... there's a difference from that and to bully him physically or psychologically. Honestly, I never noticed anything. I can't even make a judgement on that because I never experienced that situation so, it is a situation I never experienced.

SWIMMING: They have more experience, are captains, the team leaders and the rookies must understand that. Nowadays it's a little bit less ... It's not the same. I think nowadays children, probably based on the education they receive from their parents, are overprotected and become less resilient to be inserted in this kind of hierarchy. It's not necessarily better [the overprotection].

Normalization of aggression

Despite considering bullying not to occur in sport, the ex-elite athletes representing football and judo reported some exclusion of lower performance athletes in the initial period of the season, when roles within the peer group were not yet clearly defined. However, they normalized these episodes, and in some cases stated that the athletes who were initially victimized and excluded ended up being accepted by their teammates. The kind of episode reported here was also described by some of the ex-elite athletes who were involved in bullying; the main difference is that, although the ex-elite athletes who considered that bullying did not occur in sport acknowledge some sort of rejection of new incomers in the beginning of the season, they didn't consider this to be bullying, but instead some normal aggression which should easily be coped with.

FOOTBALL: (...) in the beginning of the season, there was a natural selection of the strongest ones, obviously. The strongest ones were the players who played more often. This selection was obviously made by the coach. In the end, there was a group of 15 who were always together; they were the core group and, in an initial stage, the remaining players had some difficulty in interacting with the stronger ones. However, these players were later more protected and supported than some of the players belonging to the core group. It seems a paradox but it's true. In the initial stage, there was some social exclusion and isolation, but then a further natural integration occurred and the whole peer group protected that athlete who in the initial stage was [considered] weaker.

Reasons

Although these participants referred to bullying as an important issue which should be tackled, according to their perspective and experience, they said that it did not happen in sport. When asked why that was so, a variety of different reasons were given, but each at a very low frequency. The participant representing gymnastics acknowledged the existence of bullying in school, and justified it by the mixture of youngsters with all kinds of characteristics (social, economic and personal). But when describing gymnastics, he referred to this sport as non-aggressive, and considered that the common interest of the sport being practised and the similarities between the athletes would contribute to positive relations between them.

GYMNASTICS: I think the smaller groups are somehow more homogeneous. In a school setting, there is a mixture of interests, social classes ... here [in gymnastics], there is at least one common interest and things are all related to the sport being practised.

The coach of judo considered that aggressive behaviour being enacted in this combat sport contributed to the non-occurrence of bullying. His idea was that aggressive behaviour could be properly enacted within the set of rules of the sport.

JUDO: Maybe because combat sports allow one to play or be aggressive according to a set of rules. For sports in which there isn't direct physical contact, there is probably more bullying, or maybe it can be more severe. I have never seen anything like that, or been involved or participated myself [bullying in judo].

Other types of interpersonal violence

Although these participants didn't consider bullying to happen in sport, they often reported episodes of other types of aggressive behaviours and/or interpersonal violence, which were also mentioned by some of the ex-elite athletes who were involved in bullying episodes. Besides episodes of aggression between athletes from different teams, or verbal and physical aggression among spectators (also targeting the athletes and other stakeholders), these ex-elite athletes often reported episodes of aggressive patterns of behaviours of parents and coaches towards the athletes. The participant representing swimming described the extreme pressure to win placed on many youngsters by parents and coaches. These adults focused their full attention on winning and, as a consequence, the athletes frequently felt too anxious and afraid to fail, and their performance frequently decreased as a result.

SWIMMING: [I know] many stories of athletes who haven't even started to compete yet, and are already too anxious due to an expectation for things to occur in a certain way. And the competition hasn't even started.

(1) **Narratives of ex-elite athletes who considered that bullying episodes happened and were involved**

The data collected here was divided into three categories: circumstances, roles and practical implications. Each of these categories were then further divided into sub-categories. Circumstances was divided into *frequency* and *types* of bullying, *number of athletes* involved, *location*, *crucial moments*, *feelings* towards bullying, *reasons* for its occurrence and its overlap in different *social settings*. *Other types of interpersonal violence* were also reported and analysed. We divided the category of roles into two sub-categories: *profiles* of bullies and victims, and their *social status*. Finally, the category of practical implications was divided into *consequences*, and *prevention/intervention* of bullying.

The ex-elite athletes who reported bullying episodes were mostly those representing team sports: handball, rugby and volleyball. However, athletes representing individual sports (athletics and wrestling) also reported bullying to occur. Participants who reported getting involved in bullying episodes tended to report their involvement as bystanders, with the exception of occasional aggressions: an episode of physical aggression in wrestling, a verbal provocation in handball and occasional episodes of social exclusion in rugby.

> WRESTLING: (...) and then there are other episodes in which there is a kind of bullying; in a group, there is one individual who's more popular and always has a silly idea, and attacks the weaker or awkward guy "Hey, let's make fun of A, B or C". Years later – as it happened to me and I'm not proud of that – you realize you were part of a group in which some guy was always targeted in those interactions. It's considered bullying isn't it? It included taking some belongings and hiding them (sports bag), giving him bad nicknames. I remember that whole process didn't leave me feeling comfortable ... I wasn't happy anymore. I wasn't in the mood for that anymore. It was too much, it was stupid.

Circumstances

Frequency

The participants who reported getting involved in bullying episodes as bystanders, described the bullying episodes as being very frequent, mostly on a daily basis.

> VOLLEYBALL: (...) what I remember from that time was that situation: I mean, there were some less influential [low social status] players in the peer group and also in sports performance. There were some systematic verbal provocations in the changing room ... however, I have some difficulty in interpreting these behaviours as such severe aggression; that's the reason why I asked you about the definition of bullying in the first place. We always have the tendency to ignore this kind of interaction a little bit. But I remember it was systematic, always at the end of the training sessions ... It used to occur in the changing room. During training, there was some occasional situation regarding nasty nicknames, insulting or stuff like that. But what I recall the most when performing the transition from school sport to a prestigious sports club (professional), was what tended to occur in the changing room after the training sessions. There was no physical aggression, but it was verbal aggression and mocking. That's it: I think the most accurate word is mocking.

Types of bullying

The types of bullying most reported were verbal bullying (such as mocking and insults), followed by social bullying (mainly social exclusion). Usually bullying starts mostly with provocations and/or mocking, and the targeted athlete later tends to be isolated from the rest of the peer group. Besides verbal and social bullying, these participants also referred to "disguised aggression", in which peer play is characterized by the existence of a covert aggressive behaviour. Here, the perpetrator may perform an aggressive behaviour (such as verbal mockery) and devalue it by saying it was just banter and it was the victim's fault that they were not capable of engaging in playful interaction. Here, the aggressive content has to do with the way things are said (guise), rather than what is said (content).

Number of athletes involved

All the participants who reported bullying episodes described them as being performed in a group situation, instead of a one-against-one situation. Sometimes, bullying episodes started with an attack on the victim by just one perpetrator, but quickly extended to a group dynamic, involving several athletes. Once again, the need for perpetrators to have a public audience in order to perform bullying episodes was well described.

WRESTLING: Bullying always started with the same guy being targeted [by a single bully]; and then, it quickly spread to other athletes who also bullied the victim.

Location

Although the changing room was reported as a hot spot for the occurrence of bullying episodes, the ex-elite athletes mentioned two other main locations, perhaps even more important: training areas and training centres (e.g. hotel, canteen, rooms of sports centre).

VOLLEYBALL: There were episodes in the changing room in which younger athletes, considerably less influential within the group of athletes, were targeted.

Crucial moments

Especially in team sports, the tendency for bullying episodes to reach their peak in the initial period of peer group construction was often described; it then started to gradually decrease and fade away.

Feelings

The participants who were involved in bullying episodes mostly as bystanders described bullies and victims as having different perspectives of the same episodes. The perpetrators labelled the interactions as banter and described them as funny, while the victims expressed negative feelings towards what they considered bullying. The participants themselves said that they felt bad, disliked and disapproved of the episodes, and considered them an abusive and aggressive kind of relation.

ATHLETICS: (...) they were people with a strong psychological profile based on the athlete's perspective; I mean, clearly each one of those athletes tended to pressure other peers and they created a social environment which was very aggressive towards that specific youngster. They were guys with a strong personality. The question was to know the threshold between banter and humiliation. And on many occasions, it started with banter and ended up as extreme humiliation.

Reasons

The main reasons given for the occurrence of bullying were power, hierarchy and rivalry (fundamental reasons), and also peer pressure to act according to the kinds of behaviours accepted by the peer group. Although one of the fundamental reasons highlighted by coaches and athletes was not referred to by the participants in this study, namely envy, there is a considerable consensus regarding the fundamental reasons for understanding bullying.

ATHLETICS: (...) obviously after this the group dynamic changes ... usually the behaviours within a group differ a little bit from individual behaviours. I believe that these two athletes [bully and victim] when they are alone, may have a different relationship with each other: "come on, I was just kidding, I didn't mean that ... Can't you see it was just kidding?" but it works differently: it's a humiliation. So, I think these behaviours [bullying] are based on the need to exhibit their personality and being the centre of attention in the peer group. There may be some other reasons, but I think this is the main one.

HANDBALL: (...) The funny thing is that the competition level doesn't matter because bullying is always there, and episodes occur in the same way ... Because it's purely behavioural. The problems existing in youth teams are the same ones existing in adult teams, and also in professional teams.

Social settings

The findings here were inconclusive; in some cases, participants focused mostly on personal factors in bullying, and considered that both victims and perpetrators tended to engage in bullying in other social settings as well. However, some participants also described environmental factors affecting the occurrence of bullying, specifically related to sports settings, for example the sports mentality and team group dynamics; they considered that bullies and victims enacted these roles exclusively within the sports setting.

VOLLEYBALL: I think in other social settings outside volleyball this didn't occur. No way! It was clearly in that social setting.
ATHLETICS: I think it overlaps other social settings. It's a very complex subject to analyse, but I think there is an overlap between social settings. There are some profiles of young people who can easily get involved in bullying episodes (...) I think it happens in sport as well as other social settings.

Other types of interpersonal violence

According to these ex-elite athletes, besides bullying episodes, other forms of violence and abusive behaviours clearly happen in youth sport. They reported abusive relationships between coach and athlete and also parents and athlete. There is debate about whether these should be called bullying, but they can have severe consequences for young athletes. This topic, especially the abusive relationship between coach and athlete, will be explored further in Chapter 10.

HANDBALL: (...) I've seen this happen in a team of young athletes (...) I saw a coach who grabbed the arm of a female athlete, took her off the pitch and almost beat her, screaming "you never do that again". The game ended and the guy calmed down; for some reason, I told him: "you are like a God for these children; they see you like a God. You have no idea of the consequences of what you did for the rest of their lives". I have stories of some friends of mine, who played with me when I was a young athlete (...) today I am 38 years old and a guy recently told me: "I still haven't recovered from the pressure my father used to make me suffer to play handball."

Roles

Profiles and social status

Although different personality and behavioural characteristics were mentioned by the participants, regarding the description of the victims, these highlighted "passivity" and "personality". Passivity generally refers to a tendency to avoid conflict, and personality to athletes with different ways of thinking, behaving and different interests from the remaining athletes, which makes them more prone to be targeted. Although victims tend to have lower sports performance, when describing them, most of the participants mentioned them as high performance athletes. Regardless, they were described as less popular. Another important factor highlighted by the participants in describing victims was body issues: those who diverged from the ideal athletic body (for example, by being overweight) were more prone to being targeted. Concerning perpetrators, these were usually described as being more active and high performance athletes, with a high social status among peers.

RUGBY: He used to get really angry and I remember a specific situation (...) he used to get more and more mad (...) and there were some guys there who used to tease him even more (...) but that's the real reason. These are situations with a specific player, who already had a nickname; he was older and had a reputation for being a tough player on the pitch and was very respected, but within that environment [social environment] he was teased. He wasn't from Lisbon in the first place, and was one of those physically stronger players, but he used to over-react and get really mad when he was provoked, so the other players provoked him even more.

WRESTLING: He was a very quiet, organized guy, a good student too. I think he was permissive, and being permissive ... [resulted in him being targeted].

Practical implications

Consequences

All the participants considered that bullying has consequences for those involved, especially for the victims, and – with the exception of the ex-elite football athlete – there was a general consensus that athletes tended to be likely to abandon sport early due to continued victimization. Even the athletes who considered bullying not to exist in their sport, referred to it as resulting in negative outcomes and the need for it to be tackled.

HANDBALL: (...) this topic is very complex because coaches can say repeatedly they want kids to enjoy sports practice above all, but in the end, 99% of those guys just want us to win. This mentality is a serious problem at certain ages, so I would say that I'm almost certain about the direct relation between bullying and early drop out of sport or change of sports club [to avoid victimization].

Prevention and intervention strategies

The most highlighted prevention strategy reported by the participants was the need to raise awareness about bullying. Besides sensitization campaigns, the need to educate stakeholders about bullying was highlighted.

ATHLETICS: I think the sport and educational stakeholders may have an important role to minimize some of the negative effects of bullying.

I think different stakeholders, including coaches, psychologists, sports leaders and others, should have an active role in preventing bullying.

Discussion

Bullying or banter?

The participants were divided into those who considered bullying not to exist in sport, and those who were involved (all of them as bystanders). The different perspectives between these two groups may partially be due to factors related with their sports career; for example, the sports clubs in which they practised, and the characteristics of the peer groups and coaches they had encountered. But an important aspect was the interpretation of peers' interactions, and how an individual feels and evaluates peer interactions. The interpretation of behaviours is strongly influenced by how we feel about them. Ex-elite athletes who reported on the occurrence of bullying in youth sport also expressed negative feelings towards it. In contrast, the athletes who denied the existence of bullying in youth sport still reported some occasional and isolated conflicts. These participants often normalized aggressive behaviours between peers. When describing such episodes, the athletes who were targeted were, on some occasions, described as being responsible for these. There is a subjective interpretation of bullying, which means that for the same episodes some athletes may label it as bullying and others as banter.

Circumstances

Frequency

The participants who had been involved in bullying episodes described them as very frequent, even occurring on a daily basis. It is interesting that all the participants who denied the existence of bullying in youth sport were athletes from individual sports. Although we cannot generalize with our small sample, we can hypothesize a possible relationship between type of sport (individual or team) and its influence on bullying prevalence. Such a relationship is corroborated by Evans et al. (2016), who found a higher prevalence of bullying behaviours in team sports than in individual sports. In individual sports, the number of athletes in the training group is usually lower, and each athlete develops his own work and training pattern, which he focuses on with the cooperation of the coach. This may help to explain the lower frequency of bullying behaviour in this type of sport.

Another interesting finding was that all participants who reported involvement in bullying episodes did so as a bystander or a defender.

Although they made some comments about their involvement in some situations in which athletes were targeted, their narratives were always made from a bystander perspective. Why was this? Possibly it happened by chance, given the low number of participants in this study. However, another possibility is that all these athletes had high social status in their sports clubs and successful careers which were protective factors against being victimized themselves. Yet another possible explanation could be that the participants were not comfortable admitting any involvement as a perpetrator or victim. In the context of hazing rituals in sport, Kirby and Wintrump (2002) reported difficulty in doing research because of the taboo nature of the topic.

RUGBY: Maybe some people think: "this can reflect on a good or bad image of this sport [talking about bullying in sport]". But I think it's quite important to do it, especially because of this last topic we discussed [early drop out of sport due to victimization]: if bullying is a cause for players withdrawing, it should be tackled.

Types

Verbal bullying was the most frequent type to be described, followed by the social bullying and what we labelled as "disguised aggression". This parallels the reports from athletes and coaches; there is a strong convergence that verbal bullying (especially mocking) is the most prevalent type of bullying in youth sport, followed by social bullying (especially social exclusion). These two types of bullying are intimately related, reinforce each other and promote the exclusion and isolation of the victimized athletes. The disguised aggression reported, was also reported and described by the athletes. Disguised aggression allows a perpetrator to mock the victims and, if confronted, to defend him/herself by disguising the aggressive content of the verbal message, saying he/she was just kidding. This could be considered a sub-type of verbal bullying. We will take up this topic further in Chapter 10.

Number of athletes

The bullying episodes reported occurred in a group situation. Sometimes it may have started as a one-to-one relationship, but very quickly turned into a group dynamic, with the participation of bystanders. Although bullying may start with a one-to-one attack (e.g. a perpetrator mocking one victim), generally more and more athletes get involved and contribute to the exclusion of the victim. Again we will explore this more in Chapter 10.

Location

The changing room was the main hot spot highlighted by athletes generally, including the ex-elite athletes, for the occurrence of bullying episodes. This corroborates previous research on this topic (Brackenridge, Rivers, Gough & Llewellyn, 2007; Jachyna, 2013; Roberts, 2008). However, the ex-elite athletes provided some new data about location: training areas and training centre facilities (such as hotels, high performance sports centres) were mentioned as being even more important. The experiences in training centres referred to situations in which athletes from the same team were together in a different geographic location having travelled far away from their hometown to play as visitors, or situations within national team activities in which athletes from different sports clubs spend a number of days together, training and sharing accommodation.

So far as training centres and activities are concerned, the athletes are frequently in less supervised rooms, share informal areas, and spend many hours a day together. These factors may contribute to the occurrence of bullying episodes. The changing room is also an informal and less supervised area, frequently with just the athletes in it, which makes it a likely venue for bullying. However, training areas were the most reported location for bullying occurrence by the ex-elite athletes.

Considering that these training areas are locations in which specific and controlled or supervised activities take place, and the coach is present, it is interesting to consider why this location was highlighted. The athletes spend most of their time in the training area. Besides competition, a training area is a location in which athletes practise and compete with each other (mutual evaluation). Athletes with different characteristics and social status share this area, which may contribute to the establishment of abusive relations between some of them. Still, the presence of the coach and the structured environment should hinder the occurrence of bullying. However, athletes may bully others when the coach is not looking; and we also have to bear in mind the implicit or even explicit involvement of the coach in bullying episodes, as described by O'Connor and Graber (2014), the normalization of bullying in sports settings, which may contribute to the acceptance of abusive patterns of peer interaction (Volk & Lagzdins, 2009). Although these would apply to all locations, it seems important to understand why there is such a prevalence of bullying in activities controlled by the coach.

Crucial moments

The ex-elite athletes from team sports described a tendency for bullying episodes to peak in the initial period of peer group formation, and then to gradually decrease over time. This can be understood in terms of a competition between members of the peer group to achieve social status (Pellegrini, 2003; Pellegrini & Long, 2003); aggressive behaviours, including bullying, are used to achieve dominance and establish a hierarchy (Björkqvist, Österman & Kaukiainen, 1992). Once the position of each person in the hierarchy is established, aggressive behaviours tend to decrease.

Reasons

The most highlighted reasons pointed out by the ex-elite athletes for bullying existence were abuse of perceived power, hierarchy, rivalry and peer pressure. Besides fundamental reasons (power, hierarchy, rivalry), peer pressure was also highlighted as an important reason for the occurrence of bullying. Peer pressure may exacerbate some types of behaviours (including aggressive ones) from individuals, in order to fit an accepted standard: when experiencing peer pressure to join in bullying, individuals may behave in ways which go against their personal and social values, and contrary to the way they usually behave and interact with others. An example is peer pressure and norms about masculinity. According to Jachyna (2013), athletes who do not fit the normalized understanding of masculinity tend to be victimized.

Social settings

We found little consistency regarding views on role overlap in different settings; why might this be? The individual traits approach focuses on personal characteristics of both victims and perpetrators, and hence predicts an overlap of roles in different settings. This perspective is corroborated by some research (Browitt, King & Martinez-Expósito, 2006; Courtney & Wann, 2010; Endresen & Olweus, 2005; Escury & Dudink, 2010; Volk & Lagzdins, 2009). On the other hand, these behaviours are influenced by the social environment, including the social values and the peer group in that setting (Brackenridge, Rivers, Gough & Llewellyn, 2007; Jachyna, 2013; Roberts, 2008; Stirling, Bridges, Cruz & Mountjoy, 2011; Vertommen et al., 2016). Both approaches are important for understanding bullying, and they are not necessarily in opposition.

Roles

Profiles

The ex-elite athletes mainly focused on personal factors, such as "passivity" and "personality", when describing the victims. Unlike the athletes, they did not often mention performance level, probably because the athletes they were thinking of as victims were high performance athletes too.

However, this perspective was not uniform: some participants considered that differences in sports performance partially explained the bullying episodes, and described a tendency for high performance athletes to criticize and mock lower performance peers. The perceived asymmetry regarding the ability to practise sport often provides a perceived status and power imbalance in this setting. Roberts (2008), and Escury and Dudink (2010), also indicated that high sports performance was a protective factor against victimization, as it usually gave high social status among peers. The physique of the victims was also often referred to by the ex-elite athletes, which reflected its importance in the sports setting. The image of the athlete's body is crucial in sport. Jachyna (2013) alluded to how ideas of masculinity may increase the probability of those who do not meet this ideal being victimized. Hill (2015) argues that investment in body shape through sports practice and physical activity (body capital), can be a way to increase social status in the peer group (social capital), especially among boys.

The bullies were described as more active and mostly high performance athletes. These factors are valued in sports settings and help to achieve high social status among peers (Roberts, 2008).

The participants themselves described their involvement as being a bystander. Their participation was from an outsider perspective, not involved in the perpetrator-victim dyad. They described the feelings of the victims towards bullying as negative (sad or angry). They saw the feelings of the bullies as positive (for example, seeing it as funny) and consider that they perceived their actions as mere banter or mild forms of aggression. This data is in line with the interpretation of bullying behaviours made by the participants in the research, which can be divided into two major poles: those who considered the interaction between peers as aggressive, and those who devalued it and labelled it as banter.

We do not believe that the participants who described these aggressive interactions between athletes as banter are incapable of thinking about others' feelings; indeed, some of them showed very high empathic skills. Many other factors are likely to influence the perception of the individuals about these peer interactions.

Practical implications

Prevention/intervention strategies

When participants were involved in bullying episodes as bystanders, they tended to defend the victim. This reaction is in line with the feelings towards bullying that they expressed. Several intervention proposals to tackle bullying effectively were mentioned, but there was a general consensus regarding the need to raise awareness: sensitization in which the topic of bullying is explored and discussed. This is a general intervention focused on all stakeholders, namely athletes, coaches, parents and sports leaders. By highlighting this topic, the participants seemed to consider that bullying behaviours could be efficiently dealt with by giving information about its nature, prevention and intervention, through courses for sports professionals and direct intervention with athletes and parents.

This perspective is supported by several authors who consider the need to educate sports professionals about bullying, and to provide them strategies to deal with it better (Endresen & Olweus, 2005; Escury & Dudink, 2010; Hemphill & Symons, 2009; Melim & Oliveira, 2013; Stirling, Bridges, Cruz & Mountjoy, 2011), and to change practices in this social setting (Brackenridge, Rivers, Gough & Llewellyn, 2007).

WRESTLING: (...) I think it clearly should focus on the education of the coaches: call attention, identify the cases and act. About acting: I think some cases can be dealt with in a sports court. Parents must be alert. Sometimes, parents want their child to win so badly that they may even tell him: "That's it, deal with your own problems. I don't care about it!" and sometimes they may not be aware of what is really going on and how severe the situation may be.

Consequences

There is considerable agreement among the participants in this study regarding the early drop out of sports practice due to bullying. This data is corroborated by some other researchers (Escury & Dudink, 2010; Evans et al., 2016). Even those participants who were not involved in bullying episodes during their sports careers, thought that early drop out of sport could happen due to victimization, with the exception of the ex-football player. The participants considered bullying as negative, and a factor which promotes social exclusion.

Summary and main conclusions

A considerable number of the ex-elite athletes labelled peer interaction as banter, while the remainder described it as bullying. This is a theme also found in the interviews with athletes and coaches.

Verbal bullying was considered to be the most prevalent. However, social bullying and disguised aggression were also frequently referred to. The episodes were described as very frequent (often on a daily basis), performed by a group of athletes, and tending to occur most in training areas, training centres and changing rooms.

The athletes who reported their involvement in bullying episodes described them based on a bystander perspective. When directly involved in bullying episodes, participants generally said that they defended the victim.

The participants highlighted abuse of perceived power, hierarchy and rivalry (fundamental reasons) to explain bullying, but also thought that peer pressure was an important factor to consider.

Bullies were described as more active and usually high performance athletes, while victims were labelled as more passive, with issues around physique and body image; they were considered different from other peers (not meeting the accepted standards). However, the ex-elite athletes did describe some victims as being high performance athletes as well.

The early drop out of sports practice due to victimization was very often referred to. Participants considered the need to raise awareness about bullying as a way to deal with it.

Part III

Conclusions and practical implications

Chapter 10

Discussion and conclusions on athlete–athlete bullying

This chapter articulates the major contributions of each of the four studies previously described. We summarize the results and discuss some important concepts to better understand athlete–athlete bullying in youth sport.

Conceptual issues

We start by reflecting on the concept of bullying in the sports setting. The way bullying is perceived here will exert a direct influence on its reported prevalence and our understanding of it.

Although there is a general consensus about the prevalence of bullying in many social settings, discussion of the concept of bullying is still a major topic. This is true even in the school setting, which is the most widely analysed social setting in bullying research. Considering that the sports setting is a relatively recent field of bullying research, some further challenges arise. The discussion here comes from the analysis of the complementary narratives of athletes, coaches and ex-elite athletes in the previous chapters, as well as some important contributions from other researchers.

Bullying or banter?

The conceptual discussion about bullying immediately brings up different perceptions concerning what could be considered bullying or mere banter. This topic was found in the analysis of the narratives of the athletes, coaches and ex-elite athletes, and goes in line with Brackenridge, Rivers, Gough and Llewellyn (2007) who highlight how difficult it can be for stakeholders to define a clear threshold between these concepts in the sports setting.

Victimization is a subjective experience which depends on the interpretation of those involved (Brackenridge, Rivers, Gough & Llewellyn, 2007; Escury & Dudink, 2010; Kirby & Wintrump, 2002; Volk & Lagzdins, 2009). The definition of bullying as an aggressive behaviour, based on the criteria of power imbalance, intentionality and repetition, was clearly defined to participants in our interview studies. Nevertheless, different people may have very different interpretations of the same episodes. When we interviewed teammates, they often referred to the same peers and episodes that had occurred. If we look at the victims' perspective, we can consider that bullies have a lack of empathy for those who experience victimization, and interpret bullying behaviour as an aggressive way to exert dominance over others. However, sometimes bystanders or bullies described the same episodes as the victims did previously, and perceived them differently. They considered what might be bullying behaviours between peers (and were described as such by victims) as playful and non-coercive.

Differences in interpretation may also affect those outside the peer group, for example the coach. Adolescents often talk with each other in what might seem aggressive or demeaning ways, such as calling each other gay or trading insults. But what can be considered an aggressive style of interaction from an outsider's perspective, may, at least in some cases, not reflect the real intention or meaning of such communication between athletes. We have previously discussed this as *trash talk*. Should this be considered as bullying, or as a part of the game and, in some cases, even having positive aspects such as enhancing group cohesion?

Regarding this discussion about the differences between bullying and other similar but playful (rather than abusive and coercive) interactions, Mills and Carwile (2009) argued that scholars often assume that teasing and bullying are the same concept, or just variants of the same category. But they clearly differentiated both concepts, emphasizing that teasing can be playful and fun, and a prosocial strategy of affiliation, education and influence. These authors alert us to the need to properly differentiate bullying and teasing, so that educators do not unnecessarily try to prevent the harmless, and often positive and developmentally appropriate, verbal interactions known as teasing.

While teasing is primarily verbal, what is often called *rough-and-tumble play* is much more physical, but is also often confused with aggression and fighting. Can *trash talk* in adolescents be a verbal equivalent to rough-and-tumble play in its aims and some properties?

Rough-and-tumble play and its characteristics

Rough-and-tumble play is based on play fighting. It is common in primates and other mammals in general and plays an important role in the social development of youngsters (Pellegrini & Smith, 1998). While superficially like real fighting, it differs from aggression in its components, background and consequences. In children, it is characterized by a positive relationship between participants, who often change roles (chasing/being chased, or on top/underneath in fighting) and stay friends once the interaction is finished. The lack of power imbalance here, which is so characteristic of bullying, allows peers to interchange roles within the playful interaction. Engagement in rough-and-tumble behaviours has lower injury risk for those involved than real fighting (Fry, 2004). Boys are more prone to engage in these kinds of behaviours.

Rough-and-tumble play has been found to be related to social competence (Pellegrini, 1998b). It allows participants to develop encoding and decoding skills about the intention of behaviours, as well as the management of emotions (Pellegrini, 2003). Children progressively differentiate it from real fighting as they develop their cognitive skills. This is especially so for well-adjusted children. The distinction is sometimes blurred in less socially skilled children, who may confuse playful and real fighting and tend to be socially rejected in the peer group.

The threshold between bullying, rough-and-tumble play, and trash talk: analyses of the narratives of stakeholders

We think *trash talk* (or *cross fire* as we describe it when it occurs in changing rooms) and some rough-and-tumble behaviours can have some adaptive functions and do not necessarily overlap with bullying. The way adolescents deal with it is important for establishing their social status in the peer group. However, the distinction between play and real fighting becomes a bit more blurred in adolescence, when youngsters can use rough-and-tumble play to display their strength or dominance, performing an aggressive behaviour disguised by a play component. This was frequently described by some participants in Chapter 7 (athletes) and Chapter 9 (ex-elite athletes), and we labelled it *disguised aggression*. It allows perpetrators to attack other peers without much risk to themselves, because they can always argue that it was just banter. Even so, this falls short of real fighting, or serious bullying.

Bullying, aggressiveness and assertiveness

Sport promotes the enactment of aggressive roles by athletes. In sports settings, aggressive behaviours are often legitimated (Gencheva, 2015; Krishnaveni & Shahin, 2014), and athletes who behave accordingly tend to have a high social status (García Ferrando, 1985). Some sports are characterized by high levels of aggression and even violent physical contact between the athletes (e.g. combat sports). However, these behaviours may occur within the previously established rules of the game, and be part of it, without any other intention to harm, rather than seeking to achieve sporting goals. If an athlete who performs combat sports would behave in such ways outside the sports environment, these behaviours would be considered aggression. Indeed, these behaviours of rough contact, if performed outside the sports context could sometimes be defined as criminal (Krishnaveni & Shahin, 2014). The same happens for all sports actions that demand rough physical contact (e.g. tackling in rugby); these behaviours are accepted and not considered a violent attack due to the sporting framework in which they occur, which makes them part of the game.

Although aggression is a negative form of communication, it can sometimes be adaptive depending on the social setting in which it takes place (Moral, 2005). Some sports settings often value athletes who have a confrontational attitude, and who easily strike back to any sort of provocation or attempt at intimidation (e.g. rough contact in football to intimidate opponents), sometimes in aggressive ways. These athletes are often perceived as tough, strong and with leadership skills. Many football players, especially defenders, are valued for their capacity to intimidate their opponents. In social environments in which aggressive behaviours are valued and reinforced, bullying can be more easily accepted (Martins, 2005).

Our analysis of the narratives of coaches showed that aggressiveness is considered very important and useful, and coaches tend to encourage their athletes to be aggressive in order to improve their performance. Sports practice is perceived by many coaches as a vehicle to express aggressiveness in acceptable ways, and sport is seen as a social setting that allows and encourages its expression in the proper patterns. Being aggressive does not necessarily mean being a bully; many coaches stated that they encourage their athletes to be aggressive, but to play by the rules and respect their peers and opponents.

Still, the fact that aggressiveness is encouraged by many stakeholders when practising sport should be considered. We believe this may exert some influence on the normalization of aggressive behaviours and acceptance of bullying, especially in a social environment considered very important for adolescents. In social environments in which aggressive behaviours are valued and reinforced, bullying can be more easily accepted (Martins, 2005). In sport, the exhibition of "masculinity" among boys is strongly connected with physical activity and based on athletes' performance (Roberts, 2008). Behaviours such as intimidation, provocation or dominance may be easily misunderstood as being "more masculine". Research on bullying amongst adolescent football players (Steinfeldt, Vaughan, LaFollete & Steinfeldt, 2012) demonstrated that the moral atmosphere, based on both peer influence and influential male figures, along with the adherence to male role norms, significantly predicted bullying. The strongest predictor found for the occurrence of bullying was the perception of whether the most influential male in the life of an athlete would approve of such behaviour.

Hazing rituals: bullying or play?

Hazing rituals are another important concept, which should be considered when analysing bullying in youth sport. Hoover and Pollard (2000) define hazing as a humiliating or dangerous activity expected of someone to join a group, regardless of their willingness to participate. These rituals are characterized by a power imbalance between "rookies" (newcomers) and older members of the peer group. On many occasions, the "rookies" are tested to ascertain their capacity to fit in with the group rules and norms. These rituals can lead to what are basically friendly and playful interactions, in which both rookies and older athletes enjoy the game; this contributes to attachment and bonding within the group.

However, sometimes these rituals can lead to mild or even severe forms of exclusion, discrimination or abuse. The power imbalance does not necessarily mean abuse, and athletes can in some cases benefit from participating in hazing rituals. But when the power imbalance is used as a vehicle to abuse new recruits, hazing rituals become a kind of bullying. According to Kirby and Wintrump (2002), hazing rituals in sport often become an abusive relationship and can be perceived as bullying. However, our findings in Chapter 8 suggest that hazing rituals can result in both positive and negative outcomes. Some coaches described hazing rituals as positive for the integration of the new members, while others considered these behaviours negative for the athletes and did not approve of them.

Several coaches (including some who acknowledged the existence of bullying among athletes) described hazing rituals among their athletes, including pranks and jokes, as being within a playful environment. They considered them to be helpful for new incomers to feel accepted, and as a useful way to be introduced to their peers. However, other coaches (some of whom considered bullying not to exist in youth sport), perceived hazing as abusive; they described previous episodes of abusive practices that they had later forbidden, or said that they never allowed older athletes to haze others because they considered these behaviours abusive in nature, and consequently unjustifiable. We believe hazing rituals may be a kind of interaction based on play and fun, different from bullying. However, due to the power imbalance of new incomers/rookies and older athletes, it can easily move into an abusive relation of bullying, to which coaches should be alert.

A framework to better understand bullying episodes: analysis of sports culture and the masculine ethos

The nature of sports has changed a lot in recent decades due, among other factors, to a significant effort by international institutions to integrate other populations besides able-bodied men into sports practice. These changes maybe occurred as part of a broader 'human rights' movement, and the work against bullying is a part of this. Until some decades ago, it was primarily a male social setting and the sporting ethos was deeply rooted in the traditional stereotype of masculinity (Messner & Sabo, 1990). Things have been like this for a long time, but are increasingly being challenged. Later, we explore the inequalities between men and women in sport, homophobia in sport, the participation of disabled persons in sports competitions and racism based on an historical perspective.

It seems reasonable to infer that the masculine sports culture, strongly connected with traditional sexual stereotypes, results in the acceptance of many aggressive behaviours, which may be considered normal in many sports settings. As also argued by Volk and Lagzdins (2009), bullying behaviours in sport may frequently be perceived as regular sports aggression rather than bullying. Besides helping to understand why bullying between athletes may often not be recognized or reported, this perspective can help us understand why coach–athlete bullying can sometimes happen. We give more detailed consideration to this in Chapter 11. According to previous research (Kerr & Stirling, 2012; Stirling & Kerr, 2009), ex-athletes and their parents often only recognized abusive patterns of conduct by a coach once the sporting careers of the athletes were finished.

When considering the findings from our interview studies reported in Chapters 7 and 9, we may see some supportive evidence for this. Athletes often reported occasional bullying episodes and more easily devalued their impact on the victims, while ex-elite athletes, on their recall analysis, described bullying episodes as being on a daily basis and considered that they had a strong impact on the victims. Being actively inserted in the sports setting may promote the acceptance and normalization of abusive behaviours more easily, which only later and when analysed more distantly may be perceived as aggressive and abusive.

Prevalence of bullying

Analysis of the prevalence of bullying in sports and school settings

Having analysed the concept of bullying in youth sport, we can focus on its prevalence. The bullying behaviours discussed here concern aggressive behaviours among athletes (rather than, for example, from coaches, see Chapter 11). Our survey found that a significant number of athletes reported involvement in one or more bullying roles. Our data was collected approximately two months after the beginning of the season and shows that, overall, 56% of the surveyed athletes reported having participated in bullying episodes as either victim, bystander and/or bully during the first two months of the season.

Approximately 10% of the athletes reported having been victimized since the beginning of the season, and 1% of the overall sample repeatedly. The prevalence of victimization we found was very similar to a study conducted in Spain by Ventura et al. (2019), who reported victimization among 9% of young football players of both genders. The frequency criteria in both studies was the same (being victimized at least 1–2 times since the beginning of the season), as well as the instrument used for data collection.

Comparing the sports and school settings, our survey data suggests that the prevalence of bullying behaviours in youth sport generally appears to be lower than in Portuguese schools. Here we present the prevalence of victimization reported in some of the major studies conducted in Portugal about bullying in school. This historical analysis aims to compare the prevalence of victimization in school and our data. It is well known that the prevalence rates of bullying may vary greatly by variables such as the definition presented, the time reference period, the frequency criterion, age and gender, among others. So, the results presented here should be analysed with caution, and taken as an indication only. We compare the prevalence of victimization in school and in sport because bullying in sport is a new research field, barely explored when compared to bullying in school. Some international research has also focused on this topic (Escury & Dudink, 2010; Volk & Lagzdins, 2009).

EU Kids Online conducted a survey in 2010, comparing 33 European countries including Portugal. The final report shows that in Portugal, 9% of children (9–16 years old) reported having been victimized offline in the past 12 months (this would include any setting, not only school). (www.lse.ac.uk/media@lse/research/EUKidsOnline/EU%20Kids%20III/Reports/PerspectivesReport.pdf).

The Health Behaviour of School-aged Children (HBSC) report for Portugal (2014) provided data from 5,464 pupils aged 11, 13 and 15 years. They were asked about frequency of being bullied, or bullying others, in school over the last two months. Altogether, 34.0% of the students reported having been victimized at least once a week, and 4.7% several times a week. Also, 28.3% of the students said that they bullied others at least once a week, and 2.6% several times a week (http://aventurasocial.com/arquivo/1437158618_RELATORIO%20HBSC%202014e.pdf).

A more recent report from EU Kids Online, carried out between March and June of 2018 (published in 2019) provides some further data about victimization. The results from the Portuguese team show an increase in victimization when compared to the results of their previous study in 2010. Altogether, 24.0% of the children between 9 and 17 years old who were surveyed reported having been victimized by their peers (Ponte & Batista, 2019). The children reported victimization that had occurred in the last 12 months, both off- and online. The authors thus found a very large increase in victimization when compared to the report carried out in 2010. However, no possible explanations for this are provided in the report. Their data likely covers not just the school setting, as children also reported victimization in other social settings (http://fabricadesites.fcsh.unl.pt/eukidsonline/wp-content/uploads/sites/36/2019/03/RELATO%CC%81RIO-FINAL-EU-KIDS-ONLINE.docx.pdf).

Generally, the prevalence of victimization is lower in sport than in the studies presented here on school bullying. An exception was the EU Kids Online study, reporting data from 2010; however, in the more recent version of the survey (2019), victimization had greatly increased and was clearly much higher than in our sports study.

The lower prevalence of victimization in sport was corroborated by the narratives of some athletes, especially (but not exclusively) the ones who didn't report bullying or reported only occasional episodes, who stated that the prevalence of bullying is much higher in the school setting.

Other researchers have pointed out some possible reasons for bullying being less prevalent in sport than in the school setting. Youngsters spend less time in the sports club than in school, which contributes to a lower number of bullying episodes in the former (Evans et al., 2016). Another factor may be underreporting due to a narrow conception of what is bullying; victimization in sport may be considered as part of the normal aggression existing in this social context, rather than being considered as bullying (Volk & Lagzdins, 2009), and this culture can contribute to silence about bullying and victimization, and less reporting of such cases (Stirling, Bridges, Cruz & Mountjoy, 2011).

Finally, we found that the athletes who are excluded and victims of bullying by their peers try to cope with it in various ways. Some of them try harder to improve their skills, while others simply try to ignore it. However, many athletes who are targeted tend to withdraw early from sports practice due to exposure to bullying episodes (and so would not contribute to survey statistics) in a way not easily possible in school. This early withdrawal of victims had a high consensus from the interviews with athletes, coaches and ex-elite athletes, and is in line with previous research (Evans et al., 2016). This data is also corroborated by the athletes who quit practising in a specific sport and/or sports club, but kept connected and practising somewhere else. Bullying in sport exerts negative selection processes, which can push lower performing athletes into early withdrawal (Escury & Dudink, 2010). There was a considerable prevalence of athletes who described in their narratives the change of social environment as a way to avoid victimization. These athletes didn't report being victimized in their current sports clubs, although they had been in the previous one.

However, one further explanation for the lower prevalence of victimization in youth sport than in the school setting deserves consideration. Youngsters have many extra-school activities in which they can engage and develop their skills. Although sport plays an important role for most male adolescents (even some with low performance), not all are interested in sports practice. We think that some boys who are clearly the opposite of the athletic stereotype (in body and behaviour), and who might experience more difficulty in being part of a group composed of athletes, are less prone to engage in sports activities. These adolescents are together with the adolescent athletes only in the school setting. There may be a kind of pre-selection of the type of young person who engages in sport (as well as other activities), which may automatically "exclude" the ones who don't like being part of it. Less athletic children are more likely to be victims in sport, and consequently some avoid participating in sports activities in sports clubs. Although this seems reasonable, it is only a hypothesis, which should be explored by further research.

Besides the general prevalence of bullying behaviours, it is important to remember that the victimization is mainly occasional. Although we found 1 in 10 young athletes had been victimized in the sports setting, repeated victimization was only about 10% of overall victimization (so about 1% of all). In cases of severe or repeated victimization, victimization probably leads to early drop out of sport or a change of sport and/or sports club. However, despite being targeted, some athletes may be able to cope with occasional victimization with some degree of efficiency (although not perfectly). Both athletes and coaches referred to athletes who, although victimized, kept practising and trying to improve their skills and sports performance in order to feel more integrated. The joy derived from practising sport, and the need to feel part of a group of peers may explain why these athletes keep practising sport, and why they try to fit in with the peer group, even when being victimized.

In summary, our findings showed that bullying in youth sport is not infrequent, although much of it is occasional. A significant minority of athletes, around 1 in 10, reported having been victimized. Although the prevalence of victimization is lower than in school (according to most relevant studies), it remains important to acknowledge and prevent bullying in sport. Victims suffer lower self-esteem and may leave sports practice early. Besides victims, a significant number of other athletes are involved in such episodes as bystanders and bullies.

Any comparison between studies must be analysed cautiously; variables such as the size and nature of the samples, and methods used to collect and report data, will influence the findings regarding the results about the prevalence of bullying. The major contribution of our research was to provide a baseline for a topic so far unexplored in Portugal, which shows that the prevalence of bullying in youth sport should be considered in future prevention strategies. During recent decades, considerable work has been done in the school setting, while in sports settings the research on bullying is just beginning (Nery, Neto, Rosado & Smith, 2018). There is a need to develop broad-based intervention programmes, which should include sports organizations, and also direct intervention with athletes, parents, coaches and other stakeholders. This is discussed in detail in Chapter 12.

Variables that affect the risk of being a victim

Besides focusing attention on the prevalence of bullying episodes, we also obtained a lot of useful information on factors that might or might not make it more or less likely to happen.

Firstly, some factors were not important. As it was a national study in Portugal, we were able to consider regional variations across four main geographical areas of the country. This did not significantly affect the prevalence rate of bullying. In addition we divided sports into individual, team and combat sports, and also on the basis of gender ("male", "female" and "neutral" sports). Perhaps more surprisingly, this too did not have a significant influence on the chances of being a victim. Different sports have different cultures and characteristics; we expected these variables to have some influence on the prevalence of bullying behaviours. In particular, the sports categorized as more "male", due to the accentuated prevalence of the traditional male stereotype culture, would be expected to have a higher prevalence of bullying. However, we did not find this to be the case.

What did make a significant difference was the number of good friends that a young athlete had within the peer group in the sports club. Athletes who developed more friendship relationships were less likely to be victimized. This result was expected. Victims of bullying tend to suffer from social exclusion and having more friends is a protection factor against this. Friends may also act as defenders and deter bullying. This finding is similar to that found in school settings (Smith, 2014). It has implications regarding intervention, alerting us to the need to promote friendships and peer support within the sports club.

Analysis of the main types of bullying

Three types of bullying – verbal, social and physical – are typically assessed when surveys are conducted. Although the bullying types may be further divided into sub-types (see Chapter 1), here we focus on the most common types of bullying analysed in large-scale surveys. Besides examining their prevalence in our sample, we also analyse their nature based on the data provided by the narratives of the athletes (Chapter 7), coaches (Chapter 8) and ex-elite athletes (Chapter 9).

Verbal bullying: contents and meanings

The quantitative survey clearly showed that verbal bullying was the most prevalent type of bullying in youth sport (45.9% of victims reported being victims of this – see Table 5.2). This has been found in many settings, including the school (Smith, 2014), and is corroborated in the sports setting by our research, and by Ventura et al. (2019).

The complementary qualitative approach helps us to understand better the types of verbal bullying used and their symbolic meanings. According to Rosen and Nofzlger (2018), bullying in school serves to reinforce (the sense of) masculinity among adolescents, and perpetuates the notions of masculine dominance among boys. These authors consider that many experiences of bullying are grounded in hegemonic masculinity, and consider the three key themes here to be (1) the importance of heterosexuality, (2) physical dominance and intimidation, and (3) acceptance and normalization of violence. We found all of these themes to be considerably represented in the narratives of the young athletes, coaches and ex-elite athletes.

The typical speech used by male athletes in sports settings is heavily based on the traditional stereotype of masculinity and homophobic speech, and the athletes who do not behave accordingly tend to be labelled as gay (Baiocco et al., 2018) and/or abnormal (Brackenridge, Rivers, Gough & Llewellyn, 2007). Our data showed that athletes frequently call each other gay, or make jokes about their peers' sexuality as a way to provoke and make fun. Although athletes may know that their peers are not homosexual, they keep calling them gay. Calling someone gay was frequently described as a way to pick out someone who was weak, or less athletic.

In a comprehensive analysis of the reasons why some men avoid sport, Plummer (2006) focused on homophobia. He considers it to have a particular role among male athletes, dividing those who display appropriate peer endorsed masculine behaviour, and those who show a lack of masculinity (a failure to measure up). The offensive words of homophobic speech aim to signal what a growing boy should not be.

Athletes seek to achieve physical dominance and intimidation by bullying others. A football athlete we interviewed described how bullies frequently sought out rough physical contact in training sessions, as a way to intimidate the victims and those perceived as more vulnerable. These behaviours often passed the threshold between normal sportive aggressiveness, and became violent behaviours (although disguised).

Plummer (2006) considers that, for boys, the sporting field may be where violence can be disguised as a legitimate activity; in Western cultures characterized by valuation of physical activity especially, it is almost a definitive path to manhood. In this context, it is not a surprise that sport is a setting for cultivating masculine physicality, and in which those perceived as homosexual are rejected. However, recent efforts made to promote inclusion in sport have had some positive results (Englefield et al., 2016). According to Anderson (2011, 2012), in the last three decades, there has been a progressive acceptance of male homosexuality within sport. The reasons pointed out were the improvement of conditions for sexual minorities, and the promotion of softer and more tactile and emotional forms of heterosexuality.

Both young athletes and ex-elite athletes frequently reported *disguised aggression* (verbal or physical attacks disguised as playful interaction) in their narratives. Disguised aggression may be more accurately considered verbal bullying; it's used to protect the bullies from being identified as perpetrators. When confronted, bullies can always argue that it was just banter.

Social bullying and social exclusion

We also found social bullying, especially social exclusion, to be quite prevalent among young athletes (23% of victims reported having suffered from social bullying – see Table 5.2). It was reported by athletes, coaches and ex-elite athletes. Victims tend to be left aside in training exercises, social interactions and chats. Once they are labelled as victims in this way, athletes tend to be rejected and ignored even more. Some victims reported making a considerable effort in order to integrate into the peer group and feel accepted. These athletes tried very hard to act according to what they thought their peers expected, but generally with poor results, because other athletes perceived victims as different and did not want their company.

When analysing types of bullying, Ventura et al. (2019) divided them into unidimensional (single type of bullying) and multidimensional (combination of more than one type of bullying reported by the victims). Interestingly, when analysing the types of bullying in isolation, they reported a very low prevalence of social bullying (0.8%), quite similar to cyberbullying (0.6%), and lower than physical bullying (4.6%). However, when they analysed the most frequent types of behaviours separately, among the most common were insults (34%), telling victims to shut up (30.6%), criticizing victims for sports errors (29.5%), nasty nicknames (15.3%) or rumour spreading (6.4%). Social bullying does not happen by itself in most cases. It often occurs as a continuation of verbal bullying. These results are corroborated by our analysis of the narratives of the athletes. Prejudice and discrimination is often reinforced by subtle messages.

Physical bullying and inappropriate physical contact

Although physical bullying was also reported, we found it to be much less frequent than verbal and social bullying (see Table 5.2). From the total of athletes who reported having been victimized, 8.2% of these reported physical bullying; this is a very direct type of attack, which is more difficult for the perpetrators to disguise or to label or pass off as a normal interaction. Although some physical attacks might occur without being noticed by a coach or trainer (e.g. in less supervised areas) or be disguised (e.g. during a training session, disguised as normal training exercises), these are more difficult or risky to get away with compared to verbal bullying.

This lesser frequency of physical bullying during adolescence is in line with much other research on the development of bullying and other aggressive behaviours at different ages (Björkqvist & Österman, 2000; Pepler & Craig, 1995). Whereas younger children are more prone to perform physical aggression, adolescents tend to perform more subtle forms of aggression, which allow them not to be exposed or identified as an aggressor so easily. This does not necessarily mean there is less bullying in older youngsters; in fact, there is a considerable prevalence of bullying among adolescents, but it is more difficult to identify when compared with younger children because of the different forms it takes. As a result, the harm caused by bullying is mostly psychological. This is more difficult to see than physical bruises, and makes it easier for perpetrators to devalue it, and/or define the actions causing it as banter and only part of the game (Teräsahjo & Salmivalli, 2003).

Analysis of the participants: profiles of victims and bullies

To describe the profiles of the victims and bullies, we use the perspectives of the athletes, the coaches and the ex-elite athletes, based on the analysis of their narratives. There is a considerable consensus among them in the description of the profiles of victims and bullies. Although under certain circumstances anybody can engage in bullying episodes as a victim or a bully, some individuals are more prone to become victims or bullies. It is useful to be aware of these typical profiles, to better predict and understand bullying episodes and, consequently, to be able to intervene more successfully.

Profile of the victims

Victims were generally described as being more passive, low performance athletes. They were often characterized as having body issues, such as being overweight or clumsy. These kinds of body issues are antagonistic to the ideal of the perfect athlete. These athletes are considered different from the accepted standards and, consequently, are more prone to be victimized (Jachyna, 2013; Roberts, 2008). However, this does not necessarily mean that these athletes are going to be victimized. Although the personal features of the athletes may contribute to the risk of being victimized, the relationships they have with peers are more important. Some of the athletes interviewed described overweight athletes who were well accepted among peers, and some other athletes who didn't engage in *trash talk* (*cross fire*), but were still respected and not attacked by bullies.

Some ex-elite athletes described victims who were high performance athletes. The reasons for these athletes being victimized were not based on being considered different from the others. Instead, crucial factors were how they dealt with provocations, and interacted with their peers. Less successful strategies were passively ignoring provocations, or the opposite (over-reacting). Over-reacting to provocations is often perceived as a weakness too. Those who lose their temper when provoked are more prone to be targeted because their reaction amuses the bullies.

Being passive in a social environment in which physical activity and high performance are strongly related with perceived masculinity may contribute to being an easier target for attacks. On the other hand, in a study in the UK, Hill (2015) found that youngsters may seek social capital in the peer group by investing in improving their sports performance, as well as physical capital by improving their body image, both of these being socially valued. The extra effort of some victims to improve their sports performance was generally perceived in a positive way. If under-reacting and over-reacting to provocations were frequently described as reasons to target an athlete, there are also exceptions. A coach (Chapter 8) described how some athletes were respected by their peers, and not targets of bullying, even if they were silent and introvert persons. In some cases, ignoring some minor provocations can be adaptive, because it shows that the targeted one hasn't felt affected. However, if provocation proceeds and increases, and the athlete who is targeted cannot defend him/herself, then passivity may be perceived as weakness.

Sport mentality is changing, and this social setting is becoming progressively more inclusive. Even athletes who do not fit into the usually accepted standards may end up being accepted and recognized, if they can successfully establish positive relations with their peers. Helping athletes who are excluded to develop better bonds with their peers will be positive for their integration and acceptance into the sports club (see Chapter 12).

Profile of the bullies

The bullies were generally perceived as being more physically active and high performance athletes, which was reflected in them having a high social status. In a social environment based on a tough mentality, and which plays an important role for male adolescents to display their masculinity and dominance skills over other peers, some athletes are more successful at this and use it as a means for general acceptance, demonstrating to others that they behave according to these accepted masculinity standards (Jachyna, 2013; Kirby & Wintrump, 2002; Roberts, 2008). Among competitive behaviours, there are positive interactions (banter and play fighting), but systematic abuse of those considered weaker may also occur (bullying), especially when there is a perceived power imbalance.

Bullies tend to more frequently exhibit behaviours based on the stereotypical image of masculinity. The confrontational attitude and impulsivity, which were frequently reported in the narratives of our research when describing bullies, are some of the examples of typical behavioural patterns associated with the traditional male gender stereotype.

Bullies tend to be more prone to exhibit dominance behaviours due to their personality traits, which may reflect a more pronounced need to confirm their sense of perceived power over others. Bullies (especially those who bully others in several other social settings) tend to have stable aggressive behaviour patterns. In addition, the tendency to blame others described by coaches is in line with an externalizing pattern of interaction, typical of bullies. The difficulties described by bullies in considering others' point of view and caring for them have been described by other authors in the school context, as has the tendency to blame others (Olweus, 2013).

Although personality traits are important, anyone can be a bully at certain times or in certain situations. The social environment and peer pressure also play an important role. This was clearly described by an athlete who reported his past involvement in bullying episodes, as a supporter of the bully, simply because he wanted to be part of the group of "cool" athletes. The episodes were described with regret and shame. This is just one example of the influence of the social environment on bullying among many reported by athletes, coaches and ex-elite athletes.

Analysis of the age of the victims and bullies

The quality and frequency of involvement in bullying episodes do vary by age, in both quantitative and qualitative ways. In school settings, younger children are more often victimized (at least based on self-report data); and victimization becomes less frequent as they get older (Barrio et al., 2008; Smith et al., 2004). One reason for this may be increasing development of coping skills; another is that much bullying is by older children against younger ones. Victimization tends to reach its peak at around 13 years and then to decrease gradually during later adolescence; however, the prevalence of bullying perpetration does not decrease in the same way. In this adolescent period, the consequences of bullying episodes for those who remain victims tend to become more severe (Smith, Madsen & Moody, 1999).

Type as well as prevalence changes with age. Physical bullying is more prevalent among younger children. As youngsters grow up, the frequency of verbal, social and indirect types of bullying tends to increase and become more prevalent than physical and direct types of bullying. Sexual harassment also tends to increase greatly during adolescence.

We analysed the frequency of involvement in bullying episodes as victims, or perpetrators, by age, in our sample. We divided both victims and bullies into categories based on their age and developmental stage, according to the Long-Term Athlete Development (LTAD) model (see Chapter 4). The results showed no significant relationship for either victims or bullies. Thus, in our sample, the age of the athletes was not related to the likelihood of their involvement in bullying episodes. These findings are contradictory to previous studies on school bullying (Smith, Madsen & Moody, 1999). Our sample focused mostly on adolescents. More research is needed in sports settings, with a wider age range, in order to more fully ascertain if the age of the athletes influences their likelihood of involvement in bullying.

Analysis of bullying episodes

Our survey produced many other interesting findings, including where bullying took place, whether it was done by individuals or a group, integration and crucial moments, the role of the coach, and the consistency of victim and bully roles across different settings.

Where does bullying occur?

Our quantitative data showed that the majority of bullying episodes occurred inside the sports club. The analysis of the narratives of athletes, coaches and ex-elite athletes provided further information about location, and also about the lack of communication about bullying episodes, and the fact that many coaches did not acknowledge its occurrence.

There was a considerable consensus among the athletes that bullying episodes tended to occur in the changing room. This was because of the lower adult supervision, and also because the changing room is a less structured area, more prone to informal and playful interactions. This was corroborated by the ex-elite athletes, when they reported on their involvement in bullying as young athletes. The changing room was often pointed out as the "hot spot" for bullying episodes to occur. This is in line with previous research (Escury & Dudink, 2010; Evans et al., 2016; Fisher & Dzikus, 2010; Ventura et al., 2019).

Coaches were described as often not being aware of the occurrence of bullying. Indeed, many coaches we interviewed stated that there was no bullying among their athletes, but this was frequently denied by the athletes, who reported bullying episodes mostly in the changing room, but also in other areas where adult supervision was rare or non-existent.

Bullying episodes were also frequently reported in training areas, even when the coach was physically present, but did not understand what was going on because the bullying was performed behind his back. A handball athlete described how he and a few of his teammates frequently bullied another athlete. This victim was often verbally insulted, socially excluded and even physically targeted in the changing room. He ended up dropping out of handball, despite his continued efforts to be part of the peer group. The perpetrator described one episode of bullying in the training area, in which the victim was continually teased and provoked behind the back of the coach. Finally, when the targeted athlete couldn't stand it anymore, he reacted with rage, and threw a ball towards the perpetrators; this was the only behaviour seen by the coach, who considered it as misconduct and ended up rebuking the victim for his behaviour, while the bullies laughed at what had happened.

Providing feedback about such findings may be important for both coaches and athletes. Victims tend not to share what they are going through and often feel coaches are not interested in dealing with bullying. But our data suggests that coaches are frequently just not aware of occurrences of bullying among their athletes (even if they think things are under control). Athletes (especially victims) need to know that coaches frequently don't act because they have no idea of what is going on, and not because they are not interested in tackling bullying.

One conclusion from this might be that surveillance strategies for the changing room should be stepped up in order to tackle bullying more efficiently. However, the changing room is an important area for athletes' social interaction. It is true that bullying episodes tend to occur in the changing room, and sometimes are derived from *cross fire*. However, as stated before when discussing the concept of bullying, *trash talk* may be considered a playful interaction by itself (a type of play fighting), and play an important role in peer bonding. While it may be important to develop more efficient surveillance mechanisms to tackle bullying in the changing room, we think that not allowing any kind of *cross fire* (which may be wrongly misunderstood as bullying) may not be the best solution.

The ex-elite athletes also mentioned other locations for the occurrence of bullying. In fact, for them the changing room only came in third place, after training areas and training centres. The research by Ventura et al. (2019), despite reporting the changing room (39%) as the most likely location for bullying, found a very similar prevalence of bullying behaviours (38%) for training areas, and also reported it as occurring during games (23%). Bullying episodes in training sessions are more difficult to understand, due to the physical presence of the coach. However, jokes and insults may be easily accepted in this setting, because they may be considered part of the game and normal aggression, instead of bullying behaviours.

The occurrence of bullying episodes during games reported by Ventura et al. (2019) also deserves some attention. Our data does not corroborate this. Instead, athletes described provocations and aggressions during games and even individual competitions, but these behaviours were performed by, or against opponents (not teammates). The athletes justified bullying as tactics used to undermine the confidence of the opponents, or to intimidate them in order to decrease their performance. In our research we defined bullying as occurring between peers, within their group (team or training group inside the sports club). Competition has an agonistic feature, and athletes try to defeat their opponents who are considered outsiders from their group. So, these aggressive behaviours against opponents were considered by us as another type of aggressive behaviour, rather than as bullying.

Regarding the training centres, these were described as places where athletes spend much free time and have many opportunities to engage in playful interactions (and sometimes bullying) with each other.

Individual or group bullying?

While bullying episodes may occur between individual bullies and victims, the bystanders provide an important social context. Both athletes and ex-elite athletes described bullying episodes performed within a group situation. Despite some occasional bullying just between two individuals, the majority of the episodes occurred within a group which included several bystanders. Rather than attacking secretly, bullies usually initiate bullying episodes when other peers are present and can observe their performance. Status and perceived popularity among boys is very important, especially in adolescence, and some boys value dominance over others as a way to achieve this, and bullying as a way to demonstrate this.

This data calls attention to peer group dynamics and the need to intervene with bystanders in order to more properly tackle bullying, whatever setting it occurs in (Salmivalli, 2010). If Olweus's early approach to bullying was mostly based on individual traits, later approaches have focused more on peer pressure and other group processes to better understand and prevent bullying episodes. This has important practical implications, which will be considered later on in Chapter 12.

Integration and crucial moments

The integration of newcomers to the peer group emerged as an important topic. This was not specifically addressed in the interview scripts, but it turned up frequently and ended up being included in data analysis because of its prevalence and relevance.

When newcomers or rookies arrive, the prevalence of bullying episodes is likely to increase. The new athletes do not yet belong to the peer group, and this makes them more vulnerable to victimization. A successful integration of incomers depends on many factors.

The athletes with a profile more like that identified for the victims are more prone to be excluded, and those who are more similar to the profile described for the bullies, are more easily accepted (see the section "Profiles of the victims" for more detailed information).

Although coaches stated that the integration of rookies is usually positive, factors such as these should be considered to identify the athletes with a higher risk of being victimized, who should be the focus of special attention from their coaches. Both coaches and ex-elite athletes considered that the perceived risk by older athletes of losing social status, and the consequent need to reaffirm it, may easily lead to attacks on the more vulnerable new members. This data is in line with research in school settings about this topic. Bullying episodes tend to reach their peak during the initial stages of new peer group formation, and then gradually start to decrease as social roles and status become more clearly defined and accepted (Pellegrini, 2003; Pellegrini & Long, 2003).

Consistency of victimization and perpetration across different social settings

A considerable consensus was found from the narratives of both athletes and coaches regarding the behaviour of victims and bullies in different social settings. Many athletes knew their teammates from school and other social settings (especially in small towns), and often described the same behavioural pattern of victims and bullies despite being in different social settings. Some coaches also knew athletes who were victims or bullies in sport from school, and commented on how they used to keep enacting the same bullying role in both settings.

These individuals tend to enact the same roles in different social settings, which suggests the existence of stable behavioural patterns, related to individual personality traits. Both bullies and victims tended to enact the same role in school and in the sports club. Some athletes were victims at school, and kept being victims at the sports club, and those who bully others at the sports club were often bullies at school too (even with other peers than the ones they used to be with at the sports club). Previous research has also suggested an overlap of victimization in school and sports settings (Escury & Dudink, 2010; Ventura et al., 2019).

The role of the coach in athlete-to-athlete bullying

The role of the coach in the occurrence of bullying behaviours among athletes was a topic which also came up frequently and ended up being included in the data analysis. Coaches are the adults who manage the peer group. Their attitudes and behaviours will directly reflect on athletes' behaviours. By far the most mentioned type of management adopted by coaches involved selecting athletes to enhance the chances of winning. Several athletes did however mention that their coach had a more inclusive management style, and provided equal opportunities for participation to all athletes, irrespective of their ability, skills or sports performance.

The coach can be a key factor in preventing bullying, or instead a source of concern and may even become a bully him/herself, depending on his/her personal features and coaching practices (see Chapter 11). Although athletes tended not to speak with their coaches about bullying episodes, most of them considered that they can play an important role in tackling bullying behaviours. Coaches also considered their interventions to be effective in managing bullying. Coaches' interventions can be crucial because they have a direct influence on the peer group of athletes, defining its functioning norms. They are also perceived as role models by the athletes. The combination of these factors has a strong influence on the acceptance or rejection of aggressive behaviour among peers.

Why does bullying occur?

There are a range of reasons which may help to explain why bullying happens. We have grouped them into three different categories: fundamental, peer pressure and individual characteristics.

Fundamental reasons concern (1) abuse of perceived power, (2) envy and rivalry and (3) hierarchy. *Peer pressure* involves (4) divergence from accepted standards, (5) imitation (of the behaviours of the bullies) and (6) responsibility of the victims (possible role of the victim). *Individual characteristics* include some aspects commonly associated with victims, such as (7) low sports performance, (8) body issues and (9) personality.

Although some information on the reasons for bullying was obtained from our survey questionnaire, further insight was obtained from the interviews with athletes, coaches and ex-elite athletes. The athletes provided quite detailed insights, reporting fundamental reasons, peer pressure factors and individual characteristics. Both coaches and ex-elite athletes also alluded to fundamental reasons, but only the ex-elite athletes also mentioned peer pressure as an influence.

Fundamental reasons

1. *Abuse of perceived power:* Power dynamics are at the core of many aggressive behaviours, including those that occur in the changing room (Fisher & Dzikus, 2010), and more experienced/older athletes often work to maintain their control and power over other experienced athletes. This dominance hierarchy is common in human groups, and need not be bad in itself. But it is open to abuse if a more powerful individual takes advantage of their power to hurt or abuse someone else – hence bullying as the "systematic abuse of power". Choosing more vulnerable victims to pick on enables bullies to repeatedly demonstrate their power to other peers. Often they can establish or maintain their dominant position in this way without risk of being confronted, because victims are unlikely to confront bullies, and bystanders tend to observe without intervening.
2. *Envy and rivalry:* Feelings of envy and rivalry are also related to this. Sometimes bullies feel a need to attack another because they feel their social status is threatened. This is more likely when a bully is struggling to achieve a sense of belonging among the best athletes, who are usually considered the ones with higher social status in the peer group.

GYMNASTICS COACH: : Quite often bullying occurs due to envy; here, the bullies want to be better than others, and feel they can't do it. So, the way they use to devalue the best athletes, is by bullying them. This happens because the best gymnastic athletes are commonly accepted by everybody, and everybody likes them. So, in these cases, the athletes who feel rejected may bully the best athletes with the aim that other teammates disapprove of them, and also expecting that these same others don't look at their [the bully's] own failures.

3. *Hierarchy:* Hierarchy issues were also described as a reason for bullying. Older and higher status athletes attack victims to reinforce their dominance, and/or to eliminate possible perceived threats to their status, felt by the inclusion of new athletes. A rugby athlete said that older athletes "pass the ball only between them", and exclude the new incomers by not letting them be part of the game. A football coach (who had also been a player) explained that sometimes, when a new incomer is integrated into a team, he may be a direct competitor with some high status athlete who already belongs to the team; this is because the incomer is a high performance athlete, and plays in the same position as the player who is already part of the team. In these circumstances the athlete who is already part of the team may target the incomer (often with the participation of other teammates) because this new athlete is felt as a threat to his status in the peer group.

Athletes, coaches and ex-elite athletes all described these fundamental reasons to explain bullying. These seem to play an important role in understanding bullying episodes.

Peer pressure

We divided the peer pressure category into three areas: divergence from accepted standards, imitation, and responsibility of the victims.

4. *Divergence from accepted standards:* This is commonly stated by individuals as a reason for being victimized: victims are perceived as different from other peers, in how they look, how they think, or in what is commonly expected regarding social behaviour. What is considered to be different or divergent is modulated by the social environment. Some behaviours which may be accepted or even valued in certain groups, may be strongly rejected in others.

The cultural ethos varies from one sport to another, and even among different sports clubs. In our research, no significant differences were observed when we compared different types of sports (see Chapter 5). However, some research suggests that the acceptance of violence and prevalence of bullying vary based on the characteristics of each individual sport's ethos (Browitt, King & Martinez-Expósito, 2006; Tagg, 2015). One of the reasons highlighted by the ex-elite athlete of gymnastics who was interviewed in our research (see Chapter 9) was the ethos of his sport, in which aggressive behaviours are perceived as negative and not encouraged, especially when compared with other sports. The social climate of sports club also has an influence on the expression of aggressive behaviours. In this book, we frequently refer to sports as one category; however, the difference between sports and sports clubs does need to be considered.

5. *Imitation:* This is another important aspect of peer pressure. Many athletes described how they might imitate the bullies in order to feel accepted by them and improve their own social status. Although bullies may be rejected by some peers, they are frequently perceived as "cool", or have high perceived popularity, especially among adolescents (Juvonen, Graham & Schuster, 2003). Moffitt (1993) argues that the aggressive and tough behaviours of bullies may represent challenges to adult norms and morality, which in itself leads to their acceptance among adolescents who are asserting their independence at this stage of development.

Some athletes did not particularly want to bully others; but said that they joined in the bullying as a way to achieve acceptance and proximity to high status athletes, who were frequently bullies. A handball athlete clearly expressed this, referring to his own behaviour in the past; he bullied a teammate by making fun of him. Although he regretted doing it some years later when he was interviewed, and he described this teammate as "nice and gentle", he explained how he had targeted him several times within a group situation because he wanted to feel accepted by the most popular athletes (who were the perpetrators). Previous research on school bullying has documented similar findings (Juvonen & Galvan, 2008; Olthof & Goossens, 2008; Roland & Idsoe, 2001; Witvliet et al., 2009).

Some athletes also argued that some bullies attack others, in order to disguise their personal weaknesses (e.g. making fun of a low performance athlete in order to disguise one's own low performance). A volleyball athlete mentioned that bullies tend to over-criticize the victims when they are training and/or playing. The errors of the victims are repeatedly pointed out and criticized. The athlete considered that this happens because the victims lack the capacity to defend themselves against the critics (because they feel too insecure to confront the teammate). So, the bully can attack them and thus redirect the attention of others away from their own possible mistakes and failures. By focusing attention on more vulnerable athletes, labelling them in derogatory terms and victimizing them, they are trying to escape from being victimized themselves.

It is often easier and more adaptive for bystanders to distance themselves from victims, who have low social status, to avoid their presence, and to behave like the bullies who have high social status among peers (Juvonen & Galvan, 2008). This does depend on the general attitude to bullying in the peer group, and the climate of the school or sports setting. If the injunctive norms of the peer group can be changed (i.e. what athletes think other peers approve of), this in turn can change the likelihood of defending behaviour dramatically. It is also important to mention the role of diffusion of responsibility. When bullying occurs in a group situation, many bystanders may feel that they are not responsible, and as others are doing nothing, they need not do anything either. They imitate each other's inaction. This well-known group phenomenon has important practical implications. It is important to explain to bystanders that they are part of bullying, even if it does not directly affect them.

Anti-bullying programmes should consider interventions that attempt to change athletes' attitudes about bullying. Although some bystanders consider that they are not part of bullying episodes, because they are not directly involved as perpetrators and/or victims, witnesses are very important for bullying episodes to take place, and bystanders may play a key role in intervention. If bullying is disapproved of, and bystanders tend to act on the behalf of the victims, bullying prevalence is expected to decrease. This theme is taken up again in Chapter 12.

6. *Responsibility of the victims:* This describes how some bullies and also some bystanders may consider victims as being partially responsible for bullying episodes. In fact the narratives of bullies were often marked by blaming victims for bullying ("They deserved it"). But holding victims partially responsible is not the same as blaming, and some bystanders had a deeper analysis when describing some episodes, in which they considered how the victims' behaviours and relational patterns somehow contributed to the bullying.

For example, some athletes wanted so badly to be the focus of peers' attention that they repeatedly put themselves in situations in which they were mocked by many of them. Among several such episodes described, one example came from an athlete from a volleyball team. He described one of his teammates as a person who was always saying silly jokes and behaving childishly; this made other teammates laugh at him but, instead of stopping it, he used to repeat the same behaviours. This athlete had already been previously pointed out as a repeated victim of bullying by many other teammates and also the coach. They all described very exhibitionistic behaviours and some sort of compulsion to engage in them, which clearly resulted in negative outcomes for him. The athlete describing this also stated in his interview that he knew from his own mother (who was a friend of the victim's mother), that this victim used to cry when he was at home and suffer a lot from being the butt of everybody's jokes. Still, he considered it was better to have this negative attention, than have no attention at all. Although the teammate who was being interviewed tried to persuade him to change his behaviour to a more adaptive and accepted relational pattern, he kept doing the same things over and over again.

Thus, the behaviours of victims may on some occasions contribute to the perpetuation of bullying. This is important when considering individual intervention with victims, who may need help to develop more adaptive relational patterns.

Individual characteristics

Some individual characteristics of a young athlete may make them more at risk of being a victim. These individual characteristics include low sports performance, body issues (e.g. being overweight, clumsy or too short) and personality (different ways of thinking and behaving), making these athletes be perceived as aliens in the sports setting.

7. *Low sports performance:* The athletes who have lower sports performance are more prone to be targeted. Sports skills are highly valued within peer groups in sport, and function as perceived power. In some cases, even those athletes who were not appreciated for their personal characteristics by most of their peers were still accepted and valued within the peer group due to their sports performance. This was often described by the athletes in their narratives (Chapter 7).
8. *Body issues:* The athletes who have a body that diverges from the image of the accepted sportive body in that specific sport are more likely to be targeted. The body plays an important role in sport, and being overweight or clumsy may contribute to victimization.
9. *Personality:* As happens in school bullying, those who are perceived as different are more often victimized. A rugby athlete described a previous experience in football, in which he was often bullied, and said he was totally different from the rest of his teammates. He said that he used to read manga books, was fascinated by astronomy, and described himself as a nerd. He said that these characteristics and tastes led to him being perceived as different from others, and this was a reason for making fun of him.

Any of these (characteristics 7, 8 and 9) can result in an athlete being easily made fun of, and becoming the butt of jokes. Individual characteristics like these were often mentioned by athletes, but seldom by coaches or ex-elite athletes. These findings go in line with Kimmel and Mahler (2003) who argued that bullies attack those whom they define as outside the "normal" range in terms of appearance, behaviours, musical preferences, interests and friends, among other aspects. Individual risk factors should be identified as part of prevention efforts. However, as noted above, some athletes may be, for example, overweight or lack the ability to play well, but are nevertheless quite well accepted by their peers and have good social status.

Communication, coping strategies and consequences

Communication

Do victims tell anyone about the bullying, and if so, who? Does anyone speak to the bullies? How do victims cope with their situation? And what are the consequences of bullying? These are all important topics that our findings throw some light on.

Who do victims speak with?

We found that nearly half of athlete victims (49%) do not share their experience, and remain silent. This is also commonly found for victims in other settings such as school (Smith, 2014).

There are many reasons that can explain this. Victims tend to feel shame about being victimized; among boys, being victimized is often perceived as a weakness, being unable to manage aggressive interactions by themselves. Male youngsters don't want to be associated with this feeling of vulnerability because it may damage their sense of masculinity, especially given the tough mentality of the sports setting (Stirling, Bridges, Cruz & Mountjoy, 2011). Another important reason, frequently described by the victims in their narratives (Chapter 7), was the lack of confidence in any consistent support to tackle bullying. This overlaps with the belief that bullying will always exist, and that there is nothing they can do about being victimized. These athletes often think that even if coaches intervene, their actions will not have good outcomes and bullies will keep attacking them. The victims tend to believe that adult intervention is not the answer to this problem, although they cannot deal with it efficiently by themselves.

Feeling guilt about being victimized is also quite common, and may contribute to the silence about bullying episodes. Some victims feel anger and humiliation about being victimized, and these feelings are often mixed with a sense of helplessness. When perceiving themselves as victims within the whole peer group, and looking at the popularity of bullies, some athletes may feel there is something wrong with them and feel guilty about being a victim. This sense of there being something wrong about them interferes with support seeking and makes it more likely that they will stay silent about it.

Communication systems inside the sports club must be created in order to help victims break their silence. If they keep silent about victimization experiences, it reinforces bullying and makes it hard for potential support sources (especially peers and the coach) to help the victims. Victims (and also bystanders) need to know that there is no problem talking about bullying, that they will be listened to, and that the situation is going to be dealt with consistently. So, a clear sports club policy is needed.

Although not particularly described by the athletes, we think that the fear of consequences should also be considered. An athlete who seeks coach or family support may be perceived by the peer group as someone who is weak, and who cannot handle banter. In addition to the fear of retaliation, athletes may fear an increase in rejection due to their 'betrayal' of the peer group (usually led by the bullies).

Besides not talking with the coach about bullying episodes, victims tend not to talk with their families either (less than 9% of the victims approached their families). Peers are the most frequent choice of victims to talk about bullying (26.7%). It seems easier for youngsters to talk with their peers about bullying, than with adults.

Who does support victims?

The silence of the victims towards adults about bullying, may explain why the coach was commonly (78%) reported as someone who usually does not support them. If a coach does not know what is happening, they cannot act on the behalf of the victim. For the 22% who did say that the coach took action, a majority (nearly 16%) said that the bullying decreased or stopped; many fewer (6–7%) said that it stayed the same or got worse.

Of the 10% whose families did approach the coach, more (6%) reported the bullying staying the same or getting worse, while 4% said that it decreased or stopped. This is a very worrying finding. If the occurrence of bullying is acknowledged by the family, who approaches the coach in order to help to solve the problem but his/her action is ineffective, what is wrong here? Does it have to do with the way families approach the coach (e.g. aggressively), or some lack of sensitivity of the coach, or something else? These victims feel that they have nobody who can really help them. We have no data here from the qualitative approach. This is an important topic for future research.

Peers are the ones who are more often aware of the bullying, and can be the major support source of the victims. Some 60% of victims reported that peers had approached other athletes to stop the bullying. Most of these, 46% of victims, said this resulted in a decrease of victimization; but some 14% said that the bullying stayed the same or increased. The other 40% of victims reported that none of their teammates approached other athletes to stop the bullying. Our survey data does not allow us to understand why there were these differences in outcomes, nor do the narratives of the athletes (Chapter 7) help in this respect. This is another important topic to be explored in future research about the communication and support sources of the victims.

If seeking support from peers and the coach usually has good results, why do victims so often keep silent? It is important to enhance the peer and coach support systems in sports clubs, and to tell victims they should seek help and share their feelings with others. Our data suggests that family approach did not have such good results. Athletes are more prone to approach their coach and teammates, and often feel their support is more positive than the support provided by the family in the sports setting. However, bringing families into the sports club, and enhancing their participation and cooperation with the coach, also seems important in preventing bullying. The role of the families in victimization should also be considered in future research.

Does anyone talk to the bullies?

Bullies obviously do not normally speak about the bullying to coaches or other adults. But does anyone talk to them about it, if it is noticed? Our survey suggested that in most cases (63%), nobody talks with the bullies about it. However, nearly one fifth of the bullies (17%) reported being approached by peers. Adults inside the sports club, and family members, seldom spoke to them about it.

Our survey data also showed that when bullying is individual (one-to-one situation), peers more often talked with the bully about it. However, when bullying episodes included bystanders, assistants and/or reinforcers, usually nobody talked with the bullies about their actions. Why should this be so? We hypothesize that when more peers are involved, there may be social pressure to act in conformity with the bullies (as high status athletes) and to ignore the victim (with lower social status). Even if the bystanders may not approve of the bullying, it is less risky for them to support the bullies or ignore what is happening, rather than help the rejected peer (by standing up for him, or seeking help). In particular, if bystanders do not have a general acceptance and high social status themselves among their peers, they will feel less confident in trying to help a low status victim. On the other hand, a bystander who does have high status may be more empowered to defend the victim. In the school context, this has been built on in the KiVa intervention project (Salmivalli, 2010).

The importance of working with bystanders is thus very important. They have good knowledge about bullying episodes among the athletes, and they are the ones who can talk with the bullies about it if they feel empowered to do so. So who do bystanders speak to about bullying?

Who do bystanders speak with about what they have seen?

Our survey results showed that the majority of bystanders (62%) did not like bullying, and considered the behaviours of the bullies to be wrong. The qualitative studies showed that some bystanders may intervene and defend the victim, but usually they simply observe and do nothing. Even those who talked with the bully and defended the victim tended not to talk with the coach or another adult about what was going on.

Even among bystanders, bullying seems to be considered a young person's issue, not to be shared with adults. Indeed some bystanders suggested that the resolution of bullying should be found among peers, without the interference of adults. A rugby athlete acknowledged the existence of bullying among his peers; however, he considered that adults should not interfere, and that bullying should be dealt with among athletes. Once again, there seems to be some kind of loyalty to peers, and telling the adults what's going on may be perceived as being a telltale or "snitch".

Considering that bullies usually engage in bullying without the coach knowing about it, and that victims are usually afraid of reporting it, the role of bystanders is crucial; they can act as defenders directly, or be encouraged to tell the coach or another adult. Intervention strategies should aim to increase the actions of bystanders in response to bullying episodes.

Coping strategies

Telling someone (or not) is just one of a range of coping strategies that victims may use. They struggle to escape from the bullies' attacks and to feel safer and more integrated in the peer group. Here we discuss the strategies employed by victims to deal with bullying. After that, we consider what bystanders may do, if they also do not tell anyone or confront the bully.

How do victims react to bullying?

Victims use a variety of coping strategies. One common division is between emotion-based and problem-based strategies. Emotion-based strategies are more passive; for example, feeling sad, avoiding or ignoring the issue. Problem-based strategies are more active and try to solve the problem through, for example, confronting the bully, seeking help, changing one's behaviour in certain ways.

Emotion-based strategies aim to regulate one's internal emotional state. They make it more likely that the victim will not tell anyone. This may be less adaptive from a long-time perspective, as it is not acting directly on solving the problem. However, it may be an effective response to deal with low frequency and low duration attacks. Our findings show that the majority (53%) of the victims reported using coping focused on emotion strategies to deal with bullying. This is in line with findings in sports settings from Ventura et al. (2019), who found that the most common response to bullying was to ignore the bullies (42%).

Let's look at an example: ignoring is a good example of an emotion-based coping strategy. This might be an effective strategy for incomers to cope with *cross fire* or *trash talk*. We saw before that a recent incomer is more vulnerable to suffer these kinds of provocations from other members who already know each other. The way new athletes react to such provocations is going to reflect on their general acceptance. Sometimes, provocations may lead to bullying, especially when athletes who are less prone to defend themselves are identified. However, when *cross fire* is occurring, and even when bullying occurs, an athlete who is perceived as over-reacting tends to be attacked more often. Some bullies described how they used to provoke other athletes, seeking their over-reaction which, if it occurred, led them to attack such victims more often, for the fun of doing so.

Over-reacting is perceived as losing control of one's emotions and a sign of weakness. In such situations, ignoring can be an effective strategy. If an athlete is provoked and does not counter-attack, it may be perceived as a sign of not feeling threatened (fear) and having the capacity to handle provocations and attacks from other athletes.

Nevertheless, ignoring may be less adaptive when an athlete is continually attacked; doing nothing can lead to an increasing sense of helplessness.

Avoidance is another emotion-based strategy. Avoiding the changing room and social interactions because of fear of the bullies, does not solve the problem. However, it might lead to cases in which a victim changes sport and/or sports club, and finds a new social setting in which they feel more accepted and happy. If the former social setting was clearly problematic, can this change be perceived as an effective coping strategy, or should it be considered as just a consequence of victimization?

Nevertheless, problem-based strategies, being more pro-active and aiming to change the situation, are generally more effective. This is especially so when dealing with continued bullying episodes. It is important to encourage victims to share their experience, seek help and act on the problem. All the same, negative outcomes are still possible. For example, adults may tell a bullied youngster to counter-attack, but this is a dangerous strategy as the victim is usually weaker and/or the bullies have more peer support. Even telling an adult, while generally recommended, may be counter-productive if the adult does not respond in a responsible way.

Sometimes, a victim may try to escape from bullying by bullying other peers in turn. This coping strategy is an active way to tackle victimization. However, besides the adverse consequences for the new victim(s), a danger is that these "bully-victims" experience generalized rejection by most of their peers, who consider them annoying and problematic (Juvonen, Graham & Schuster, 2003).

The theoretical splitting between emotion-based and problem-based strategies does not necessarily mean that these two cannot be combined. Each type of coping style has its pros and cons. What is most effective depends on the particular situation and context.

How do bystanders react to bullying?

Although bystanders who reinforce bullying may be in a minority, they are crucial for bullying to take place. Some reinforcing behaviours that they may show are very subtle. A good example of this is quiet laughing about the bullying, or even just staying and observing. These behaviours send a message of general acceptance of the bully's behaviour, and can be seen as encouraging it. This way of engaging in the bullying allows them to excuse themselves if confronted, by saying they had nothing to do with it.

A handball athlete described a situation in the changing room, in which an athlete was physically attacked for no apparent reason. This youngster had been previously verbally and socially victimized for a long time. Over this period, bystanders did nothing or even reinforced the bullying by laughing and discreetly engaging in bullying in other ways. The athlete, now 18 years old, also took part in this, and described these episodes with guilt and shame, explaining his behaviour by the need to feel accepted by the most popular athletes in the peer group (the bullies in this case).

Some athletes withdraw, or passively participate in bullying by observing and not intervening, because they feel fear of the bully and the consequences of getting involved; this can be so, even if they disapprove of bullying and tend to feel distress about it. According to Gini, Albiero, Benelli and Altoe (2008), these individuals may have empathy towards the victims, but lack confidence or feelings of self-efficacy about how to defend them. Intervention with bystanders should not only focus on their attitudes towards bullying, making them feel part of what is going on, and explaining how their behaviour will reflect on bullying episodes, but also give them the confidence and skills to intervene effectively.

The results from the quantitative approach suggest that the bystanders who dislike bullying more often defended the victims. However, in their narratives, the athletes described several episodes of bullying, and even when they didn't approve of it, they didn't interfere. Also, the bystanders often considered that their actions on behalf of the victims were effective, while the victims felt the opposite (Chapter 7). These results seem contradictory. This may be due to a disjunction between reported attitudes and actual behaviour from the bystanders.

Consequences

Consequences of athlete-to-athlete bullying

We know the negative consequences of bullying in school settings, from much previous research (Chapter 1). The narratives of the athletes demonstrated that, as with school bullying, victims tend to suffer from anxiety, low self-esteem, social rejection and isolation. The experience of being victimized by peers has short-term consequences, along with considerable impact on the youngsters' social development. It is harder for victims – usually low performance athletes – to improve their skills because they feel huge pressure from their peers, which reflects in a generalized feeling of anxiety, along with lack of confidence and being unsafe.

The continued rejection and being the butt of jokes from peers reflects on the self-esteem of the victims. Athletes, coaches and ex-elite athletes all agreed that victims in sports clubs tend to drop out of sport early. They do so in order to escape from being victimized, even when they enjoy their sport. Some athletes move to another sports club, or change the sport practised as a way to avoid the bullying. The interviews held with athletes who were previously victimized in other clubs and/or sports showed that, in some cases, this shift in the social environment works well, and athletes adapt and enjoy the new experience and peer group. A rugby athlete who was previously a football goalkeeper described how things changed positively when he quit football and integrated into a rugby team, in which he felt accepted and welcome by his new peers.

However, even when the new social setting is perceived positively, the experience of being victimized usually leaves scars. Victims described the painful experiences they have been through, and often expressed shame and anger. These feelings remained after many years, and recalling bullying episodes is still difficult for some victims. Here we give two examples of men who suffered from bullying as youngsters, and became coaches in adulthood.

A coach of athletics described his painful experience when he was a handball athlete. He kept practising handball because his parents insisted. He went to the sports club, where he suffered from verbal, social and even physical bullying. He used to attend training sessions until he couldn't handle it anymore because of being victimized. Even now, it was still difficult for him to talk about it. He reported that everything changed when he dropped out of handball and started practising athletics. This shift was felt as very positive, and allowed him to stay involved in sport.

A coach of judo also described his experience of being victimized when he was a young athlete. Besides verbal bullying, he suffered from physical aggression from older athletes, who attacked him with no reason or previous provocation. He kept training in order to improve his skills and performance, and ended up achieving a high level of performance and being respected for it among judo athletes. This felt like a victory against the bullies. However, his speech was marked by anger and feelings of injustice. Now, he does not allow any kind of bullying behaviours among his athletes and wants them to have a different kind of sporting experience from that which he suffered from.

Although early drop out from sport is a common consequence of victimization, coaches also gave other reasons for athletes withdrawing from sports practice, which tends to occur mostly when they go to college. Excessive pressure from parents for the athletes to become successful was often mentioned by the coaches as a factor that contributes to youngsters dropping out of sports. Obviously, bullying is not the only reason for athletes' early drop out of sports practice. However, it is an important issue, and coaches need to know that early drop out of sport and/or changing sports club may be a strategy employed to avoid bullying. Although athletes may more easily talk about being victimized later on, they may not readily reveal this as the real reason to quit practising sport at the time.

The national coverage of our research meant that we collected data from sports clubs in very distinct places in Portugal. A youngster who lives in one of the major cities can easily choose one sports club among the many nearby, and often does not have any previous relationships to his peers in the sports club because they come from many different schools. However, in small towns there are frequently only one or two sports clubs, and athletes are more likely to have previous knowledge of each other derived from sharing the same school setting. Some athletes from small towns argued that some bullying episodes had already started in the school setting, and continued in the sports club. In some cases, if an athlete doesn't fit in the only sports club existing in his/her town, it becomes difficult for him/her to practise sport anywhere nearby. In such a case, dropping out of sports practice is an option with more serious consequences.

In summary, bullying in sport seems to have both short- and long-term consequences for victims. Besides interfering with the athlete's performance, it also reflects on the athlete's social development. Many highly talented athletes may have abandoned their promising careers due to victimization, and there is a considerable amount of evidence, corroborated by previous research (Escury & Dudink, 2010; Evans et al., 2016), that many youngsters have a low-quality sports experience, and end up dropping out of sport due to social rejection and bullying.

Summary and main conclusions

Bullying is a universal form of behaviour, due to the existence of power dynamics in every social relationship and the consequent potential for abusive patterns. However, sports have a particular culture which must be considered in order to tackle bullying more effectively in that setting. We have been concerned with athletes at the beginning of their careers – training in sports clubs. In this chapter, we considered the differences between bullying, teasing and banter, and described the sports culture and athletic mentality, which often functions as a framework to justify abusive patterns of behaviours.

The description of bullying episodes from multiple perspectives (athletes, coaches and ex-elite athletes) allowed us to better understand peer systematic abuse in youth sport. We presented a baseline for the prevalence of victimization in sports settings, compared it to school research and discussed the reasons for a possibly lower prevalence of bullying in sport than in school settings. We also discussed the main types of bullying behaviours seen in sports clubs: verbal, social and physical bullying. The rates for cyberbullying were very low and, as a consequence, not considered here.

The profiles of the victims and bullies were described, and we explored their contribution to the understanding of bullying episodes. We also focused on several other variables such as their location, the number of youngsters involved, reasons for why it happened, overlap of bullying behaviours in other social settings, and the role of the coach. We discussed the reasons for its occurrence in some detail. Bullying episodes tend to occur mainly in the changing room, and are mostly performed by a group of athletes rather than individually. Within the sports club, the coach has an important role regarding the prevalence of bullying among athletes. The behaviour of the coach may promote bullying, or on the contrary decrease aggression among youngsters (see Chapter 11).

The sports culture influences the expression of bullying behaviours. However, the victims tend to be also targeted in other social settings besides sports clubs, such as school, which may indicate the contribution of their own behaviour and relationship patterns to the understanding of bullying. Besides the topics covered by the interview scripts, some others also came up frequently and were important in understanding bullying episodes. Examples of these are the crucial moments when bullying is more prone to occur, the description of the integration of incomers and the factors which may facilitate it, and the consequences of bullying for the athletes.

There are several reasons to explain bullying behaviours; these were divided into fundamental reasons, peer pressure and individual characteristics. All seem to provide complementary insights into understanding the motivations of the perpetrators.

Victims often remain silent about the bullying and mostly cope with it by ignoring the bullies. Bystanders often contribute to the bullying by their inaction or passive encouragement; however, their reaction is related to how they perceive bullying. Those who disapprove are more likely to defend the victim, while a minority of athletes tend to join the bullies. However, the majority of bystanders watch bullying episodes and don't do anything about it.

Bullying has consequences for those involved, especially for the victims. Besides the negative feelings associated with being victimized, they also tend to suffer from early drop out from sports practice.

Strengths and limitations

The national coverage of our quantitative survey is a very positive factor. It has a sufficiently large sample to make the findings generalizable, at least for male athlete trainees in Portugal at the time of giving the survey (2013 and 2014). Considering the lack of this kind of research in Portugal, it has been important to provide a general report about bullying in youth sport, to function as a baseline. In fact, until now this has been a rather neglected topic internationally.

The complementary qualitative approach is also positive. Although anonymous questionnaires are considered appropriate to collect data about sensitive subjects, a reliance on self-report data would be a limitation. Standard questionnaires restrict the information collected and do not allow a deeper comprehension of the topic that qualitative investigation can bring. We performed a considerable range of interviews, with different stakeholders (athletes, coaches and ex-elite athletes), which allowed us to compare their perspectives, and to achieve deeper insights into bullying in sport.

A major limitation is that our research only studied male athletes. Further research is needed in order to understand bullying in female sports training, and to compare findings for male and female athletes. Different results are expected for girls; our research suggests that bullying in sport among boys is influenced (among other factors) by the male ethos. It seems important to understand how girls perceive sports culture, and how it influences their behaviour. Also, although bullying phenomena seem fairly similar at least in Western countries (Smith, Kwak & Toda, 2016), our findings here are limited to the Portuguese context.

Only the traditional types of bullying were deeply analysed. Although cyberbullying was considered in our survey, this type of bullying got less attention than the traditional types. Even in the narratives of the athletes, cyberbullying was not mentioned by them (Chapter 7). Although we collected and analysed data about the role of the coach in athlete–athlete bullying, coach bullying was not considered in our research. Finally, although we describe some of the consequences of bullying, it lacks direct assessment of its effects, especially on bullies and bystanders.

Chapter 11

Coach abuse

The coach-athlete relationship

The relationship between coach and athlete is one of major importance and has a strong influence on the quality of the youngster's sport experience (Stirling & Kerr, 2008a). Many youngsters who practice sport spend more time of their week with their coaches, than they do with their parents. The majority of the coaches care for the children's welfare, and play an important positive role in their lives. It is common for adults to evoke pleasant memories of the relationship with a former coach, and how important he/she was for them at that period of their lives. Most of the coaches also have an important educational role outside of the school. Sports activity and a good coach have certainly helped many youngsters who found little or no motivation at school, or lacked a supportive environment at home.

During training, coaches should care about other aspects, more than just improving training skills. The interpersonal relations and developmental stages of the athletes must be considered, in order to promote healthy and enjoyable experiences for them. Coaches should be positive and inspiring role models. They need to be alert to any misconduct of the athletes, and not tolerate any bullying behaviours. However, some coaches may become a source of conflict, rather than a way to deal with it. A minority of coaches are abusive, and the close relationship established with the young athletes may result in negative outcomes for them.

Youth sport settings are very competitive and a winning-at-all-cost mentality tends to prevail among the majority of the coaches, who are frequently perceived as the way to achieve success by the athletes they work with. This gives them considerable influence among youngsters and their parents. Some coaches may have good intentions when performing what are actually abusive styles of training, not being aware of the negative outcomes of those practices. They may adopt an autocratic style of leadership, based on the power imbalance between them and the athletes, and frequently shout at and insult athletes as a way to make them "tough" and "improve their resilience", or to punish inadequate performances and/or behaviours (Stirling & Kerr, 2008a).

Sometimes concerns have been raised in national media. In January 2018, the Washington Post published an article entitled "Why we still allow bullying to flourish in kids sports", that explored the abusive nature of some coaching practices with young athletes, and raised concerns about its normalization (www.washingtonpost.com/news/posteverything/wp/2018/01/02/why-we-still-allow-bullying-to-flourish-in-kids-sports/?noredirect=on&utm_term=.8adf2476506e).

In January 2019, the British Broadcasting Corporation (BBC) aired a program about abusive coaching practices and sexual abuse that occurred in one of the top tennis centres. They pointed out the repeated warnings that had been made, which were missed by the Tennis Centre in the UK (www.bbc.com/sport/tennis/46973925).

In this chapter, we focus on this minority of coaches, discussing their abusive coaching practices and its negative outcomes. In the second half of the chapter we focus on sexual harassment and abuse in sports by coaches to athletes. Although this is also an abusive behaviour, it is not part of abusive coaching practices as such, and it has some particular features that justify analysing it separately.

Systematic abuse from coach-to-athlete. should we call it "coach bullying"?

Our own research has focused on peer bullying, among young athletes. The role of the coach was analysed within this framework. However, the systematic abuse of the athletes by the coach is an important topic that should also be discussed in this book. To do so, we describe some findings from research by other authors who focused specifically on this topic.

By some definitions (see Chapter 1), systematic abuse is only considered bullying when it occurs between peers. This would mean that in youth sports settings it would be restricted to athlete-to-athlete relationships. However, some coaches establish abusive relations with their athletes, based on the power imbalance existing between them and the athletes who they are responsible for. Some authors have labelled this *emotional abuse* rather than bullying (Kerr & Stirling, 2012; Stirling, 2013). However other authors, such as Swigonski, Enneking and Hendrix (2014), do consider that a pattern of abuse by the coaches towards the athletes should be labelled as coach bullying. According to them, the inherent imbalance of power within an abusive relationship makes it bullying, even if it is not performed between peers.

As Stirling and Kerr defined it, "Emotional abuse refers to a pattern of deliberate non-contact behaviours by a person within a critical relationship role that have the potential to be harmful to an individual's emotional well-being" (2008b, p 178). In their research they aimed to define and categorize emotional abuse by the coaches in sport, and their findings were similar to those in research on school bullying, which suggests a considerable overlap of these concepts, with examples of verbal, social and physical bullying.

The World Health Organisation considers both bullying and emotional abuse. It uses Olweus' definition when considering bullying (see Chapter 1), and defines emotional abuse as

> acts towards the child that cause, or have a high probability of causing, harm to the child's health or physical, mental, spiritual, moral or social development, including restriction of movement, patterns of belittling, denigrating, scapegoating, threatening, scaring, discriminating, ridiculing or other non-physical forms of hostile or rejecting treatment .
> (WHO, 1999)

The Canadian Red Cross definition also suggests similarities between both concepts. Here, emotional abuse is defined as a pattern of behaviour performed by adults towards children, in which adults criticize, threaten and/or dismiss the youngsters, resulting in damaged feelings of self-worth and self-esteem. Examples of these behaviours include rejecting, degrading, isolating, terrorizing or exploiting. Bullying is defined by mean, cruel, hurtful behaviour, that involves using power in a negative way to hurt others.

The discussion around the definition of bullying, and the boundaries separating it from other abusive patterns of relationship with considerable conceptual overlap is still quite active. Although there may not be a consensus among experts regarding this specific conceptual issue, here we consider any abusive pattern of relationship performed by coaches to the athletes as a type of bullying. The nature of the aggressive behaviours may include several types, such as verbal (e.g. yelling or ridicule), physical (e.g. throwing objects, using forced physical contact) relational (e.g. abusive coaching practices) or even sexual (e.g. sexual harassment and abuse).

The traditional youth sport training triangle is composed of the athlete, the parents and the coach. Obviously one could ask about systematic abuse performed by athletes to the coaches, or by athletes' parents to both athletes and their coaches. These forms of aggression should also be analysed and described. However, there is very little knowledge in these areas. Due to the specific features of the social setting we are considering, as well as the similarities between athletes bullying and coach abuse, here we are only going to consider the systematic abusive relationship between coach and athletes as a type of bullying.

Encouragement or coach-bullying?

If bullying among athletes is frequently misinterpreted as banter, bullying performed by coaches may be easily mis-labelled as encouragement. Athletes and parents, among other stakeholders, may believe that belligerent coaches do not intentionally hurt their athletes, but instead only intend to bring out better performances (Fisher & Dzikus, 2010). However, real encouragement is based on a pedagogical relationship and aims to fulfil the athletes' personal objectives, while coach bullying is an abusive pattern of relationship, in which abuse is ignored, or perceived as justifiable to achieve success. When encouragement prevails, the relation between athlete and the coach is characterized by positive feelings and trust, and the coach approach to training is based on the development of the athletes' skills. On the other hand, in coach bullying the relation between coach and athlete is based on negative feelings or neutrality (based on the normalization of the abuse), and winning at all cost is the basis of all the training work.

Coach bullying differs greatly from encouragement, because it is a relationship based on dominance and control from the adult, in which the athletes' personal wishes and aims are ignored and all training and competition is based on the coach's own desires and personal aspirations. In these cases, the relationship with the coach is frequently recalled later by athletes as abusive, especially after abandonment of sport and/or competition (Stirling & Kerr, 2007). For coaches, aggressive behaviours such as bullying and hazing may appear to result in better enhancement of performance in the short-term, but they have negative consequences to the athletes in the longer-term (Fisher & Dzikus, 2010).

Types of behaviours

The abusive behaviours by a coach may be verbal, physical, social, and sexual (Gervis & Dunn, 2004; Kerr & Stirling, 2012). Some examples of bullying behaviours performed by coaches are:

- Verbal:
    - shouting, insulting, injuring, making demeaning or degrading comments and belittling;
    - humiliating an athlete, especially if he or she is weaker, socially rejected and/or more vulnerable;
    - threatening (by gestures or verbal expressions)
    - using sarcasm or other insulting types of language;
    - mocking the look or background of the athlete.

- Physical:
    - physically attacking or using any form of undesired physical contact;
    - throwing objects;
    - punching walls.

- Social/indirect:
    - making athletes feel incompetent, below expectations and devalued;
    - denying assistance when it is necessary;
    - demanding more than the athlete can do, without considering limitations, difficulties and/or age.
    - punishing the athlete for mistakes related with skill development and learning to train;
    - intentionally ignoring and excluding the athlete
    - denying participation or involvement in the activities organized by the sport club;
    - refusing to provide adequate feedback.

- Sexual:
    - sexual abuse or harassment [discussed later].

Estimated prevalence of coach-bullying

The Minnesota Amateur Sports Commission (www.mnsports.org/) reported a study on child abuse in sport in 1999, which included surveying coaching abusive practices. The results are reason for concern. Verbal aggression was highly prevalent. In total, 45% of young athletes had been called names, yelled at, or insulted while participating in sports, and 8% were called names with sexual connotations while participating in sports. Physical abuse was also reported: 21% of the youngsters were pressured to play with an injury, 17.5% were kicked, hit or slapped by their coaches while playing sports, and 8% were intentionally pressured to harm others while playing sports. Although this study was made 20 years ago, subsequent studies have indicated that it is still a serious problem.

Shields, Bredemeier, LaVoi and Power (2005) carried out research in the USA to estimate the prevalence of good and poor sport behaviours, from the perspectives of young athletes, parents and coaches. In total, 803 young athletes (fifth through eighth grades) representing ten sports were surveyed, as well as 189 of their parents and 61 of their coaches. The analysis of coach behaviour, based on the perspectives of the young athletes and the coaches themselves, showed that verbal abuse was highly reported, including the coach making fun of a team member. Both athletes and coaches stated that over a third of all coaches yelled angrily at children for making mistakes. 45% of children reported verbal misconduct by coaches, including name-calling and insulting them during play. Regarding physical abuse, 4% of the young athletes reported having been hit, kicked, or slapped by their coaches.

A study conducted in Scotland by Alexander, Stafford and Lewis (2011), interviewed more than 6,000 young adults from 18 to 22 years about their experiences in sports earlier in adolescence. They found that three-quarters of the athletes reported at least one incident of emotional harm, and nearly one-third of these reported their coach as the main source of harm.

All these results suggest that coach abuse is not infrequent, and must be considered and addressed. However, they should be analysed with caution; each study has its own limitations, and the percentage of behaviours reported will considerably vary depending on the definition used, the time reference period, and frequency cut-off, among other variables. These findings should only be considered as indicative, but they clearly point to the need to focus attention on these issues. Most coaches do have a positive role in the lives of young athletes; but a minority may abuse this. These kinds of behaviours in sports settings, including their prevalence, are clearly a reason for concern (Kirby, Greaves & Hankivsky, 2000).

Reasons for coach bullying

Abusive coaching practices are often normalized as a means to achieve sporting success (Gervis & Dunn, 2004), and are under-acknowledged (Swigonski, Enneking & Hendrix, 2014). The prevalence of emotional abuse can be related to styles of coaching. An autocratic style of coaching is based on a power imbalance between coach and athlete, and uses tactics like yelling and or making disparaging comments aiming to promote athletes' toughness or enhance their resilience (Palframan, 1994). Similarly Stirling (2013) describes two reasons for the employment of emotionally abusive coaching practices: the expressive and the instrumental. In expressive abuse, the abuse is an end by itself, while in instrumental abuse, coaches employ abusive coaching styles to achieve a desired end (e.g. athletes' development). Emotionally abusive coaching practices are based on fear of the coach (Kerr & Stirling, 2012), and an autocratic type of coaching results in increasing burnout among athletes.

Risk factors for coach-bullying

There are some risk factors for coach bullying, which should be considered to plan effective intervention programmes (guidelines will be discussed later in Chapter 12).

In their research on emotional abuse by coaches, Kerr and Stirling (2012) analysed the narratives of parents of ex-elite athletes, and identified 5 phases that describe the progressively increasing control of the coach over the athletes, and how parents felt about it; (1) *talent Identification*: when the child is identified by the coach or other sport stakeholders as talented; (2) *relinquishing of control by the parents*: at an early stage of the sports career, parents were asked to trust the coach's expertise, and were expected to pass control of their children over to the coach; (3) *growing concern by the parents*: in the first couple of years working with the coach, the demands of the training and competition increased greatly, and parents were asked to make sacrifices (e.g. not allow their children to participate in school sport team so he/she can totally focus on sport club sportive activities, to schedule family vacations based on the competition schedules of their children). Parents expressed concern, but complied for the sake of their child's sporting success; (4) *acceptance/acquiescence by the parents*: when the athlete reaches the peak of his/her career, parents expressed pride for the accomplishments of their child, but acknowledged that the process of reaching there had negative consequences, and generated distress; (5) guilt of parents: this occurred when the athletes retire from their sporting careers. The coach practices generally accepted by the parents in the past, are now often perceived as negative and unacceptable. Parents feel guilt, remorse and self-doubt about having allowed the abuse to occur and continue.

The growing involvement of parents in their children's sporting lives that often occurs, could be a protective factor against coach bullying. However, on many occasions it can result in a progressive acceptance of the sport culture, based on the "tough mentality" and "winning-at-all-cost approach" which is quite prevalent in youth sport (Woolger & Power, 1993). When this happens, parents often become silent bystanders towards any abuse by the coach (Kerr & Stirling, 2012). According to Fisher and Dzikus (2010), the cultural values in sport setting may promote an "ends justify means employed" approach, which can more easily justify bullying behaviours and abusive hazing rituals. This may lead to intellectualized justifications of some coach bullying behaviours (Stirling & Kerr, 2007), especially when parents were also athletes of that particular sport.

The high performance of the athletes helps to justify and legitimize emotional abuse by their coaches; during the bulk of the sports careers of the athletes, the experience of emotional abuse is often normalised as part of the elite sport culture, because athletes are socialized into this culture from an early age. However, a "stage of rebellion" by the athletes often occurs near the end of the career, in which they call into question and criticize the behavioural patterns that their coach had used. Stirling and Kerr (2007, 2008a) argue that coaches often behave in ways that would not be allowed in other settings such as school; if teachers in school threw objects at or insulted their students, they would probably face serious consequences.

The methods of the coach being perceived as a way to achieve success may also contribute to a submissive attitude of the athletes towards abusive conduct, such that bullying can be ignored because the coach is the one who can make athletes achieve the final objective: sporting success. The age of the coach, his or her knowledge about the sport and past successful experiences as a coach should also be considered. If the coach is older, has worked in this particular sport for a long time and has had many successes in the past, his or her authority, methods and pattern of relationship with athletes are less likely to be questioned. The high status of the coach partially protects him or her from being confronted by others, especially the athletes (Stirling & Kerr, 2009). Gender is also an important factor when analysing abusive coach relations towards athletes, especially when male coaches work with female youngsters, which may facilitate sexual abuse and harassment. However, cases of male coaches sexually abusing boys (e.g. in football) should also be considered.

Abusive coaches frequently state that they work based on the athletes' best interests, but on many occasions, they depend on athletes results for their own success, which results in guiding the training and competition based on their own priorities and aims rather than considering the athletes' wishes and welfare. This pressure may facilitate coaching practices that are not fully compatible with the well-being of the athletes (Stirling & Kerr, 2009). The power of the abusive coach frequently overlaps other domains of the life of the athletes like nutrition, weight, sleep patterns, interpersonal relations. Coaches become pseudo doctors, psychologists, nutritionists, resulting in an increasing control over the athletes' life (Tomlinson & Yorganci, 1997). Both athletes and their parents are more prone to accept the abusive behaviours, and to normalize them, especially during the competition stage and when the performance achieved is high.

High performance can be reached without abusive coach practices. A considerable amount of effort and abnegation from the athletes are needed to achieve success in elite sport. However, hard work and discipline do not justify abusive coaching practices. There are numerous stories of coaches who helped the athletes they worked with to achieve high performance, and still had a humanized and positive relationship with them.

Defensive strategies and intellectualized justifications for coach-bullying:

Intervention regarding coach abuse is not easy. One difficulty is knowing at which threshold the coach crosses accepted limits. The difference between legitimate criticism about training progress, and bullying or abusive behaviours, may not always be obvious. However, there is a difference between a guiding and constructive feedback toward the performance's success, and an insulting criticism. The limit may be defined by the existence of a persistent pattern of behaviour which harms rather than helps the athlete's development.

Coaches may use some defensive strategies to excuse their abusive behaviour (Field, 1996):

- Moral justification: defending a behaviour as being common and widely accepted: "All coaches lose their rag once in a while" or "We have always done like that and we have sports success".
- Backhand apology: minimizing the impact of behaviour on the victim and justifying it in the name of a supposed greater good: "I am sorry I lost my temper a bit, but I had to do it if we wanted to win".
- Inappropriate comparisons: justifying abusive behaviours by comparing them with even more serious ones. "I screamed at the athletes but I never laid a finger on them".
- Escalation: increasing the pressure until the person gives up complaining. "If you don't like my methods, you can leave".

Reasons for silence of the athletes about coach-bullying

Just as with bullying among athletes, when coaches develop a systematic abusive pattern of relationship with an athlete, the athlete tends to keep silent about it. Some of the reasons for silence about coach bullying, pointed out by Kerr and Stirling (2012), are:

- The tough mentality in youth sport (acceptance of negative strategies).
- Normalization of the abusive behaviours (e.g. watching other athletes accepting the coach behave this way);
- Considering coach bullying as a normal and acceptable path to achieve sporting success;
- Fear of the coach;
- Being afraid nobody will believe them (considering the reputation and social status of the coach);
- Fear of the possible consequences breaking silence may have on the athletes' sport career;
- Coaches interfere in the communication between athlete and their parents about what happens in the sport club;
- Intimidation of the athlete and his/her parents.

Consequences of coach-to-athlete bullying

If the power of the coach is used to abuse (rather than to promote development), the young athlete may suffer long-term psychological damage. He or she may progressively assimilate what adults say about them and, if the coach is a bully and the abuse is chronic, it may destroy the motivation of the athlete and result in a huge impact on his or her self-esteem. The comments of "encouragement" made by some coaches to improve the sport performance of their athletes may have the opposite effect. The verbal and psychological abuse can result in extremely negative harmful effects for the athletes. Here are some examples (**Stirling, 2013; Stirling & Kerr, 2007**):

- Low mood, anxiety and depression
- Anger;
- Feeling devalued;
- Low self-esteem;
- Poor body image;
- Impaired focus, reduced enjoyment and energy;
- Decrease of motivation and sport performance;
- Being over-afraid of committing errors;
- Experiencing social exclusion and isolation;
- Depleted coping resources;
- Early drop-out of sport practice;
- Change of social setting (sport practice and/or sport club) in order to avoid bullying.

These consequences are those likely to result from being systematically exposed to bullying behaviours from the coach. The negative effects are frequently reported as resulting from athletic competition, and because they are not as obvious as physical and/or sexual harm, tend to be ignored. Nevertheless, they are severe failures in the sporting codes of conduct, and should not be tolerated by sport clubs.

Sexual harassment and abuse in youth sports

Recent occurrences of major incidents of sexual harassment and abuse (SHA) in sports have called the attention of researchers and sports stakeholders to this important topic. Here are some examples:

Larry Nassar, who was the former doctor for the USA gymnastics team and a member of Michigan State's Sport Medicine staff, was sentenced to 40 to 175 years in prison after admitting he molested athletes while he was supposedly treating their injuries (www.nytimes.com/2018/01/24/sports/larry-nassar-sentencing.html). More than 150 women and girls complained about his behaviour, as far back as the 1990's.

Andy King was sentenced to 40 years in prison for molesting young female athletes (15 and younger) training at San Jose Aquatics Club (www.espn.com/olympics/swimming/news/story?id=4872192). Two years before, the coach Brian Hindson from Central Indiana Aquatics, was sentenced to 33 years in prison, after pleaded guilty of distribution, production and possession of child pornography. He was accused of setting up hidden cameras in locker rooms (www.justice.gov/archive/opa/pr/2008/October/08-crm-934.html).

In the UK, a major scandal occurred in football; in 2016 a group of former players broke silence, and talked about the sexual abuse they had suffered at the hands of their coaches. These complaints resulted in a police investigation of non-recent child sexual abuse in football. The number of victims reached 839, with an age range from 4 to 20 years old when the abuse occurred. The former coach Barry Bennell pleaded guilty to several crimes (www.bbc.com/news/topics/cpml0mvd3wpt/barry-bennell-child-sex-abuse-case).

In 2010 36 swimming coaches were banned for life for sexual abuse practices, and that list has grown to 150 since then (www.d2l.org/abc-news-investigation-usa-swimming-coaches-molested-secretly-taped-dozens-of-teen-swimmers/).

In August 2019, Chelsea Football Club released the results of a report about sexual abuse of young athletes during the 1960´s and 1970´s. The independent investigation revealed that the former scout of the club, Eddie Heat, had sexually abused many young players, and that other stakeholders within the sport club might have known what was happening, but ignored it (www.itv.com/news/2019-08-06/chelsea-issues-unreserved-apology-over-historical-child-sex-and-racial-abuse/).

These episodes of SHA may occur in any country, and are clearly a breach of Human Rights. Such episodes have severe consequences for the victims, and also the organization in which they take place. Research and intervention on sexual harassment and abuse in sport are topics of major importance, and a growing number of international entities that regulate sport and/or focus their attention on the welfare of the athletes have contributed to this. The International Olympic Committee and UNICEF are two examples of entities who have been working on SHA in sport: describing it, sensitizing stakeholders, and creating guidelines (IOC Medical Commission, 2007; UNICEF, 2005). Here, we mention research developed internationally about this topic. The data presented here was not collected by us. Both theoretical contributions and guidelines (see Chapter 12) are the result of the work developed by other researchers who have focused their attention on studying SHA in sports.

SHA exists in all sports and levels of competition; the athletes are targeted by members of the technical team, namely coaches or health professionals, among others (Fasting, Brackenridge & Sundgot-Borgen, 2013). Athletes from both genders may suffer from SHA (Fasting, Chroni, Hervik & Knorre, 2011). The situations of sexual abuse in sport often involve the manipulation of the victim, who ends up feeling trapped by the perpetrator (Marks, Mountjoy & Marcus, 2012). SHA in sport must be perceived as a structural and cultural problem, rather than an individual one. Besides perpetrators and victims, it is also necessary to consider the structure of the sports club, to analyse the underpinnings and moral standards accepted in it, as well as its culturally accepted practices. When sexual harassment occurs, it means something may be wrong within the sports club. Both sexual harassment and sexual abuse are severe faults regarding the moral values that sporting activity is based upon.

The process of the coach-athlete relationship in SHA

The coach has a "power position" regarding the athlete, which consists of an imbalance of power between the two in this social setting. The perverse exploitation of this may result in the occurrence of SHA cases. Here, the perpetrators seek to establish a trust relationship with the victim, with whom they apparently share common goals. Considering that most of the cases of SHA involve a grooming process, these coaches seem to have a prior motivation to execute SHA, rather than performing an isolated act (Brackenridge, 2001).

The process of grooming made by the perpetrators towards the victim consists of the use of coercive strategies, aiming to establish dominance over the victim, as a way to initiate and perpetuate the abuse. According to Marks, Mountjoy and Marcus (2012) this process divides into 4 main phases:

1. Identify the isolated and vulnerable victim: choose the most isolated athletes, who suffer from some kind of emotional vulnerability;
2. Grooming: establish a trust relationship with the athlete: make the targeted athlete feel special and unique (e.g. offer gifts). These privileges are frequently used to ask for favours in return in the future;
3. Enhance control and loyalty, by limiting the contacts of the athlete with his or her support network (family, friends etc.). In this phase, the perpetrator tends to gradually break the acceptable boundaries, and abuse the victims by violating his/her personal space by using expressions of verbal familiarity, or physical contact;
4. Ensure secrecy: blackmail may be used to ensure compliance; emphasising secrecy gives a higher sense of security to the perpetrator; it can also produce greater cooperation from the victim, because the victim frequently ends up feeling responsible for the abuse (feeling that he/she caused it).

These strategies may be used for years, without the full consent of the victim about the abusive relation. The victims feel trapped, without any ability to fend off the sexual urges of the perpetrator (Brackenridge, 2001).

According to Leahy (2010), the perpetrator uses strategies to make victims feel powerless, while he or she presents him/herself as omnipotent. He or she tends to impose his or her version of the reality, and to isolate the victim from potential support sources. This external control is complemented by an internal control, achieved by manipulation, psychological abuse and the creation of training environments which are psychologically abusive. The traumatic attachment with the perpetrator, as a result of sexual abuse, frequently results in a shift in the locus of control; the youngster often feels bad, and responsible for what is happening to him/

her. This mechanism allows the victim to maintain the illusion of controlling the situation, and to idealize the perpetrator, which contributes to the victim remaining silent and not sharing the abusive experience.

Key concepts in SHA

SHA behaviours may be verbal, non-verbal and/or physical. Examples of each are given here:

- *Verbal*: intimate and undesirable questions about one's body, clothes or private life. Degrading comments about bodies and sexual activities, and offensive name calling. "Jokes" of sexual content, invitations or demands to perform acts or get involved in sexual intercourse. Unwanted phone calls or text messages with sexual contents.
- *Non-verbal*: exhibitionism (photography or objects with sexual allusions), exposure of children to pornography.
- *Physical*: unwanted and unnecessary physical contact (with a sexual connotation) such as pressing the body of the perpetrator against the body of the victim, forced attempt to kiss, touching, fondling, masturbation, sexual penetration (oral, vaginal or anal with objects or any part of the body, performed by the perpetrator or by another victim who does it under coercion), rape.

The adults in the sport club who are responsible for the wellbeing of the young athletes may have different perceptions regarding SHA. This is particularly important in sports settings, because there is natural and frequent physical contact between people (e.g. the coach explaining a movement or technique to an athlete). The behaviours of SHA vary along a continuum with different degrees of severity, from *sexual exploitation*, through to *sexual harassment*, and finally *sexual abuse* (Marks, Mountjoy & Marcus, 2012).

Sexual exploitation is a broad concept that includes sexual harassment and abuse, but also harassment based on gender, hazing rituals (frequently with sexualized contents) and homophobia.

Sexual harassment refers to sexualised verbal, non-verbal or physical behaviour, which may be legal or illegal. These behaviours are based on the abuse of power and trust, and are felt by the victim or bystander as unwanted, intrusive and/or coercive. Sexual harassment should not be confused with flirting, which is often reciprocal and is felt as positive and pleasant by both individuals. Sexual harassment includes three categories of impermissible behaviour (1) *sexual coercion*: this refers to implicit or explicit attempts to make work conditions contingent upon sexual cooperation (e.g. "have sex with me or you won't play"), (2) *unwanted sexual attention*: this consists of unwanted touching, stroking, kissing or repeated advances for sexual intercourse. Sexual overtures in youth sports may not be sexual harassment; to be considered harassment, the sexual advances must be felt as unpleasant and not desired by the person who is targeted, and must be sufficiently severe or pervasive to create an abusive training environment. Unwanted sexual attention can include sexual assault and rape. Finally (3) *gender assault*: this consists of denigrating people based on gender. It is mostly sexist (e.g. considering women not-suited for leadership and sports, or men for childcare).

It is important to note that these actions constitute sexual harassment because they are sex-based, and not necessarily because of the existence of sexual involvement between those involved. When there is sexual involvement, the situation is likely to be one of sexual abuse.

Sexual abuse: this is a very severe form of mistreating children, mainly used to describe behaviour towards children, not adults. It involves coercive sexual and genital acts in which the victim is imprisoned by the perpetrator, or sexual intercourse with a person against his or her own will (rape), without consent. It is also considered sexual abuse when the targeted person does not have the capacity to consent (e.g. if they are too young, or intellectually disabled) (Leahy, 2014). This is a violation of another person rights and a crime.

Prevalence

It is hard to make an accurate estimative of the prevalence of SHA. These behaviours are often ignored for years, and only acknowledged much later, when a victim decides to break silence. A broad spectrum of research to establish a baseline, and to allow comparisons between different countries regarding the rates of SHA, is needed.

Risk factors

Research on SHA in sport has identified several risk factors. The victims are often younger athletes, who may feel distant from their parents, have low self-esteem and suffer from social exclusion (Brackenridge, 1997). The perpetrators are usually male individuals, who have an authority or a caregiver role towards the victims (Leahy, 2014; Marks, Mountjoy & Marcus, 2012). Those with such a role are the coaches, referees, other athletes or health professionals such as psychologists, physical trainers and doctors. Although SHA in youth sport may be perpetuated by any of these, considering the role of the coach and his/her proximity to the athletes, we focus on SHA perpetrated by the coaches to young athletes.

The episodes of sexual abuse tend to occur in isolated areas such as the changing room, the car or the house of the coach, during journeys to competitions (Kirby, Greaves & Hankivsky, 2000), or in social settings which involve alcohol consumption (Waldron, Lynn & Krane, 2011). The lack of conduct codes and procedures to report SHA situations within the sport clubs are also considered risk factors (Brackenridge, 1997).

Silence

Prevention and intervention in sports clubs in very important, in order to promote an environment that rejects SHA. If procedures to report and tackle SHA were improved, it would be much easier for athletes to break silence. However, even when this is done, some episodes may occur, which lead victims to employ coping strategies to deal with it. The athletes seldom report these kinds of occurrence to an adult. The most used strategies are sharing the experience with other athletes, and/or avoiding some areas, so as not to be there alone with the coach.

It can happen that other athletes and/or members of staff block or discourage the exposure of SHA episodes they suspect or are aware of. This has a negative effect because it contributes to maintaining the silence of the victims and the continuation of the abusive relationship. It is important to create a support system for the athletes, which they can rely on if they get involved in SHA episodes. Victims need a safe way to report any SHA episodes, so that they can be acknowledged and properly tackled. Victims must know who they can speak with, and what to do (see guidelines in chapter 12).

Consequences

The World Health Organisation considers abuse and violence as public health issues, which have severe consequences for those involved. Sexual abuse has physical, performance and mental health consequences (Leahy, 2014; Marks, Mountjoy & Marcus, 2012). Besides the repercussions felt by the victims, SHA episodes also have a negative effect on bystanders, which can last for many years.

Sporting consequences:

- Decrease of attentional focus
- Decrease in performance (training sessions and work)
- Obsessive training to cope with anxiety, which can result in burn-out
- Negative impact on other family and sport club members
- Deterioration of coach-athlete relationship
- Early drop-out from sport practice.

Symptoms and mental health consequences:

- Insomnia
- Anxiety, depression
- Physical reactions to stress
- Post-traumatic stress
- Eating disorders
- Drug consumption
- Low self-esteem
- Difficulties to trust other people
- Difficulties in intimate relationships
- Negative effect on social activities
- Feelings of guilt and shame
- Self-harm behaviours
- Suicidal ideation.

Athletes who suffered from sexual abuse from another person whom they used to trust, experience difficulties to rely on their own judgement of the situation. The guilt and shame can be very powerful, because the athletes had had a long cooperation process with the coach to achieve success. This may contribute to the feeling that they are responsible for what happened.

Summary

Most coaches are positive role models for young athletes, and greatly assist their sporting development. But it can happen that their power over a young athlete is abused. Coach bullying is a pattern of abuse between the coach and the athletes. It can often be misinterpreted or defended as encouragement, and an autocratic style of coaching is often justified as a way to improve the performance of the athletes.

There are some risk factors for the occurrence of coach bullying, such as the acceptance of a sport culture based on winning-at-all-cost, and the normalization of aggressive behaviours by many stakeholders in this setting. The coach is frequently perceived by the athletes as a way to achieve success, which facilitates the acceptance of his or her possible abusive behaviours. When the coaches are getting positive sporting results, or when they have a high status within the sport based on his or her previous results, it makes it harder for athletes and parents to question his or her methods.

When abusive coaches are confronted by the parents of the young athletes about their behaviours, they often use defensive strategies to justify their behaviour. The athletes who are targeted by their coaches often remain silent about it due to many reasons, such as the tough mentality in sport, the normalization of the aggressive behaviours, or the fear of the coach. But coach bullying has negative consequences for the athletes, and contributes to impairments in their social development.

Sexual harassment and abuse (SHA) is a particular concern in youth sports. It involves a process by which the coach identifies a likely victim, grooms him or her, enhances control and loyalty, and ensures secrecy. Risk factors includes younger athletes who feel distant from their parents and suffer from social exclusion. The episodes tend to occur in less supervised areas. When SHA occurs, the athletes who are victimized often remain silent about it. SHA may result in severe sporting and mental health consequences for the victims.

Chapter 12

Practical implications, and guidelines for athletes, parents and coaches

Introduction

Tackling bullying: the work previously developed in school settings

To tackle bullying effectively, different variables and levels of intervention must be considered. Research has been carried out at the individual level, mostly by psychologists, aiming to understand the profiles of the victims and bullies, and their families' ways of functioning. Other perspectives have considered the social dynamics of bullying within a group context (Salmivalli, 2010), class and school level factors (Thornberg, 2011), and transitions between school levels (Pellegrini & Long, 2002). Besides these variables, others within a macro level should also be considered, related to general society at a national level. This ecological approach to bullying (see Chapter 2) is useful when designing intervention programmes and developing national and international anti-bullying policies. For recent intervention work in schools and the impact it is having, see the book edited by Smith (2019a, 2019b).

Tackling violence and abuse in sport

Aggressive behaviours and violence in sport must also be tackled and prevented with a multi-level approach. The UNICEF report from 2010 titled "Protecting Children from Violence in Sport. A Review with a Focus on Industrialized Countries" (www.unicef-irc.org/publications/pdf/violence_in_sport.pdf) describes different types of aggressive behaviours (including bullying), and focuses on the prevention of these behaviours at different levels, and by involving several sports agents and stakeholders.

Psaaji and Schailée (2019) used the socio-ecological framework to understand the nature of what they labelled as unsanctioned aggression and violence in amateur sport. They considered violent behaviours as multifaceted, and proposed an approach based on four levels along a continuum from individual, to situational, contextual and sociocultural factors.

- The individual level is divided into personal values, obsessive passion (perceived as the degree to which an athlete identifies with the culture of sport practised) and demographic factors (age and gender);
- The situational level is divided into conflictual interactions, bystanders and situational dominance;
- The contextual level considers the type and level of sport;
- The sociocultural level includes social learning, moral atmosphere, moral disengagement and masculinity values within the society.

The levels described here correspond to the micro-, meso-, exo- and macro-levels of Bronfenbrenner's Ecological Systems Theory. This review calls attention to the need to combine several approaches to better understand aggressive and violent behaviours in sport. Some of these levels of prevention and intervention were considered when we performed the analysis of bullying episodes earlier in this book. In their research on emotional abuse by the coach towards athletes, Stirling and Kerr (2014) also presented an ecological systems approach to understanding and preventing it, which considers a micro-, exo- and macro-approach, and includes several stakeholders.

Describing prevention and interventions of bullying in youth sport by system levels

Bullying cannot be tackled by a few random strategies. To decrease the prevalence of bullying behaviours and build a more inclusive environment among young athletes, consistent policies must be developed, which require time and effort by those who work on them. To create a social environment which promotes inclusion, acceptance and tolerance, and improves both motor and emotional development of the athletes, is a substantial task to be developed over time.

The different and complementary levels of intervention work best in combination. Besides the need to raise general awareness and to educate sports agents, some procedures inside the sports club, as well as group and individual interventions, must be considered. Although each sports stakeholder can play an important role in successfully developing and implementing an antibullying policy, some interventions, namely some specific individual work with bullies and victims, should be conducted by a specialized professional.

Figure 12.1 shows different levels of intervention of bullying in sport, based on the Ecological Systems Model. Here we summarize some bullying prevention and intervention measures, and divide these interventions into levels, describing their targets, as well as delineating general and specific intervention measures. We also provide a brief description of each measure.

Conclusions and practical implications

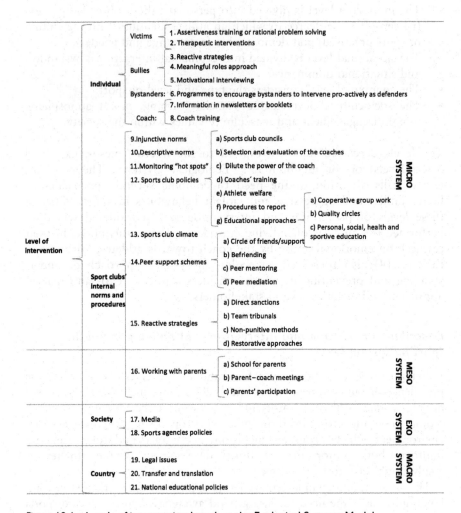

Figure 12.1 : Levels of intervention based on the Ecological Systems Model.

Micro-level

The micro-level approach refers to the policies and measures developed within the sports club. It includes individual and group intervention with different stakeholders. Here we include:

TARGET

Sports clubs;
Sports stakeholders (athletes, parents, coaches and sports leaders).

GENERAL INTERVENTIONS

- *Coaches and sports leaders:* training and education on violence, abuse and discrimination (how to develop a club policy);
- *Internal policies:* develop prevention and intervention programmes, which include an anti-bullying policy, attitudinal change towards violence and abuse, peer group norms, moral atmosphere, an athlete-centred approach, codes of conduct and ways to report occurrences of bullying;
- *Athletes:* establish individual and group management approaches to bullies, victims and bystanders (prevention and intervention of bullying when it occurs);
- *Parents:* educate parents about their role in their children's sporting activities within the club, and ask them to acknowledge the sports club rules and policies, and means of communication with the coach and other stakeholders.

SPECIFIC INTERVENTIONS

Individual intervention with victims

1. Assertiveness training or rational problem solving (improve coping strategies), to help victims improve their social skills and become more included in the peer group;
2. Therapeutic interventions (reduce anxiety and depression): victimization and depression are strongly related. In some cases, a therapeutic intervention is needed to help victims. Both interventions 1 and 2 should be conducted by a psychologist and/or psychotherapist;

Individual intervention with perpetrators

3. Reactive strategies: these interventions aim to tackle bullying when it has occurred. Their main goal is to reduce the action of the perpetrators. Different approaches are considered (see more detail in item 16 below);
4. Meaningful roles approach: to give the perpetrators some meaningful role within the sports club (e.g. team captain, responsible for helping the coach in some actions, to help the integration of younger athletes). It may help perpetrators to feel respected and valued, and find some other motivation rather than targeting victims. This approach needs to be taken with care to ensure that the perpetrators do not abuse their new positions, but may be a way of changing their behaviour towards more pro-social ends;
5. Motivational interviewing: this consists of a directive, client-centred style of counselling, which aims to change behaviour by helping the person to explore and resolve it. It works as a facilitative style for interpersonal relationships, and can be a powerful resource for working with the bullies.

Both interventions 4 and 5 aim to change perpetrators' motivation to bully.

Individual intervention with bystanders

6. Bystanders often feel they are not involved in bullying episodes, because they are neither perpetrators nor victims. However, their acceptance or rejection of bullying will reflect on the prevalence of these behaviours. It is important to work with bystanders in order to encourage them to reject bullying, and act on behalf of the victims more often. Thus, programmes to encourage bystanders to intervene pro-actively as helpers or defenders can be useful.

Individual intervention with coaches

7. Information in newsletters or booklets: pedagogical materials are important to sensitize coaches about bullying. These should contain information such as signs of victimization, how to help victims to cope with bullying, if children are bullies or bystanders to discuss the harm caused by bullying and the need to stop it, how parenting style may impact on bullying, and advice on the use of the internet;
8. Coach training (e.g. within general training on sports bullying or specific intervention programmes): coaches should be educated about bullying; the nature of the behaviours, their role within the sports club, how to prevent it, and how to cope when it occurs.

Sports clubs' internal norms and procedures

9. Injunctive norms: these refer to what behaviours are commonly expected by other athletes within the training sessions. Codes of conduct are helpful ways to define and standardize the behaviours expected from stakeholders within the sports club, to define what is acceptable and what is not, and to tackle the normalization of abusive behaviours;
10. Descriptive norms: these refer to the perception of what most athletes in the training sessions actually do. It is important to work on the social climate within the sports club. An individual's behaviour is influenced by the social environment. The way training sessions are organized, and peer relationships managed, will influence the behaviour of the members of the group;
11. Monitoring "hot spots": bullying is more prone to occur in less supervised areas, especially the changing room, but also other areas within the sports club. Monitoring these areas is important to decrease the prevalence of bullying. Surveillance can be done directly (e.g. by the presence of an adult), or indirectly (e.g. the team captain may have the responsibility to help victims and report bullying episodes to the coach);

12. Sports club policies: define bullying, state everyone's responsibilities, and clearly explain what actions will be taken to prevent bullying and deal with incidents if these occur.

    a. Sports club councils: an assembly of stakeholders is a good way to discuss any problems among athletes within the sports club. Besides acknowledging them, it can also enable discussion of individual and group approaches to their resolution;
    b. Selection and evaluation of the coaches: other criteria besides training skills should be considered when selecting coaches. Coaches should be evaluated on their interpersonal skills, and their capacity to promote the welfare of the athletes. Checks should be made for any criminal record;
    c. Share the power of the coach with other stakeholders: most of the coaches use their perceived power to promote the development of their athletes. However, abusive coaches often control other areas of the athletes' lives, including their interpersonal relations. Sharing out the coach's management of the athletes (e.g. including other sports stakeholders in the process such as nutritionists, sports psychologists) may be an important preventative measure;
    d. Coaches' training: coaches should be encouraged to make continuous efforts to improve their skills and knowledge by attending courses. Sports clubs should organize workshops for coaches to discuss their activity, and to foster feedback on their activity provided by peers;
    e. Athlete welfare: a sports club should have a sports psychologist, who is responsible for monitoring the development of welfare policies within the sports club, and who can deal directly with issues regarding bullying. He/she should work with coaches to help them prevent bullying, and act effectively if it happens;
    f. Procedures to report: sports clubs must have a clear policy regarding bullying, which includes explicit means to report possible occurrences;
    g. Educational approaches: besides the training issues, sports clubs should have a pedagogical approach to the athletes, which includes fostering healthy relations between them, and a positive social climate. Possible means include:

        i. Cooperative group work: this involves small groups, within which participants work together to capitalize on their various abilities. Athletes work together to enhance their own and one another's skills. This promotes positive interdependence and integration;

ii. Quality circles: a small group of athletes perform a similar task, and meet regularly to identify and discuss their problems. Nobody knows what happens between athletes better than themselves. Quality circles can improve sense of belonging, communication among peers and human relations;
iii. Personal, social, health and sporting education: this may be delivered formally or informally. Coaches should adopt a pedagogical attitude towards athletes that goes far beyond sports skills, and includes issues such as interpersonal relations;

13. Sports club climate: the moral atmosphere within a sports club directly influences the behaviours of the athletes. It is important to foster positive relations among everyone within the sports club, to provide structure and supportiveness;
14. Peer support schemes: there are several kinds of peer support schemes, each having their own pros and cons. The common factor is that peer supporters are trained to help other athletes, without direct adult intervention. This may be useful, especially because some athletes consider that adults should not be involved in solving bullying occurrences. However, there needs to be adult training of peer supporters in all these methods. It is important to consider various factors: the type of scheme needed; how peer supporters are selected; how they are trained and monitored; and the facilities provided by the sports club. The different peer support schemes below are taken from those used in school settings.

   i. Circle of friends/support: the coach promotes discussion among a group of athletes about feelings, how to develop creative methods to foster positive relationships, and empathic skills. It helps rejected athletes to feel less isolated;
   ii. Befriending: also known as Buddy Schemes, offers support from peers to those athletes who feel isolated (being victimized or new to the peer group). A designated peer is assigned to help others to feel more integrated and adjusted;
   iii. Peer mentoring: older pupils may help to train younger ones. Good coach supervision is needed here, because the power given to the older peer might be used to bully, rather than fostering integration.

Circle of friends, befriending and peer mentoring are all useful methods to help rejected athletes, and also to prevent bullying in crucial periods, when incomers are integrated into the peer group.

   iv. Peer mediation: this is a problem-solving strategy in which an athlete meets with a peer mediator, is encouraged to identify the problem, to discuss possible options to deal with it, to negotiate a plan of action, and finally to evaluate outcomes over time.

15. Reactive strategies: what to do if a bullying situation occurs.

   a. Direct sanctions: this is a direct behavioural response to bullying perpetration, by some negative consequence or punishment for such behaviour. The aim is to demonstrate its unacceptability, and be a deterrent to doing it again;
   b. Team tribunals: meeting with athletes and coaches to discuss any occurrence of bullying (what happened, why, who was involved and how to cope with it). The aims are to discuss what happened, how to solve the problem and how to prevent it from happening again;
   c. Non-punitive methods: there are several non-punitive methods, including the Method of Shared Concern and the Support Group Method (which have both been used in school settings). These aim to change the aggressive behaviours, but also to avoid doing so through punishment. Here we present only a brief description of each:

      i. Method of Shared Concern: also known as the Pikas Method, this involves several meetings (individual and group) between the sports psychologist (or counsellor), and those who were involved in bullying episodes. It is appropriate if a group of athletes are involved in the bullying. Step 1) *individual talks with the suspected perpetrators*. Non-confrontational interviewing, in which bullies are told that there is a problem, and that teammates saw an athlete being bullied. Bullies are asked about what they could do to improve the situation. Step 2) *individual talk with the victim*. For passive victims, it is important to reassure them and let them know that the bullies have agreed to change their behaviour. For provocative victims, the sports psychologist should help them to understand that their own behaviour contributes to their problems. Step 3) *preparatory group meeting*. The sports psychologist meets with the perpetrators together, asks if they have kept their agreements and if they can say something positive and friendly when the victim joins them. Step 4) *summit meeting*. In this meeting, all those involved are assembled together to discuss how they should behave in the future, and how to maintain that behaviour (cooperative work). Step 5) *follow-up*. Athletes are brought together again, so that the sports psychologist may monitor the progress. This strategy does need someone skilled in counselling techniques.

ii. Support Group Method: this encourages assistance to the victim by sharing knowledge of his/her negative feelings at a meeting that includes the perpetrators and other peers who offer to support the victim. It fosters breaking silence, and calls on empathy from the perpetrators, who are asked to accept responsibility to help solve the problem. It is run by an adult facilitator (coach or sports psychologist), and includes seven steps. Step 1) *talk with the targeted athlete*. Collect information about what happened, and assure them that no one will get into trouble. Step 2) *convene a group meeting*. Put six to eight athletes together in a meeting, including those implicated by the victim in Step 1, but also bystanders and friends of the victim (who is not included here). Say that the bullied athlete has a problem, and they were the ones chosen to deal with it. Step 3) *Tell the group members how the victims feels*. The adult tells the other athletes how the victim feels about their actions. Previous permission from the victim is needed, and the athletes should not be blamed. Step 4) *share responsibility*. In a non-judgemental atmosphere, seek out problem-solving strategies – encourage the group to accept joint responsibility for the situation and to act. Step 5) *Elicit helpful suggestions*. Obtain suggestions from the group about how to tackle the problem. Step 6) *Hand over responsibility to the group*. Each member of the group is given responsibility to implement some actions, and it is agreed that one week later they will meet again for a follow-up on progress. Step 7) *Individual meetings with participants*. The adult responsible interviews each athlete individually (including the victim) to evaluate the success of the intervention, and the contribution of each person to it;

d. Restorative approaches: these strategies aim to repair damaged relationships by bringing a sense of remorse to the perpetrators, along with forgiveness by the victim. They have three principles: 1) *responsibility* – bullies learn to accept responsibility for their behaviour; 2) *reparation* – by involving the victim, reparative strategies are discussed and applied; 3) *resolution* – end the conflict, and allow athletes to interact in a more positive way. The sports psychologist or counsellor should focus on the unacceptable behaviour, rather than anyone's personality or moral character.

Meso-level

With the meso-level approach we can aim to improve the communication between the parents and the sports club. The role of the parents must be considered when addressing bullying. Here we include:

TARGET

Interrelation of family (parents) with the sports club.

GENERAL INTERVENTIONS

- *Parent–coach relationship:* develop standardized and well-established means of communication between parents and coaches.
- *Family attitudes:* develop a school for parents and sensitizing campaigns within the sports club.

SPECIFIC INTERVENTIONS

16. Working with parents:
    a. School for parents: some sports clubs already have a "school for parents". This should be managed by a sports psychologist, who is able to inform parents about the importance of the parent–coach relationship, appropriate level of involvement of parents, the nature of bullying and other forms of abuse and violence, and how to contribute to improve the training process from the parents' perspective;
    b. Parent–coach meetings: many clubs seldom meet with parents. It is important to schedule regular meetings with parents (individual and group) to discuss the sporting plan, the pedagogical approaches used, to foster the cooperation of parents, and to promote support from them in case of any relationship difficulties;
    c. Parents' participation in the sports activities of their children: to enhance the involvement of the parents in sports club activities (e.g. helping in training activities, accompanying athletes in sports club travels). The activities and roles must be chosen carefully, and should not aim to replace the coach or other stakeholder. It can be an important preventive factor for bullying.

Exo-level

Through the exo-level approach we can consider the intervention of governmental sports entities. These must make a connection with more local sporting entities, such as the federations and sports clubs. Here we include:

TARGET

> Sports community norms and policies;
> Mass media and the sports industry.

GENERAL INTERVENTIONS

- *Relationship with media and the sports industry:* the media and sports industry can be powerful resources to send positive messages to those involved in sport. This channel of communication should be used to spread positive examples;
- *Sports agencies and policies:* the governmental organizations responsible for regulating sports activities must be involved in national policy, and foster the participation of sports federations, sports clubs, faculties and others in improving the welfare of athletes.

SPECIFIC INTERVENTIONS

Society

17. Media and industry: used to send messages condemning violence and discrimination in sport:
    a. Campaigns: develop campaigns to change attitudes, and to tackle violence, abuse and discrimination in sport (e.g. fair play episodes performed by successful athletes, positive stories of coach–athlete relationships, anti-discrimination campaigns);
18. Sports agencies policies: these organizations should finance and support research, prevention and intervention projects, as well as campaigns against bullying and abuse in sport:
    a. Intervention projects (funding programmes to tackle violence, abuse and discrimination in sport): these programmes should allow access to online information such as definitions/indicators/ signs and symptoms of bullying, guidelines for stakeholders, risk management strategies, education on how to deal with such problems and how to create a positive youth sports experience;
    b. Coach educational programmes: violence, abuse and discrimination issues should be included in undergraduate and graduate sport science curricula, continuing education/certification should be promoted, and regional workshops held;
    c. Creation of independent sport units dedicated to athletes' welfare: organizations autonomous from the sports clubs, with specialized professionals, should be created to support sports stakeholders

regarding issues of violence, abuse and discrimination. These units should also help in developing child protection sports policies.

Macro-level

The macro-level approach aims to change the social environment. The repercussions of these measures are wider, and expected to influence all other levels of intervention. Here we include:

TARGET

Culturally accepted violence and aggression;
Winning-at-all-costs mentality.

GENERAL INTERVENTIONS

- *Legal issues:* discuss the existing legal framework on child abuse, and the need to include sanctions for some forms of bullying;
- *Translation:* define and clarify the meaning of bullying;
- *National educational policies:* develop national policies to tackle bullying, violence and discrimination, and promote the welfare of the athletes. These are necessary as a framework for more local intervention.

SPECIFIC INTERVENTIONS

Country

19. Legal issues: some countries have developed anti-bullying laws (e.g. Brazil; some states in the USA), while other countries do not have specific laws on bullying, but do have laws on various forms of abuse (e.g. racial harassment, in the UK). It is important to develop laws to appropriately tackle violence, abuse and discrimination in sport. Without a good legal framework, it is difficult to develop further effective intervention;
20. Translation: although some countries also use other words to define peer abuse (see Chapter 1), the word "bullying" has been generally adopted internationally. It is important to define what bullying is, and clarify how it differs from banter or acceptable forms of criticism;
21. National educational sports policies:
    - Develop child protection policies: youngsters can be exposed to different types of abuse in sport. Youth sport must have child protection policies, focused on the well-being of the athletes;

- Promote the duty to report: violence and abuse in sport are frequently normalized, and there is a lack of means to report such behaviours. It is important to promote the duty to report, but also to develop support structures to do so;
- Change cultural norms and beliefs about violence and aggression: the culture and the social values strongly influence the behaviour of the citizen. In sports settings, the sports mentality, the habits, the influence of the traditional sexual stereotypes, and the high prevalence of performance-based values contribute to the acceptance and normalization of some forms of abuse. Intervention here is needed, by using social learning and educational programmes;
- Fund scientific research on issues such as:
  - Prevalence of societal risk factors for increasing violence;
  - Violence, abuse and discrimination in sport;
  - Effectiveness of prevention programmes.

Guidelines for stakeholders

Above, we presented general guidelines, varying from a micro- to a macro-level of intervention. These are helpful to understand the need for a comprehensive, global set of interventions to prevent and tackle bullying effectively. Here, we present more specific guidelines, designed for athletes, parents and coaches/sports leaders, divided into two sections: athlete-to-athlete bullying, and coach-to-athlete bullying.

The interventions proposed are based on the results of the research described in this book, on previous research about bullying, abuse and violence (Escury & Dudink, 2010; Evans et al., 2016; Fisher & Dzikus, 2010; Kerr & Stirling, 2012; Kirby & Wintrump, 2002; Rivers, 2010; Salmivalli, 2010; Stirling, 2009, 2013; Stirling, Bridges, Cruz & Mountjoy, 2011; Stirling & Kerr, 2007, 2009, 2010, 2013, 2014; Swigonski, Enneking & Hendrix, 2014; Vertommen et al., 2016; Volk & Lagzdins, 2009), and on the authors' own experiences. The contents are intended as a guide only.

Athlete-to-athlete bullying: guidelines for parents

Generic information

Bullying in sport has specific characteristics. Parents should be aware of the following aspects:

- It is important to detect possible signs of the athlete being victimized;
- Youngsters talk less with parents about bullying episodes that occur in sports clubs than they do about bullying in school;

- In the periods corresponding to integration into an older group of peers, and when an athlete changes club or sport (and becomes a new incomer), an athlete is more prone to be victimized.

What to do: preventive measures

Show yourself as being interested in the sports life of your child. Talk regularly with your child about his/her sports life and try to keep informed about what happens at the club. Asking your child directly if he/she is being a victim of bullying may not be the best approach. However, some indirect information might provide you with an insight of how well integrated into the club he/she is, and also about the possibility of being victimized. The following are some ideas for questions:

- Whether your child enjoys being at the sports club and being part of the team (or group of athletes, in the case of individual sports);
- How training and competitions are organized;
- If there are close friends in the group of athletes and who they are;
- If he/she has ever seen someone being bullied or teased/mocked at the sports club;
- Who the coach is;
- What the coach is like with the athletes;
- If he/she is happy about their own relationship with the coach (if not, ask why).

Your involvement in the sports life of your son/daughter creates proximity and opens up space for the sharing of experiences. If you suspect that your son/daughter may be a victim of bullying, be aware of the possible signs and do not ignore the situation! Ask him/her about relationships with other athletes, and create conditions so that silence can be broken.

How to identify if your child may be a victim of bullying: signs that young athletes may be suffering from bullying in sport

- Sudden behavioural changes without apparent reason;
- The athlete is more irritable than normal or is feeling sad/apathetic;
- The athlete no longer wants to participate in sports activities he/she likes, displaying a sudden lack of interest in the club or the sport;
- The athlete doesn't want to be with his/her colleagues and friends of the club, or with some of them in particular;
- The athlete presents complaints such as head-aches, stomach-aches or upsets, etc., or makes excuses not to be involved in the activities when the time for training or for participating in the club's initiatives arrives. They may say they feel unwell or show anxiety when it is time to go to

the club. Don't take just one of these signs too seriously, but be alert to a combination of a few of them. Parents don't like to think that their sons/daughters might be involved in bullying episodes, but victims tend to keep silent about the topic. A parent's first reaction may be to feel a need to tackle it quickly and to get involved directly. However, this type of reaction may not be beneficial in the long run.

How your child may feel if they are bullied

Sports practice, especially among children, should be based on having fun. Being bullied may lead to demotivation, and often culminates in early sports drop out, even in those cases in which the athlete likes the activity. It is not desirable that sports start to be felt as an obligation or a task. Parents may speak with someone in charge at the club, but should try to keep calm and think about the impact this may have on their son/daughter in the future. Try to find out, together with your son/daughter, how he/she would feel if he/she was to have a conversation with his/her coach or other adult inside the sports club. Often, athletes don't break silence due to being ashamed and feeling weak about doing so, being afraid of retaliations from their colleagues or from their coach, or because of disbelief in the capacity of the club and of those in charge of it to help overcome the problem.

Direct intervention with victims at home

- *Listen*: if your son/daughter has told you that he/she is being a victim of bullying, it is important that you listen without judging him/her or becoming annoyed, and allow him/her to have a say on the action to be taken. Understand and respect that his/her concerns and fears are real for him/her, and they need a sensitive and adequate response. Show him/her that you listened to what was said by repeating what you just heard. If requested, it is important to allow some time before responding, but not to postpone the response for too long, since over time the problem tends to escalate. Victims may be concerned about what is going to happen; for example, being afraid of continuing to be victimized, being expelled from the team or continually substituted;
- *Collect information*: make a detailed record about the frequency of episodes, what happened and where, who was involved, and your son/daughter's reaction. Try not to make moral judgements, and be precise;
- *Support*: when victims break silence and talk about what they are going through, they tend to feel more able to deal with the problem. The adults' reply may be very effective, but only if it is supportive. Therefore, if your son/daughter complains, don't undervalue this and act in a consistent way. It is important that you support your son/daughter throughout this process, giving attention and listening to him/her,

creating a secure space for him/her to express and share their feelings. Make it clear that your son/daughter is not to blame; there is a prevalent idea that bullying victims are to be blamed for what is happening and they often feel ashamed. This aspect links to yet another false belief that is frequently present, that being a victim is a sign of weakness, while being a bully is a sign of strength. It is important to demystify these ideas;

- *Discuss a solution*: in case your son/daughter is being a bullied by a teammate or by the coach, think together about a solution, rather than wanting to solve everything by yourself. In case your son/daughter tells you to not become directly involved in the issue, discuss with him/her which strategies he/she thinks might help to solve the problem. In this way, you will be fostering the learning of how to handle adversity, and you are helping him/her to develop problem resolution thinking independently. Monitor with him/her the way the situation evolves and check if everything is going well. Try to understand and help your son/daughter to think about what is happening and why, and in what way he/she can change their behaviour to deal with the situation more effectively. If the situation escalates and becomes intolerable, then it is time to intervene directly: talk to your son/daughter about this issue and decide how it should be done.

What to avoid

When children tell parents that they are being bullied, there are some frequent parental reactions that are best avoided. Even if these possible reactions are based on good intentions, they tend to be counter-productive and to aggravate the situation.

- Don't act impulsively. It is normal that you may feel rage, guilt or helplessness when your child speaks with you about being bullied. However, think twice before you act, otherwise your action may become an obstacle instead of an aid;
- Don't demand to confront the coach or talk to the bullies' parents immediately. This reaction is often feared by victims and excludes them from the resolution of the problem;
- Don't advise counter-attacking in the same way your child is being targeted. Victims tend to lack confidence, and their reaction may bring about more bullying behaviours;
- Don't underestimate what your son/daughter is telling you. Usually, victims don't tell anyone about what is going on. If, when doing so, he/she is disregarded or left to deal with the problem on his/her own (e.g. parents say that bullying is banter and that it is part of growing up), then your

son/daughter will receive the message that bullying should be tolerated rather than being tackled;
- Don't feel bad if your son/daughter seeks out other people to talk to (psychologists, friends, other adults), or if he/she seeks outside help to solve a problem that might be difficult to handle. Such a request does not make you a bad father or mother, and sometimes it is easier for youngsters to talk with someone outside of the family, without this meaning that they don't like or don't trust you.

Support from the club

Beyond the measures at home and taken together with your child, others can be carried out at the club to help deal with the situation. Nevertheless, before you talk to the coach or to other managers, bear in mind the following points:

- Before you head to someone in charge at the club, collect detailed information about what has happened, who has been involved, when it occurred, who witnessed it, anything your son/daughter may have done that may have provoked the incident;
- Do not show up at the club without warning, arrange a meeting with the coach and/or the sports manager in advance;
- Focus on managing the problem with the club, making it clear that you are looking for the club's help to find a solution;
- Avoid accusations. Coaches are often not aware of what is going on, since bullying tends to occur out of their sight or in a dissimulated way;
- Be patient and allow time for the club to act on the problem, keeping in touch with those in charge, and arrange a subsequent meeting to establish how the problem is being dealt with, and to evaluate progress.

The coach is the adult who is responsible for managing the group of athletes, and has an important role in the creation of a safe and inclusive sports environment. His/her action can be decisive in intervening as regards bullying between athletes.

What if my child is a bully?

When parents are told that their son/daughter has been involved in bullying episodes as a perpetrator, they usually feel negative feelings such as rage, shame or guilt. Bullies are usually seen as bad, which goes against the way parents like to perceive their child. It's important to know that every child may be a bully at some point, and bullying is explained by many factors. The most important thing is to know what is going on, and how to manage the situation.

What to do

- Collect as much information as possible and know what is really going on. Sometimes, there are other things going on like isolated conflicts as opposed to bullying. Avoid making criticisms or accusations too quickly, and focus your efforts on clearly understanding the situation;
- Find out why your child is involved in bullying episodes and what role he/she performs (e.g. ringleader, or follower or bystander who supports the bullying). It is usual for a youngster to diminish or even deny their involvement;
- Don't allow your child to devalue the situation. Bullies commonly consider that the interaction was just banter rather than bullying, and deny that it has any consequences for the victims. Explain clearly that you don't tolerate bullying behaviours, that they can be truly harmful, and talk about the differences between bullying and banter;
- Try to help your child to think about what the victim may be feeling (fear, humiliation) and ask him/her if he/she would like others to make him/her feel the same way;
- Condemning bullying behaviours is not the same as condemning your child. Explain that you don't approve of bullying behaviours but that you do support your child in changing their behaviours and stopping involvement in bullying episodes;
- Think together how your child can change his/her behaviour and establish more positive relations with peers and achieve a better social position without engaging in bullying episodes;
- Teach your child to respect peers and their differences.

Explain that if bullying continues, it may have consequences for your child. Punishment should never be physical; that would in itself be an abusive behaviour and may increase bullying. Accept your child but not his/her behaviour.

Athlete-to-athlete bullying: guidelines for athletes

Bullying vs. banter

Bullying is an aggressive, repeated and intentional behaviour between peers, characterized by a power imbalance between perpetrator and victim. Although bullying and banter tend to be misinterpreted as the same by many, there are important differences between them, especially regarding intentions and how things are said or done. The threshold between bullying and banter is sometimes not easy to establish and define. But when the targets of "jokes" are always the same, if those athletes don't like how they're treated by their peers and this tends to occur repeatedly, we are more likely to be talking about bullying. It's common for athletes who are victims of this to feel that they are worthless, and to have low self-confidence. Their motivation to continue to be part of the sports club, training and competing, tends to decrease.

How to tell bullying and banter apart

There are important differences between bullying and banter. To evaluate if what is going on inside the peer group is banter or bullying, you should ask yourself the following questions:

- What do you think the targeted athlete feels? Victims tend not to speak about what they are going through because they feel ashamed, or believe that nobody will be able to help them. Often they try to deal with the victimization alone, which demands considerable effort and tends to result in negative outcomes. You can always ask directly when both of you are alone ...
- Why is it that a specific athlete is targeted? Think about the possible reasons for this. Does he/she have something different, or is it a random choice?
- Is the behaviour always directed toward the same target? Think whether the jokes and provocations tend to be directed to the same person over and over again, and if the targeted athlete is unable to respond in a positive social climate. Although anybody can be bullied occasionally, usually bullying is directed at certain specific peers who are less able to defend themselves;
- What do you feel about it? Trust in your intuition! Take a moment to think about how your teammates behave and relate to each other. Do you think it's OK? Is some behaviour wrong? You can compare what you think with the opinions of other peers or even someone outside the peer group ... .

Guidance for if you are victimized

IMPORTANT POINTS YOU SHOULD KNOW

- Anyone can be a bully or a victim: bullying can happen to you for a variety of reasons. Besides any personal features, these include the social environment you are in;
- Bullying does not have to be tolerated: bullying behaviours are harmful, especially for the victims, and should not continue. There is no reason to accept these behaviours;

- Bullying can be tackled: bullying is a severe problem, but can be effectively tackled. When interventions are well designed and structured they provide a an good solution to the problem. You have the right to demand that sports leaders and coaches in the club recognize and deal with the problem.

WHAT TO DO

If you are being bullied by your teammates, there are several actions to consider. It's important that you make the first move to solve the problem:

- Speak to your parents, a responsible person inside the sports club, or another adult you can trust. Sharing your concerns with an adult will help you and they can discuss the situation, and how to deal with it. Remember to keep speaking up until someone helps you; sometimes, the first approach may not be enough and the response of adults may not be consistent. This doesn't necessarily mean they don't care, but maybe that they have misjudged what is happening and think it's not as important as it is for you – in that case, keep trying until your voice is heard. Coaches are frequently not aware of bullying among athletes; bullying tends to occur in disguised ways and in less supervised areas, and coaches usually have no idea of what is going on. However, if alerted, their intervention is usually effective;
- Ask your parents to speak with the coach and to explain the situation. Parents may be an important help, and can facilitate reaching the coach effectively;
- Record what happened (when, where, who was there and what they did) in a diary or notebook. These written accounts will help you to explain what happened when speaking to someone about a sensitive topic;
- Speak with your friends so that they can support you. Sometimes, some teammates don't get involved because they are afraid of being victimized themselves, or because they have no idea of the harm that is happening. This does not necessarily mean that they don't care or cannot help you;
- Try to stay calm, avoid counter-attacking and instead project confidence. Many times, victims try to react but feel so helpless and lonely that it makes them more vulnerable and less able to deal with the bullying effectively. Bullies usually enjoy watching the victims' over-reaction and it encourages more bullying. Try to show confidence, because bullies tend to attack those who are perceived as afraid.

If the problem is still not dealt with, your parents should ask the coach or the sports leaders for a copy of the regulation and codes of conduct of the sports club.

CYBERBULLYING: WHAT TO DO ABOUT IT

Cyberbullying is bullying using digital means (social networks, text messages, etc.) and sometimes it's difficult to identify who the bullies are. It is best not to reply or retaliate directly. In such cases there are other types of measures that can be taken:

- Block the bully (in chats or social networks);
- Save the messages and/or print them as evidence (text messages, emails, etc.);
- Local internet service providers and authorities may be helpful partners in tackling the bullying;
- Speak with a friend about what is going on;
- Tell an adult you trust about the cyberbullying.

Guidance for bystanders if you see bullying happen

WHAT TO DO

- Be aware: bullying is very harmful for victims, they often cannot deal with it properly, which contributes to its continuation. Sadness, helplessness and being socially isolated are very frequent outcomes among cyber victims;
- Don't ignore it: if you do nothing, you are also part of the bullying! Bullying is everybody's problem, and bystanders are also a part of it if they consent to it happening. The way you act may be decisive in dealing with the problem effectively;
- Defend the victims: athletes can support each other and report bullying. Victims usually don't speak with adults about bullying but instead seek peer support and, given the right response, this can strongly enhance the capacity of the victims to deal with the bullying;
- Don't participate: the way you act makes a big difference. Bystanders can contribute to increasing or decreasing bullying. What you do when you observe a bullying episode may have a strong effect, and influence the behaviours of other athletes. If you support bullying, even if "just" by laughing a little bit or doing nothing, the bullying tends to get worse. On the other hand, if you support and defend the victim, you are contributing to stopping the bullying. What if you were the victim? Think about it and what you would want another teammate to do …;
- Talk about what is going on: talking with adults is the right thing to do. Talk with one of the responsible adults inside the sports club. It is an important (and sometimes crucial) way to solve the problem. It doesn't turn you into a "snitch", but instead someone who is proactively trying to solve a problem.

Athlete-to-athlete bullying: guidelines for coaches and sports leaders

Generic information

Banter is quite common among youngsters. These behaviours can have positive outcomes on the social environment and the development of the athletes; however, there is a thin line between banter and bullying. If the target of "banter" is frequently and repeatedly the same person, it may become bullying, especially in those cases in which the targeted person expresses negative feelings towards it, and his/her motivation to be in the club, to train and compete decreases, as well as his/her self-esteem, confidence and performance. It is important to encourage, support and foster cohesion among peers, rather than negative behaviours.

Research on youth sports bullying alerts us to the need for coaches and sports leaders to consider the following:

- Bullying can exist in any sports club;
- Coaches are frequently not aware of bullying among athletes: it occurs in less supervised areas and it is often disguised by the bullies, and in addition victims frequently keep silent about it;
- Many athletes consider bullying behaviours to be normal, and "part of the game", which contributes to hiding it;
- The victims of bullying tend to drop out of sports practice early;
- The younger athletes who are being integrated into the group of older ones, and other new incomers to the peer group, are those more at risk of being victimized. The integration of new peer members leads to a redefinition of social roles, and the incomers usually lack social support inside the peer group, which makes them more vulnerable to being targeted.

What to do about bullying

Coaches are responsible for creating a healthy environment for young athletes, which promotes their harmonious development. The coach's intervention strongly reflects on the social climate of the sports club. Coaches are one of the main support sources for the victims, and when their action is well guided, it may play an important role in decreasing bullying prevalence.

Anti-bullying policy for coaches and sports leaders

An anti-bullying programme to tackle bullying in youth sport must combine both preventive and reactive measures. Sensitizing sports agents (athletes, parents, coaches, sports leaders, other staff members) combined with the creation of codes of conduct contribute to promote an anti-bullying culture, which is essential to the success of any global intervention. These measures provide guidelines for positive conduct and guide sports leaders in their intervention efforts. More accurate supervision of areas and activities in which bullying is most prone to occur should also be carried out.

General preventative measures within the sports club

Sports leaders and coaches must act in order to tackle bullying in sport, and make clear to everybody inside the sports club that these kinds of behaviours are not tolerated. The education of sports agents about this topic is essential to correctly identify, prevent and intervene if bullying occurs.

- Ensure norms and codes of conduct in the sports club are delivered to whom they were designed for, and the information is available to everybody concerned;
- Ensure all members of the sports club base their actions on the codes of conduct which promote basic rights and individual dignity;
- Ensure adequate supervision of spaces and activities, especially areas of low supervision in the sports club, such as the changing room and other areas in which young athletes may spend a considerable amount of time without much adult presence;
- Encourage young athletes to negotiate and cooperate with each other, especially new incomers and people perceived as different;
- Reinforce the existence of an anti-bullying culture, which encourages breaking silence about bullying episodes, and fosters an effective answer from stakeholders to the problem.

All stakeholders should sign a declaration which attests that they understand and accept the content, norms of conduct and procedures embedded in the policy. An anti-bullying policy involves the athletes, their parents, coaches and other staff members, and it contributes to clarifying the role of each in creating a positive climate of relationships inside the sports club. This policy must be clear, and it must be easily accessible to everyone involved in the club.

What to do about bullying if it happens

GUIDELINES FOR SPORTS LEADERS

Sports leaders must create the conditions to develop an anti-bullying programme inside the sports club. Their intervention should aim to create a structure which sustains the development of the activities and measures of the programme.

- Educate the staff: all adults in the sports club, especially the sports leaders, must assume an active role in the educational organization of the club. All staff should be educated about the topic, providing them tools to effectively identify and deal with bullying episodes;
- Develop procedures to tackle bullying: describe the specific procedures to be followed by athletes and staff members to tackle bullying. It is important to designate a person responsible for the welfare of the athletes, such as a sports psychologist, who has specialized skills for the task, ensures the privacy of sensitive subjects discussed with youngsters, and acts in order to deal with any problems exposed by working with athletes, coaches and parents;
- If bullying occurs and episodes are reported, ensure the anonymity of those involved as far as possible. It is important to differentiate formal and informal procedures;
- If bullying occurs, the sports leaders within the club should support the coaches and other staff members in their efforts to resolve the problem.

GUIDELINES FOR COACHES

The youth sports coach is the adult responsible for the activities with the athletes, and is a highly specialized professional who has the duty to:

- Promote an educational and sporting environment free of bullying. Youth sports training should be based on a developmental approach. Training sessions and competition should rely on the process of learning and development, rather than winning at all costs;
- Have knowledge about bullying, which allows him/her to foster an anti-bullying culture, to know how to behave as a coach and to prevent and act properly if bullying occurs. The coach should have access to educational guidelines to guide their actions, and be able to ask for support from a sports psychologist when confronted with any situation for which he/she lacks adequate skills to deal with;
- Deal with bullying episodes if these occur. Coaches should not ignore or devalue bullying episodes; preferentially adopt a non-punitive or support group approach instead of punishment.

Intervention strategies with athletes

Intervention with athletes includes prevention, supervision and reactive strategies. Possible interventions are given for each group of strategies described.

PREVENTATIVE STRATEGIES FOR COACHES

- Assembly of athletes: regular meetings of the athletes aiming to promote psychosocial development of the youngsters and discussion of problem resolution strategies. The sports psychologist may be helpful here;
- Cooperation (peer support network): isolated athletes and incomers (especially younger athletes) may benefit from the support of other peer members. The creation of a "sponsor", who is responsible for helping the designated athlete to positively integrate into the peer group, may be a helpful approach. The "sponsors" themselves may also benefit from performing this role. However, it is important to consider the personalities and characteristics of the athletes in order to make a good choice of the "sponsors". If the wrong athlete is chosen, an abusive relation may be promoted instead of a developmental one, due to the imbalance of power between the two athletes. "Sponsors" should have high prosocial skills and use them to promote peer development;
- Support chain: the incomers from the younger team may achieve a gradual integration into the older peer group, by occasionally participating in their training sessions and other activities during the previous season. If this process of integration is done gradually and over time, it tends to be more successful. This strategy may be done together with the nomination of "sponsors";
- Awards: having awards, based on the values which sustain the inclusive culture within the sports club (e.g. fair play, cooperation, support, dedication, skill development and evolution, companionship). The athletes and coach may vote for the awards, in order to distinguish the athletes who act according to the sports club values. These awards aim to reinforce adaptive and desirable behaviours, and encourage athletes to value other important features than popularity and sports performance.

SURVEILLANCE STRATEGIES

- Team captain: these athletes may be a key element in monitoring bullying among athletes, because they are integrated inside the peer group and have easy access to changing rooms (especially useful when the coach's gender is different from the athletes') and other less supervised areas. Nobody knows better than the athletes themselves what is going on between peers. If well chosen, the team captain may play an important role in cooperating with the coach to tackle bullying;
- Supervision: bullying episodes tend to occur in less supervised areas. It is important to identify these "hot spots" and to reinforce adult supervision;

- Culture (social climate): if there is a general rejection of bullying and other anti-social behaviours, these are more effectively dealt with. An anti-bullying culture has an indirect effect on monitoring disruptive behaviours; these become supervised by everybody in the sports club.

REACTIVE STRATEGIES

Record: Report any concerns about athletes to the sports psychologist and the sports leaders within the club. These notifications will start the procedures to deal with bullying. Keep a record about what has been said (what happened, who was involved, etc.). Be aware that any intervention within the sports club setting itself has limitations. If the sports club has difficulties in dealing with bullying episodes, then professional help should be sought. In particular, mental health issues, and criminal issues, are out of the range of action of the sports club. If you are aware of somebody who could seriously hurt him/herself, or is mentally disturbed, search for professional advice and refer the athlete to external support (e.g. mental health services, psychiatrist). Don't try to go beyond your scope of action. Equally, if actual criminal activity is going on, it should be dealt with by police rather than stakeholders within the sports club.

If bullying occurs, you should always:

- Inform all members of the sports club about the procedures being undertaken;
- Keep a written record of what is going on;
- Keep alert to what the bullies are doing, and make sure the behaviours don't still occur in more disguised ways.

INTERVENTION WITH THE WHOLE GROUP OF ATHLETES

If bullying occurs, understand and deal with the situation – don't be exclusively focused on punishing. Focus your attention mainly on trying to change the behaviours of the athletes, instead of punishing the bullies.

In the group meeting, explain to athletes that:

- Peers may support each other and report bullying;
- Telling an adult about bullying is the right thing to do and does not make you a "snitch".

Emphasize that:

- Bullying is not tolerated;
- Bullying episodes will be investigated, and a solution will be found.

Manage the situation by:

- Using a non-punitive or support group approach (if possible), and avoiding punishment. This approach tends to be more effective, involves the whole peer group in problem resolution and calls attention to the role played by each athlete in bullying (victims, bullies and bystanders);
- If bullying persists even after a non-punitive approach, sanctions or punishment measures can be discussed with the athletes. The sanctions should aim to stop the bullying rather than humiliate the bully, and should be realistic, fair, easily understood by all, and easy to implement.

The sports leaders should be informed about the procedures in order to:

- Monitor the situation;
- Support the coach and other adults involved in the intervention to solve the problem (e.g. for example through counselling);
- Reformulate the policies and procedures of the club if necessary.

INDIVIDUAL INTERVENTION

Besides the group intervention strategies just described, some individual action may also take place with the victims, bullies and bystanders. Each of these roles contributes differently to bullying episodes and has specific characteristic needs, which require a particular intervention.

Victims The individual intervention with victims should be based on supportive measures, combined with procedures to ensure confidentiality, and also strategies aiming to help them cope better with the bullying.

Support and confidentiality aim to deal with any feelings of helplessness and fragility of the victims. Talking about bullying, trusting in a mediator adult and the support of peers can increase the capacity of the victims to deal with bullying. The measures which aim to ensure confidentiality are justified by the common fear felt by the victims about how bullying will be tackled, and the possible consequences derived from the action taken. The measures to cope more effectively with bullying aim to promote more adaptive styles of interaction.

Support:

- Help victims to break silence and to talk about the bullying episodes;
- Provide immediate support to the victim. Victims often feel helpless, and support is needed for them to feel more capable of contributing to a solution;

- Tell the victims there is nothing wrong with them, and that the bullying is not their fault. If dealing with 'provocative victims', help them realize that they contribute to the bullying and that they need to change their own behaviour, as well as the bullies changing theirs. Even in those cases, victims don't want to be targeted, and usually don't understand why bullies attack them;
- Reinforce the positive personal features of the victims, as well as the positive contributions they provide to the peer group and other athletes generally.

Confidentiality:

- Ensure victims can trust you, and that you will help them to deal with bullying. However, make it clear that you may eventually need to talk with somebody else about it.

Behavioural change (assertiveness training):

- Help the victims to cope more efficiently with bullying, by understanding which are the most frequently strategies used by them, and by exploring possible alternatives.

Cyberbullying:

- If cyberbullying occurs, you should advise athletes to:
    - Not answer or retaliate;
    - Block the bully (in chats and social networks);
    - Save the messages and/or print them (messages, emails, etc.);
    - Utilize local internet service providers and authorities who may be helpful partners in tackling bullying;
    - Speak with a friend;
    - Tell an adult who they can trust.

Bullies There are several possible ways to intervene individually with bullies, namely direct discussion, strategies aiming to increase empathy or change of behaviour, and sanctions.

Direct discussion strategies aim to show the bully that bullying is not acceptable within the sports club, and will not be tolerated. An empathic approach consists of making efforts to increase the insight of the bullies about the consequences of their actions, as well as the feelings of the victim, in order to change their behaviour. If the bully or bullies persist with their behaviour and keep justifying their own aggressive behaviour, or perceiving others as responsible for it, some behavioural change measures and sanctions should be considered. Sanctions aim to decrease bullying behaviours by punishing them.

Examples of the different kinds of actions are presented here.

Direct discussion:

- Speak with each bully separately from any others;
- Be certain of what is really going on;
- Confront the bullies with the facts as you know them;
- Point out that their behaviour is unacceptable and against the written policy of the sports club. Request the bullies to undertake some positive action towards the victims (e.g. apologize);
- Be clear with them about the sanction(s) to be considered, if bullying behaviours persist;
- Carry out a follow-up of the process, to evaluate progress after confronting the bully.

If there is no immediate danger for the athletes involved, give bullies a chance to justify their earlier behaviours in terms of not realizing what they were doing and the consequences for the victim(s). Explain that:

- Their behaviour is wrong;
- Now they are aware their behaviour is wrong;
- Their behaviour will not be further tolerated and, if it persists, it will be sanctioned.

Empathic approach:

- Encourage the bullies to apologize to the victim(s);
- Ensure that the bullies give back anything that they took or "borrowed" from the victims and, if appropriate, to compensate them;
- Encourage bullies to change their behaviours.

Sanctions/punishment:

- Sanction if needed (e.g. verbal warning, withdrawal of privileges, suspension if bullying continues, or being expelled from the club). Penalties are used as a deterrent to prevent further bullying;
- If the sports club lacks the capacity to deal effectively with more severe cases, report to external authorities. Although sports clubs are responsible for what happens inside their facilities, they lack the legal authority to deal with some situations. The cases in which bullying behaviours include breaking the law (e.g. taking money/theft) are beyond the legal liability of sports clubs. In these cases, police action should be considered.

If you think the behaviour of the bullies is unacceptable and continued, it may be important to talk with their parents. However, be sensitive and make a careful judgement regarding telling the bullies' parents about bullying; put the athlete in the centre of your concerns before acting and think about the consequences and advantages of speaking with his/her parents or, on the other hand, if it will result in more problems for the youngster. The parents of the bullies may become angry and/or annoyed with acknowledging their child's behaviour and react aggressively themselves. If that is the case, be clear regarding the sports club's policy about bullying. If you opt to hold meetings with the families of the bullies, it's important to provide regular feedback to them about the progress achieved.

Bystanders The bystanders have a very important role in preventing bullying. For one thing, peers are generally the most sought after support source by the victims. But beyond that, the way bystanders participate in bullying episodes may increase its prevalence or, on the contrary, decrease it and help to tackle bullying episodes more effectively.

- Attitudes towards violence and bullying. When attitudes towards these are negative, the bystanders tend to act on behalf of the victim, and feel more confident in doing so. It is important to act on attitude change towards bullying, to promote peer support, and the defence of the victims by speaking up, getting help and helping the targeted athlete. Quiet bystanders give bullies the audience they desire. Once bystanders acknowledge the negative effects of bullying on victims, they are more prone to act on their behalf. Bystanders also need to feel confident to act – those of higher popularity or status in the peer group are more likely to do so and to be more effective;
- Make bystanders feel responsible, by saying that bullying is everybody's problem and not just victims' and bullies'. Otherwise, the diffusion of responsibility inside the peer group may contribute to the lack of action by bystanders during bullying episodes, which results in continuation of the cycle of aggression;
- Although the intervention of the bystanders may not be direct, the way they behave when bullying episodes occur is very important. Raising awareness about ways they can intervene provides bystanders with more effective tools to tackle bullying.

Things to avoid in general:

- Don't encourage victims to seek revenge from bullies when targeted;
- Don't label athletes as bullies or victims. This procedure may result in negative outcomes. Explain the situation in a pedagogical way that they can understand;

- Don't tell a victim to ignore the bullying. This will promote the feeling that bullying is acceptable;
- Don't use sanctions which result in large periods of isolation or make the bullies look silly;
- Don't try to solve the problem all by yourself. Report what is going on to sports leaders and to those responsible for the welfare of the athletes. If bullying becomes more severe, seek professional help.

Coach-to-athlete bullying: a guide for parents

Generic information

Most of the coaches have an important role in the life of the athletes they work with. This is typically a very positive role, as they encourage young athletes to develop their potential and abilities in their chosen sport. However, a minority of them may bully athletes by using abusive patterns of coaching. Coach bullying is an abusive pattern of coach-to-athlete relations based on power imbalance, repetition and intentionality. There is a threshold between persuasive or strong encouragement, and actual coercive behaviour or bullying by the coach. This can be misunderstood by coaches, and in some cases also by parents. Some coaches use coercive or abusive patterns of coaching to improve the athletes' skills and performance. However, ends don't necessarily justify the means used. Coaches who bully athletes often train them based on their own personal wishes and goals, rather than the athletes' own needs and subjectivity. Parents who observe coach bullying without interfering also become part of it, just like passive bystanders in episodes of athlete-to-athlete bullying. It is important for you as a parent to know what to do, and to act on behalf of the young athlete.

Guidance for parents

- Pay attention to how your son/daughter's coach behaves, find out about what is going on in the sports club changing room and observe the behaviour of the coach during the games;
- In case you want to explain that you are worried about the behaviour of the coach, make sure you focus on his/her actions. This helps avoid a defensive attitude from the coach (in which they may often be supported by the club);
- Write a report: file a written complaint about the bullying behaviours to the club managers. The coaches should be held accountable for any inappropriate conduct, given that such behaviours have a negative impact on the emotional balance of the young athletes. This should be a later step; other actions should be considered first.

Action guidelines

Parents should actively participate in the activities of the sports club in which their child is enrolled. You can address the club's sports leaders in order to push forward the implementation of an anti-bullying policy. Involving them is important to create an inclusive environment in which bullying is not tolerated.

- Ask your son/daughter about their relationships within the sports club (peers, coach and other stakeholders);
- Don't be a passive observer if your son/daughter is a victim of bullying behaviours by their coach. If the behaviour seems harsh and inappropriate, talk with the coach about it;
- Increase your participation at the sports club (e.g. help coaches accompanying the athletes when travelling, go to the meetings);
- Watch some training sessions to observe the behaviour of the coach towards the athletes.

An approach centred on the athletes should focus on their needs and rights while undergoing their sporting experiences. If a parent is evaluating a coach, they should do so not solely on the basis of their success in promoting sporting achievement but also on how they encourage companionship and fair play, and foster healthy development of the athlete in social and emotional ways as well as physical prowess.

Coach-to-athlete bullying: guidelines for athletes

Important points you should know

- If an athlete complains about coach bullying, it should be considered by the board of the sports club. The coach should not:
  - Devalue what the athlete may have felt;
  - Blame the athlete for feeling bad about how they have been treated by the coach.

This doesn't mean that the coach should not have a chance to defend him/herself. Occasionally, accusations may be malicious or unfounded. A safe environment – created by an adequate policy – protects athletes from abuses, but also coaches from false accusations. This may be especially important in cases of sexual harassment, where false accusations may cause considerable damage to the reputation of the coach.

- The coach is a professional in sport, and the adult in the sports club is responsible for training sessions. When he/she is working with young people, he/she has the duty to:

- Keep an educational and athletic social environment free of bullying and harassment;
- Prepare training sessions and competition plans adapted to the age of the young athletes;
- Focus mainly on the learning and development of skills rather than on winning at all costs, and not to ask athletes to do more than they are capable of;
- Treat the athletes respectfully and be a positive role model;
- Treat athletes on an equal basis and help them to develop their sports skills, even those who might have less physical ability.

- Coaches should base their behaviour on the codes of conduct of the sports club, which promotes the rights and individual dignity of the athletes;
- Although some coaches may say that their behaviour is well-intended (e.g. believing that sporting success can only be achieved through some abuse and suffering), this is a mistaken belief. Coach bullying is bad for the bullied athlete, and for the club generally, and it should not be tolerated.

What to do

ALL ATHLETES

- Don't join in or approve of any bullying: some coaches believe that sports practice is only for tough guys, and that any means can be employed to justify success, including coach bullying. These ideas are false and totally lack evidence to sustain them. If everyone accepts coach bullying, it becomes "normal". This contributes to victims feeling guilty, and thinking that they are the ones who are wrong. It makes it more difficult to identify when abuse occurs and to tackle it effectively;
- Don't ignore what is going on: coach abuse cannot be tolerated; these professionals have an obligation to treat you well and consider your best interests. If you see coach bullying, make a record of it and talk about it with someone you trust:
  - Record and describe what happened (when, where, who was there and what they did ...). Keep this written record and use it when you speak with a responsible adult. It can help you to explain more accurately what happened;
  - Speak with an adult you can trust, who may be your parents/carers, another adult inside the sports club or even an adult outside the

sports club. Sharing your personal concerns with somebody older helps you to identify the problem and act to solve it.

Coach-to-athlete bullying: guidelines for coaches and sports leaders

Important things to bear in mind

- There is a difference between fair criticism and humiliation. Fair criticism aims to help the athletes to acknowledge their mistakes in order to improve their performance. However, ends don't justify the means. When athletes are insulted or ridiculed, the "encouragement" becomes abuse. Although an autocratic style of coaching may result in enhanced performance in the short term, these are unacceptable tactics and have long-term negative effects (both emotionally and by decreasing performance);
- A sports culture which openly or tacitly accepts aggressive behaviours contributes to their normalization and considers breaches of the codes of conduct as "part of the game". Then, athletes tend not to speak about coach bullying because they are afraid of the consequences, or because they think nobody is going to believe or help them. The fact that athletes usually keep silent about it does not mean that there is no coach bullying in youth sport, or make these behaviours any more acceptable.

Prevention of coach bullying

GUIDELINES FOR SPORTS LEADERS

- Disseminate the codes of conduct of the sports club, which should describe the procedures to deal with any abusive or bullying behaviours;
- Educate coaches who work with young athletes to base their practice on a developmental approach, which considers the athletes' different stages of physical and emotional development, and promotes their participation in planning their sporting experience. It focuses on the needs and welfare of the athletes;
- Hold practical workshops which aim to increase good practice among coaches;
- Share responsibilities and the power to decide, rather than leaving everything to the individual coach: promote the involvement of athletes and their parents in the activities of defining objectives and monitoring the progresses and goals achieved. Other stakeholders (e.g. sports psychologist, nutritionist) should also share responsibilities regarding the training process of the athletes;

- The evaluation of the coach should not be based strictly on sports results; it should also take account of his/her capacity to promote the emotional development of the athletes, by considering aspects such as companionship, fair play and promotion of the healthy development of the athletes;
- Reduce situations in which coaches are alone with some athletes inside the sports club (e.g. training and changing rooms), and also when coach and athletes are doing sporting activities outside the sports club (e.g. travels, hotel rooms).

GUIDELINES FOR COACHES

- Discuss the challenges of being a coach with sports leaders and other colleagues;
- Be sure you are familiar with the codes of conduct of the sports club;
- Learn about power dynamics, how to model and reinforce positive behaviours among athletes, how to promote a reflective examination of their own behaviours and discuss the pressures of focusing on winning;
- Take account of the individual personalities of the young athletes you are training; some may tolerate being pushed hard in their training, others may have lower self-esteem and need to be treated more gently;
- Seek regular feedback about your way of dealing with athletes and conducting training sessions.

References

Ajzen, I. & Fishbein, M. (2005). The influence of behavior on attitudes (pp. 173–222). In D. Albarracín, B. T. Johnson & M. P. Zanna (Eds.). *The Handbook of Attitudes*. New York: Psychology Press.

Alexander, K., Stafford, A., & Lewis, R. (2011). *The Experiences of Children Participating in Organised Sport in the UK*. Edinburgh, Scotland: The University of Edinburgh/NSPCC Child Protection Research Centre. www.research.ed.ac.uk/portal/files/7971883/experiences_children_sport_main_report_wdf85014.pdf.

Allison, S., Roegen, L., & Reinfeld-Kirkman, N. (2009). Does school bullying affect adult health? Population survey of health-related quality of life and past victimization. *Australian and New Zealand Journal of Psychiatry*, 42, 163–70.

Allodi, M. (2010). Goals and values in school: A model developed for describing, evaluating and changing the social climate of learning environments. *Social Psychology of Education*, 13, 207–35.

Alsaker, F. D. & Nägele, C. (2008). Bullying in kindergarten and prevention (pp. 230–52). In D. Pepler & W. Craig (Eds.). *An International Perspective on Understanding and Addressing Bullying*. PrevNet publication series. Volume I. Kingston, Canada: PREVNet.

Alvariñas-Villaverde, M., López-Villar, C., Fernández-Villarino, M. A., & Alvarez-Esteban, R. (2017). Masculine, feminine and neutral sports: Extracurricular sport modalities in practice. *Journal of Human Sport and Exercise*, 12(4), 1278–88. DOI: 10.14198/jhse.2017.124.14.

Anabel, R. & Anna, S. (2009). School violence in Spain: Notes in its emergence as a problem and on research approaches. *International Journal of Violence and School*, 10, 71–96.

Anderson, E. (2011). Masculinities and sexualities in sport and physical cultures: Three decades of evolving research. *Journal of Homosexuality*, 58, 565–78. DOI: 10.1080/00918369.2011.563652.

Anderson, E. (2012). The changing relationship between men's homosexuality and sport (pp. 35–45). In G. B. Cunningham (Ed.). *Sexual Orientation and Gender Identity in Sport: Essays from Activists, Coaches, and Scholars*. College Station, TX: Center for Sport Management Research and Education.

Andrews, J. & Andrews, G. (2003). Life in a secure unit: The rehabilitation of youth people trough the use of sport. *Social Sciences and Medicine*, 56, 531–50.

Arseneault, L. (2018). Annual Research Review: The persistent and pervasive impact of being bullied in childhood and adolescence: Implications for policy and practice. *Journal of Child Psychology and Psychiatry*, 59, 405–21.

Bacchini, E., Esposito, G., & Affuso, G. (2009). School experience and school bullying. *Journal of Community & Applied Social Psychology*, 19, 17–32. DOI: 10.1002/casp.975.

Baiocco, R., Pistella, J., Salvati, M., Ioverno, S., & Lucidi, F. (2018). Sports as a risk environment: Homophobia and bullying in a sample of gay and heterosexual men. *Journal of Gay & Lesbian Mental Health*. DOI: 10.1080/19359705.2018.1489325.

Balyi, I., Way, R., & Higgs, C. (2013). *Long Term Athlete Development*. Champaign, IL: Human Kinetics Publishers.

Barboza, G. E., Schiamberg, L. B., Oehmke, J., Korzeniewski, S. J., Post, L. A., & Heraux, C. G. (2009). Individual characteristics and the multiple contexts of adolescent bullying: An ecological perspective. *Journal of Youth and Adolescence*, 38, 101–21. DOI: 10.1007/s10964-008-9271-1.

Barrio, C., Martin, E., Montero, I., Gutiérrez, H., Barrios, A., & Dios, M. (2008). Bullying and social exclusion in Spanish secondary schools: National trends from 1999 to 2006. *International Journal of Clinical and Health Psychology*, 8(3), 657–77.

Bibou-Nakou, I., Tsiantis, J., Assimopoulos, H., Chatzilambou, P., & Giannakopoulou, D. (2012). School factors related to bullying: A qualitative study of early adolescent students. Social psychology of education. *An International Journal*, 15(2), 125–45. DOI: 10.1007/s11218-012-9179-1.

Björkqvist, K. (1994). Sex differences in physical, verbal and indirect aggression: A review of recent research. *Sex Roles*, 30(3/4), 177–88.

Björkqvist, K., Lagerspetz, K., & Kaukiainen, A. (1992). Do girls manipulate and boys fight? Developmental trends in regard to direct and indirect aggression. *Aggressive Behavior*, 18, 117–27.

Björkqvist, K. & Österman, K. (2000). Social intelligence – empathy = aggression? *Aggression and Violent Behavior*, 5(2), 191–200.

Björkqvist, K., Österman, K., & Kaukiainen, A. (1992). The development of direct and indirect aggressive strategies in males and females (pp. 51–64). In K. Bjorkqvist & P. Niemela (Eds.). *Of Mice and Women Aspects of Female Aggression*. San Diego, CA: Academic Press.

Blakemore, S.-J. & Mills, K. L. (2014). Is adolescence a sensitive period for sociocultural processing? *Annual Review of Psychology*, 65, 187–207.

Blaya, C. & Debarbieux, E. (2003). *Gender and violence in schools*. Paper commissioned for the EFA Global Monitoring Report 2003/4. The Leap to Equality.

Bond, L., Carlin, J., Thomas, L., Rubin, K., & Patton, G. (2001). Does bullying cause emotional problems? A prospective study of young teenagers. *British Medical Journal*, 323, 480–84.

Bordens, K. (2002). *Research Design and Methods: A Process Approach*. Boston, MA: McGraw-Hill.

Boulton, M. (2012). Associations between adult's recalled childhood bullying victimization, current social anxiety, coping and self-blame: Evidence for moderation and indirect effects. *Anxiety, Stress & Coping: An International Journal*, 26(3), 270–92.

Boyle, D. E., Marshall, N. L., & Robeson, W. W. (2003). Gender at play: Fourth-grade girls and boys on the playground. *American Behavioral Scientist*, 46, 1326–45.
Brackenridge, C. H. (1997). "He owned me basically ... " Women's experience of sexual abuse in sport. *International Review for the Sociology of Sport*, 32(2), 115–30.
Brackenridge, C. H. (2001). *Spoilsports: Understanding and Preventing Sexual Exploitation in Sport*. London: Routledge.
Brackenridge, C. H., Rivers, I., Gough, B., & Llewellyn, K. (2007). Driving down participation. Homophobic bullying as a deterrent to doing sport (pp. 122–39). In C. Aitchison (Ed.). *Sport & Gender Identities. Masculinities, Femininities and Sexualities*. London: Routledge.
Braz, J. (1998). Olimpismo, mensagem de uma ética para o desporto (pp. 73–86). In J. Proença & J. Constantino (Eds.). *Olimpismo, Desporto E Educação*. Lisboa: Universidade Lusófona.
Breakwell, G. (1995). Interviewing (pp. 1–19). In G. Breakwell, S. Hammond & C. Fife-Schaw (Eds.). *Research Methods in Psychology*. London: Sage.
Brislin, R. W. (1970). Back-translation for cross-cultural research. *Journal of Cross-Cultural Psychology*, 1(3), 185–216.
Brofenbrenner, U. (1979). *The Ecology of Human Development*. Cambridge, MA: Harvard University Press.
Brofenbrenner, U. (1996). *A Ecologia Do Desenvolvimento Humano: Experimentos Naturais E Planejados*. Porto Alegre: Artes Médicas.
Browitt, J., King, S., & Martinez-Expósito, A. (2006). Introduction to the theme of masculinity and violence in Spain and Latin America. *Journal of Iberian and Latin American Research*, 12(2), 1–3.
Burnard, P., Gill, P., Stewart, K., Treasure, E., & Chadnick, B. (2008). Analysing and presenting qualitative data. *British Dental Journal*, 204, 429–32.
Buss, D. M. (2007). *Evolutionary Psychology: The New Science of the Mind* (3rd ed.). New York: Allyn and Bacon.
Campbell, M. & Bauman, S. (Eds.). (2018). *Reducing Cyberbullying in Schools*. London: Elsevier.
Canadian Institute of Health Research Bullying Statistics. (2012). Canadian bullying statistics. www.cihr-irsc.gc.ca/e/45838.html.
Carvalhosa, S. (2008). *Prevention of Bullying in Schools: An Ecological Model*. Norway: University of Bergen.
Carvalhosa, S., Moleiro, C., & Sales, C. (2009). Violence in Portuguese Schools: National Report. *International Journal of Violence and School*, 9, 57–78.
Cashmore, E. (1996).*Making Sense of Sports* (2nd ed.). New York: Routledge.
Catalano, R. F., Haggerty, K. P., Oesterte, S., Fleming, C. B., & Hawkins, J. D. (2004). The importance of bonding to school for healthy development: Findings from the Social development research group. *Journal of School Health*, 74(7), 252–61.
Chalabaev, A., Sarrazin, P., Fontayne, P., Boiché, J., & Clément-Guillotin, C. (2013). The influence of gender stereotypes and gender roles on participation and performance in sport and exercise: Review and future directions. *Psychology of Sport and Exercise*, 14, 136–44. DOI: 10.1016/j.psychsport.2012.10.005.

Clandinin, J. & Caine, V. (2008). Narrative inquiry (pp. 541–44). In L. Given (Ed.). *The SAGE Encyclopedia of Qualitative Research Methods*. London: Sage Publications.

Cohen, R. (2002). *By the Sword: A History of Gladiators, Musketeers, Swashbucklers, and Olympic Champions*. New York: Random House.

Coie, J., Dodge, K., Terry, R., & Wright, V. (1991). The role of aggression in peer relations: An analysis of aggression episodes in boys' play groups. *Child Development*, 62, 812–26.

Constantino, J. (1998). Olimpismo e educação (pp. 53–61). In J. Proença & J. Constantino (Eds.). *Olimpismo, Desporto E Educação*. Lisboa: Universidade Lusófona.

Cook, C. R., Williams, K. R., Guerra, N. G., Kim, T. E., & Sadek, S. (2010). Predictors of bullying and victimization in childhood and adolescence: A meta-analytic investigation. *School Psychology Quarterly*, 25, 65–83.

Cooper, L. & Nickerson, A. (2012). Parent retrospective recollections of bullying and current views, concerns and strategies to cope with children's bullying. *Journal of Child and Family Studies*, 22(4), 526–40.

Council of Europe. (2001). Committee of Ministers. Recommendation No R (92) 13 REV of the Committee of Ministers to Member States on the Revised European Sport Charter. Available online: https://rm.coe.int/16804c9dbb (accessed on 19 September 2018).

Courtney, J. & Wann, D. (2010). The relationship between sport fan dysfunction and bullying behaviours. *North American Journal of Psychology*, 2(1), 191–98.

Cowie, H. & Smith, P. K. (2010). Peer support as a means of improving school safety and reducing bullying and violence (pp. 177–93). In B. Doll, W. Pfohl & J. Yoon (Eds.). *Handbook of Youth Prevention Science*. New York: Routledge.

Crick, N. R. & Grotpeter, J. K. (1995). Relational aggression, gender, and social-psychological adjustment. *Child Development*, 66, 710–22.

Cunningham, N. (2007). Level of bonding to school and perception of the school environment by bullies, victims, and bully victims. *The Journal of Early Adolescence*, 27(4), 457–78.

Cunti, A., Bellantonio, S., & Priore, A. (2016). Sport, gender differences and sexuality between social stereotypes and educational needs for recognition of subjectivities. *Studia UBB Educatio Artis Gymn*, LXI, 77–84.

Cuyler, P. (1979). *Sumo: From Rite to Sport*. New York: Weatherhill.

Daniels, D., Gabel, R., & Hughes, S. (2012). Recounting the K-12 school experiences of adults who stutter: A qualitative analysis. *Journal of Fluency Disorders*, 3, 71–82.

Debarbieux, E. (2004). La violence à l'école: Une mondialisation? *Ville-école-intégracion Enjeux, Hors*, 8, 11–31.

Demirel, D. H. & Yıldıran, I. (2013). The philosophy of physical education and sport from ancient times to the enlightenment. *European Journal of Educational Research*, 2(4), 191–202.

Denison, E. & Kitchen, A. (2015). Out on the fields: The first international study on homophobia in sport. Nielsen, Bingham Cup Sydney 2014, Australian Sports Commission, Federation of Gay Games. Accessed through: www.outonthefields.com.

Dietz-Uhler, B., Harrick, E. A., End, C., & Jacquemotte, L. (2001). Sex differences in sports fan behavior and reasons for being a sport fan. *Journal of Sport Behavior*, 23, 219–31.

Due, P., Holstein, B., Lynch, J., Diderichsen, F., Gabhain, S., Scheidt, P., & Currie, C. (2005). Bullying and symptoms among school-aged children: International comparative cross sectional study in 28 countries. *European Journal of Public Health*, 15(2), 128–32.

Dunning, E. (1999). *Sport Matters: Sociological Studies of Sport, Violence and Civilization*. London: Routledge.

Einarsen, S., Hoel, H., Zapf, D., & Cooper, C. L. (Eds.). (2003). *Bullying and Emotional Abuse in the Workplace: International Perspectives in Research and Practice*. London: Taylor and Francis.

Elgammal, M. (2008). The ancient Egyptian Sports during the Pharaoh dynasties & its relations to the ancient Greek Sports. 16th International Seminar on Olympic Studies for Postgraduate Students.

Endresen, I. & Olweus, D. (2005). Participation in power sports and antisocial involvement in preadolescent and adolescent boys. *Journal of Child Psychology and Psychiatry*, 46(5), 468–78.

Englefield, L., Cunningham, D., Mahoney, A., Stone, T., & Torrance, H. (2016). Sport, physical activity & LGBT. A study by pride sports for sports England. www.sportengland.org/media/11116/pride-sport-sport-physical-activity-and-lgbt-report-2016.pdf.

Escury, A. & Dudink, A. (2010). Bullying beyond school: Examining the role of sports (pp. 235–48). In S. Jimerson, S. Swearer & D. Espelage (Eds.). *Handbook of Bullying in School: An International Perspective*. New York: Routledge.

Espelage, D. & Swearer, S. (2003). Research on school bulling and victimization: What have we learned and where do we go from here? *School Psychology Review*, 32(3), 365–83.

Espelage, D. L. & Swearer, S. M. (Eds.). (2004). *Bullying in American Schools: A Socio-ecological Perspective on Prevention and Intervention*. Mahwah, NJ & London: Erlbaum.

Evans, B., Adler, A., MacDonald, D., & Cote, J. (2016). Bullying victimization and perpetration among adolescent sport teammates. *Pediatric Exercise Science*, 28, 296–303.

Farrington, D., Loeber, R., Stallings, R., & Ttofi, M. (2011). Bullying perpetration and victimization as predictors of delinquency and depression in the Pittsburgh Youth Study. *Journal of Aggression, Conflict and Peace Research*, 3(2), 74–81.

Farrington, D. P., Lösel, F., Ttofi, M. M., & Theodorakis, N. (2012). *School Bullying, Depression and Offending Behaviour Later in Life: An Updated Systematic Review of Longitudinal Studies*. Stockholm: Swedish National Council for Crime Prevention.

Fasting, K., Brackenridge, C., & Sundgot-Borgen, J. (2013). Experiences of sexual harassment and abuse among Norwegian elite female athletes and nonathletes. *Research Quarterly for Exercise and Sport*, 74(1), 84–97. DOI: 10.1080/02701367.2003.10609067.

Fasting, K., Chroni, S., Hervik, S. E., & Knorre, N. (2011). Sexual harassment in sport toward females in three European countries. *International Review for the Sociology of Sport*, 46, 76–89.
Field, T. (1996). *Bully in Sight: How to Predict, Resist, Challenge and Combat Workplace Bullying: Overcoming the Silence and Denial by Which Abuse Thrives.* Wantage, Oxfordshire, UK: Success Unlimited.
Fields, S., Collins, C. L., & Comstock, R. D. (2010). Violence in youth sports: Hazing, brawling and foul play. *British Journal of Sports Medicine*, 44, 32–37.
Fink, A. (1985). *How to Conduct Surveys. A Step-by-step Guide.* Beverly Hills, CA: Sage.
Fisher, L. & Dzikus, L. (2017). Bullying in sport and performance psychology. *Oxford Research Encyclopedia of Psychology*. DOI: 10.1093/acrefore/9780190236557.013.169.
Fisher, L. A. & Dzikus, L. (2010). Bullying and hazing in sport teams (pp. 372–81). In S. J. Hanrahan & M. B. Andersen (Eds.). *Routledge Handbook of Applied Sport Psychology*. London and New York: Routledge.
Folkman, S. & Lazarus, R. S. (1985). If it changes it must be a process: Study of emotion and coping during three stages of a college examination. *Journal of Personality and Social Psychology*, 48, 150–70.
Fontaine, R. (2003). *Psychologie De L'agression*. Paris: Dunod.
Foucault, M. (1966). *The Order of Things. An Archaeology of the Human Sciences.* London and New York: Routledge.
Francisco, M. & Libório, R. (2008). A study on bullying victimization among peers in elementary and junior high school. *Psicologia: Reflexão E Crítica*, 22(2), 200–7.
Freeman, M. (2008). Autobiography (pp. 45–48). In L. Given (Ed.). *The SAGE Encyclopedia of Qualitative Research Methods*. London: Sage Publications.
Freischlag, J. & Schmidke, C. (1980). Violence in sports: Its causes and some solutions (pp. 182–85). In W. Straub (Ed.), *Sport Psychology: An Analysis of Athlete Behaviour* (2nd ed.). Victoria: Mouvement Publications.
French Department of Sport. (2000). *La France Sportive. [The Active France]*. Paris: Statistical Commission of the Department of Sport.
Fry, D. (1993). The intergenerational transmission of disciplinary practices and approaches to conflict. *Human Organization*, 52(2), 176–85.
Fry, D. (1998). Anthropological perspectives on aggression: Sex differences and cultural variation. *Aggressive Behaviour*, 24, 81–95.
Fry, D. (2004). Rough-and-tumble social play in children (pp. 54–88). In A. Pellegrini & P. K. Smith (Eds.). *The Nature of Play: Great Apes and Humans*. New York: Guilford Publishers.
García Ferrando, M. (1985). *Agresión Y Violencia En El Deporte: Un Enfoque Interdisciplinario*. Madrid: Instituto de Ciencias de la Educación Física y del Deporte.
García Ferrando, M. (1987). *Interpretações Sociológicas Da Violência No Desporto*. Lisboa: ME/DGD.
García Ferrando, M. (1990). *Aspectos Sociales Del Deporte: Una Reflexión Sociológica*. Madrid: Alianza Editorial.

Gencheva, N. (2015). Aggression in youth athletes. *Research in Kinesiology*, 43(2), 205–9.
Gervis, M. & Dunn, N. (2004). The emotional abuse of elite child athletes by their coaches. *Child Abuse Review*, 13, 215–23.
Gini, G., Albiero, P., Benelli, B., & Altoe, G. (2008). Determinants of adolescents' active defending and passive bystanding behavior in bullying. *Journal of Adolescence*, 31, 93–105.
Giroux, H. (2001). *Theory and Resistance in Education*. London: Bergin & Garvey.
Golden, M. (2008). *Greek Sport and Social Status*. Austin, TX: University of Texas Press.
Gonçalves, S. & Matos, M. (2007). Bullying in schools: Predictors and profiles. Results of the Portuguese health behaviour in school-aged children survey. *International Journal of Violence and School*, 4, 91–108.
Gonzalez, J. (2008). El Acoso Escolar – Bullying: Una Propuesta de Estudio desde el Análisis de Redes Sociales (ARS). *Revista d'Estudis De La Violència*, 4, 1–17.
Griffin, P. (1998). *Strong Women, Deep Closets: Lesbians and Homophobia in Sport*. Windsor, Ontario: Human Kinetics.
Guilbert, S. (2004). Sport and violence: A typological analysis. *International Review for the Sociology of Sport*, 39, 45–55.
Guilbert, S. (2009). Violences sportives., milieux sociaux et niveaux scolaires. Distribution "socioculturelle" des formes de violence dans le champ des pratiques sportives de terrain. *International Journal of Violence and School*, 8, 24–40.
Gutiérrez, H., Barrios, A., Dios, M., Montero, I., & Barrio, C. (2008). The incidence of peer bullying as multiple maltreatment among Spanish secondary school students. *Psychology and Psychological Therapy*, 8(2), 247–57.
Guttman, A. (2004). *From Ritual to Record. The Nature of Modern Sports*. New York: Columbia University Press.
Habashi, Z. (1976). King Tutankhamun sportsman in antiquity (pp. 71–83). In R. Renson, P. Paul de Nayer & M. Ostyn (Eds.). *The History the Evolution and Diffusion of Sports and Games in Different Cultures*. Brussels: Bestuur voor de Lichamelijke Opvoeding, de Sport en het Openluchtleven.
Hamby, S., Blount, Z., Smith, A., Jones, L., Mitchell, K., & Taylor, E. (2018). Digital poly-victimization: The increasing importance of online crime and harassment to the burden of victimization. *Journal of Trauma and Dissociation*, 19, 382–98.
Hamed. (2015). Sport, leisure: Artistic perspectives in Ancient Egyptian temples (part II). *Recorde*, 8(1), 1–28.
Harwood, A. & Lavidor, M. (2017). Reducing aggression with martial arts: A meta-analysis of child and youth studies. *Aggression and Violent Behavior*, 34, 96–101.
Hawkins, D. L., Pepler, D. J., & Craig, W. M. (2001). Naturalistic observations of peer interventions in bullying. *Social Development*, 10, 512–27.
Haynes, S. (2001). Clinical applications of analogue behavioral observation: Dimensions of psychometric evaluation. *Psychological Assessment*, 13(1), 73–85.
Heinemann, P. (1972). *Mobbning. Gruppvåld Bland Barn Och Vuxna*. Stockholm: Naturoch kultur.

Hemphill, D. & Symons, C. (2009). Sexuality matters in physical education and sport studies. *Quest*, 61(4), 397–417.

Hernández, D. & Recoder, G. (2015). *Historia De La Actividad Física Y El Deporte. Bases Conceptuales. Premisas Ordenadoras*. Mexico: Síntesis. Literatura.

Hill, J. (2015). "If you miss the ball, you look like a total muppet". Boys investing in their bodies in physical education and sport. *Sport, Education and Society*, 20 (6), 762–79.

Hill, M. & Hill, A. (2005). *Investigação Por Questionário* (2ª). Lisboa: Sílabo.

Hong, J. & Espelage, D. (2012). A review of research on bullying and peer victimization in school: An ecological system analysis. *Aggression and Violent Behavior*, 17(4), 311–22.

Hoover, N. C. & Pollard, N. (2000). *Initiation Rites in American High Schools: A National Survey*. New York: Alfred University.

Hoyle, R. (2002). *Research Methods in Social Relations* (7th ed.). Toronto: Wadsworth.

Huitsing, G. & Veenstra, R. (2012). Bullying in classrooms: Participant roles from a social network perspective. *Aggressive Behavior*, 38, 494–509.

Humphreys, A. & Smith, P. K. (1987). Rough and tumble, friendship and dominance in school children: Evidence for continuity and change with age. *Child Development*, 58, 201–12.

Instituto Nacional de Estatística. (2015). *Estatísticas Oficiais*. https://ine.pt/xportal/xmain?xpgid=ine_main&xpid=INE.

International Olympic Committee. (2007). *Consensus Statement on Sexual Harassment and Abuse in Sport*. Lausanne, Switzerland: International Olympic Committee.

IOC Medical Commission. (2007). *Consensus statement on sexual harassment and abuse in sport*. https://bjsm.bmj.com/content/50/17/1019.

Ireland, J., Archer, J., & Power, X. (2007). Characteristics of male and female prisoners involved in bullying behavior. *Aggressive Behavior*, 33, 220–29.

Jachyna, P. (2013). Boys' bodies: Speaking the unspoken. *Sport, Education and Society*, 18(6), 842–46.

Jimmerson, S. R., Swearer, S. M., & Espelage, D. L. (Eds.). (2010). *Handbook of Bullying in Schools. An International Perspective*. New York: Routledge.

Jolliffe, D. & Farrington, D. P. (2011). Is low empathy related to bullying after controlling for individual and social background variables?. *Journal of Adolescence*, 34, 59–71.

Justiciano, A. (1998). Olimpismo como projecto cultural e social (pp. 19–40). In J. Proença & J. Constantino (Eds.). *Olimpismo, Desporto E Educação*. Lisboa: Universidade Lusófona.

Juvonen, J. & Galvan, A. (2008). Peer influence in involuntary social groups: Lessons from research on bullying (pp. 225–44). In M. Prinstein & K. Dodge (Eds.). *Peer Influence Processes among Youth*. New York: Guilford Press.

Juvonen, J., Graham, S., & Schuster, M. (2003). Bullying among young adolescents: The strong, the weak and the troubled. *Pediatrics*, 112, 1231–38.

Kerr, D. C., Gini, G., & Capaldi, D. M. (2017). Young men's suicidal behavior, depression, crime, and substance use risks linked to childhood teasing. *Child Abuse and Neglect*, 67, 32–43.

Kerr, G. A. & Stirling, A. E. (2012). Parents' reflections on their child's experiences of emotionally abusive coaching practices. *Journal of Applied Sport Psychology*, 24, 191–206.

Kidd, B. (2013). Sports and masculinity. *Sport in Society*, 16(4), 553–64. DOI: 10.1080/17430437.2013.785757.

Kilby, E. (1976). Ancient Tyre: Its hippodrome and other athletic facilities (pp. 96–104). In R. Renson, P. Paul de Nayer & M. Ostyn (Eds.). *The History of the Evolution and Diffusion of Sports and Games in Different Cultures*. Brussels: Bestuur voor de Lichamelijke Opvoeding, de Sport en het Openluchtleven.

Kim, Y.-S., Leventhal, B., Koh, Y.-J., & Boyce, W. T. (2009). Bullying increased suicide risk: Prospective study of Korean adolescents. *Archives Journal of Adolescent Mental Health*, 20, 133–54.

Kimmel, M. S. & Mahler, M. (2003). Adolescent masculinity, homophobia, and violence. *American Behavioral Scientist*, 46, 1439–58.

Kirby, S., Greaves, L., & Hankivsky, O. (2000). *The Dome of Silence: Sexual Harassment and Abuse in Sport*. London: Zed Books.

Kirby, S. & Wintrump, G. (2002). Running a gauntlet: An examination of initiation/hazing and sexual abuse in sport. *Journal of Sexual Aggression*, 8(12), 49–68.

Krippendorff, K. (1980). *Content Analysis: An Introduction to Its Methodology*. Newbury Park: Sage.

Krishnaveni, K. & Shahin, A. (2014). Aggression and its influence on sports performance. *International Journal of Physical Education, Sports and Health*, 1 (2), 29–32.

Kvale, S. (1996). *Interviews: An Introduction to Qualitative Interviewing*. Thousand Oaks, CA: Sage.

Lazarus, R. (1991). *Emotion and Adaptation*. New York: Oxford University Press.

Leahy, T. (2014). Sexual abuse in elite sport (pp. 852–61). In A. G. Papaioannou & D. Hackfort (Eds.). *Routledge Companion to Sport Exercise Psychology. Global Perspectives and Fundamental Concepts*. London: Routledge International Group.

Leedy, P. & Ormrod, J. (2009). *Practical Research: Planning and Design* (9th ed.). Boston, MA: Pearson Education International.

Lentillon, V. (2009). Les stéréotypes sexués relatifs à la pratique des activités physiques et sportives chez les adolescents français et leurs conséquences discriminatoires. *Bulletin De Psychologie*, 499(1), 15–28. DOI: 10.3917/bupsy.499.0015.

Leonard, W. (1996). The odds of transitioning from one level of sports participation to another. *Sociology of Sports Journal*, 13, 288–99.

Lereya, S. T., Samara, M., & Wolke, D. (2013). Parenting behavior and the risk of becoming a victim and a bully/victim: A meta-analysis study. *Child Abuse & Neglect*, 37, 1091–108.

Lincoln, Y. & Guba, E. (1985). *Naturalistic Inquiry*. Newbury Park: Sage Publications.

Lippe, G. (2002). Media image. *International Review for the Sociology of Sport*, 37 (3–4), 371–95.

Litwin, M. (1995). *How to Measure Survey Reliability and Validity*. Thousand Oaks: Sage.

Lomas, C. (2007). La escuela es un infierno? Violencia escolar e construcción cultural de la masculinidad. *Revista De Educación*, 342, 83–101.

Lombardo, M. P. (2012). On the evolution of sport. *Evolutionary Psychology*, 10 (1), 1–28.

López-Albalá, E. (2016). Mujeres deportistas espa-olas: Estereotipos de género en los medios de comunicación. *Sociologiados. Revista De Investigación Social*, 1(2), 87–110. DOI: 10.14198/socdos.2016.1.2.04.

Lorenz, K. (1966). *On Aggression*. London: Methuen & Co. Ltd.

Losel, F. & Bender, D. (2011). Emotional and antisocial outcomes of bullying and victimization at school: A follow-up from childhood to adolescence. *Journal of Aggression, Conflict and Peace Research*, 3(2), 89–96.

Luiggi, M., Travert, M., & Griffet, J. (2018). Temporal trends in sport participation among adolescents between 2001 and 2015: A French school- and territory-based study. *International Journal of Environmental Research and Public Health*, 15, 1335. DOI: 10.3390/ijerph15071335.

MacDonald, C. A. (2014). Masculinity and sport revisited. A review of literature of hegemonic masculinity and men's ice hockey in Canada. *Canadian Graduate Journal of Sociology and Criminology*, 3(1), 95–112.

Marivoet, S. (1998). *Aspectos Sociológicos Do Desporto*. Lisbon: Livros Horizonte.

Marks, S., Mountjoy, M., & Marcus, M. (2012). Sexual harassment and abuse in sport: The role of the team doctor. *British Journal of Sports Medicine*, 46, 905–8. DOI: 10.1136/bjsports-2011-090345.

Martins, M. (2005). Agressão e vitimação entre adolescentes em contexto escolar: Um estudo empírico. *Análise Psicológica*, 4(23), 401–25.

McClung, L. & Blinde, E. (2002). Sensitivity to gender issues: Accounts of women intercollegiate athletes. *International Sports Journal*, 6, 117–33.

Melim, F. & Oliveira, B. P. (2013). Prática desportiva, um meio de prevenção do bullying na escola? *Porto Alegre*, 19(2), 55–77.

Messner, M. (2002). *Taking the Field: Women, Men, and Sports*. Minneapolis, MN: University of Minnesota Press.

Messner, M. (2011). Gender ideologies, youth sports, and the production of soft essentialism. *Sociology of Sport Journal*, 28, 151–70.

Messner, M. & Sabo, D. F. (Eds.). (1990). *Sport, Men, and the Gender Order: Critical Feminist Perspectives*. Champaign, IL: Human Kinetics Publishers.

Mills, C. B. & Carwile, A. M. (2009). The good, the bad, and the borderline: Separating teasing from bullying. *Communication Education*, 58(2), 276–301. DOI: 10.1080/03634520902783666.

Mishna, F. (2003). Learning disabilities and bullying: Double jeopardy. *Journal of Learning Disabilities*, 36, 336–47.

Moffitt, T. (1993). Adolescence-limited and life-course-persistent antisocial behavior: A developmental taxonomy. *Psychological Review*, 100, 674–701.

Monks, C. & Coyne, I. (Eds.). (2011). *Bullying in Different Contexts*. Cambridge: Cambridge University Press.

Monks, C., Smith, P. K., Naylor, P., Barter, C., Ireland, J., & Coyne, I. (2009). Bullying in different contexts: Commonalities, differences and the role of theory. *Aggression and Violent Behavior*, 14, 146–56.

Moral, M. (2005). Actitudes socioconstruidas ante la violencia bullying en estudiantes de secundaria. *Anuario De Psicología*, 36(1), 61–81.

Mora-Merchán, J. (2006). Las estrategias de afrontamiento. Mediadoras de los efectos a largo plazo de las víctimas de bullying? *Anuario De Psicología Clínica Y De La Salud/Annuary of Clinical and Health Psychology*, 2, 15–26.

Morita, Y., Soeda, H., Soeda, K., & Taki, M. (1999). Japan (pp. 309–23). In P. K. Smith, Y. Morita, J. Junger-Tos, D. Olweus, R. Catalano & P. Slee (Eds.). *The Nature of School Bullying: A Cross-national Perspective.* London: Routledge.

Mutz, M. & Baur, J. (2009). The role of sport for violence prevention: Sport club participation and violent behaviour among adolescents. *International Journal of Sport Policy and Politics*, 1, 305–21. DOI: 10.1080/19406940903265582.

United Nations. (2007). *Women 2000 and Beyond: Women, Gender Equality and Sport* (Report). New York: Division for the Advancement of Women, Department of Economic and Social Affairs. United Nations. www.un.org/womenwatch/daw/public/Women%20and%20Sport.pdf.

Naylor, P., Cowie, H., & Del Rey, R. (2001). Coping strategies of secondary school children in response to being bullied. *Child Psychology & Psychiatry Review*, 6 (3), 114–20.

Nery, M., Neto, C., Rosado, A., & Smith, P. K. (2018). Bullying in youth sport training. A nationwide exploratory and descriptive research in Portugal. *European Journal of Developmental Psychology*, 16(4), 447–63. DOI: 10.1080/17405629.2018.1447459.

Nishina, A. & Juvonen, J. (2005). Daily reports of witnessing and experiencing peer harassment in middle school. *Child Development*, 76, 435–50.

O'Connor, J. & Graber, K. (2014). Sixth-grade physical education: An acculturation of bullying and fear. *Research Quarterly for Exercise and Sport*, 85(3), 398–408.

Ólafsson, K. (Ed.). (2006). *Sports, Media and Stereotypes: Women and Men in Sports and Media.* Iceland: Centre of Gender Equality.

Olthof, T. & Goossens, F. (2008). Bullying and the need to belong: Early adolescents' bullying-related behavior and the acceptance they desire and receive from particular classmates. *Social Development*, 17, 24–46.

Olweus, D. (1973). *Hackkycklingar Och Översittre: Forskning Om Skolmobbning [Whipping Boys and Bullies: Research on School bullying].* Stockholm: Almqvist & Wiksell.

Olweus, D. (1978). *Aggression in Schools: Bullies and Whipping Boys.* Washington, DC: Hemisphere.

Olweus, D. (1986). *The Olweus Bully/Victim Questionnaire.* Mimeo. Bergen, Norway: Research Center for Health Promotion, University of Bergen.

Olweus, D. (1993). *Bullying at School: What We Know and What We Can Do.* Oxford, UK: Blackwell.

Olweus, D. (1995). Peer abuse or bullying at school: Basic facts and a school-based intervention programme. *Prospects*, 25(1), 133–39.

Olweus, D. (1999). Sweden (pp. 7–27). In P. K. Smith, Y. Morita, J. Junger-Tos, D. Olweus, R. Catalano & P. Slee (Eds.). *The Nature of School Bullying. A Cross-National Perspective.* London & New York: Routledge.

Olweus, D. (2010). Understanding and researching bullying: Some critical issues (pp. 9–33). In S. Jimerson, S. Swearer & D. Espelage (Eds.). *Handbook of Bullying in Schools: An International Perspective*. New York: Routledge.

Olweus, D. (2013). School bullying: Development and some important challenges. *Annual Review of Clinical Psychology*, 9, 751–80.

Olweus, D. & Limber, S. (2010). The Olweus Bullying Prevention Program. Implementation and evaluation over two decades (pp. 377–402). In S. Jimerson, S. Swearer & D. Espelage (Eds.). *Handbook of Bullying in Schools: An International Perspective*. New York: Routledge.

Olweus, D. & Limber, S. (2019). The Olweus Bullying Prevention Program (OBPP): New evaluations and current status (pp. 23–45). In P. K. Smith (Ed.). *Making an Impact on School Bullying: Interventions and Recommendations*. London: Routledge.

Ortega, R., Mora-Mérchan, J., Lera, A., Singer, M., Smith, P. K., Pereira, B., & Menesini, E. (1999). *Final report of the working group on general survey questionnaires and nomination methods concerning bullying*.

Österman, K., Björkqvist, K., Lagerspetz, K., Kaukiainen, A., Landau, S., Frączek, A., & Caprara, G. (1998). Cross-cultural evidence of female indirect aggression. *Aggressive Behavior*, 24, 1–8.

Ostvik, K. & Rudmin, F. (2001). Bullying and hazing among Norwegian army soldiers: Two studies of prevalence, context, and cognition. *Military Psychology*, 13, 17–39.

Palframan, D. (1994). Expert deplores emotional abuse in sport. *Coaches Report*, 1 (2), 3–5.

Patton, M. (1990). *Qualitative Evaluation and Research Methods*. Thousand Oaks, CA: Sage Publications.

Patton, M. (2002). *Qualitative Research & Evaluation Methods* (3rd ed.). London: Sage Publications.

Pedersen, D. (2007). Perceived aggression in sports and its relation to willingness to participate and perceived risk of injury. *Perceptual and Motor Skills*, 104, 201–11.

Pellegrini, A. (1998a). Bullies and victims in school: A review and call for research. *Journal of Applied Developmental Psychology*, 19(2), 165–76.

Pellegrini, A. (1998b). Elementary school children's rough-and-tumble play and social competence. *Developmental Psychology*, 24(6), 802–6.

Pellegrini, A. (2003). Perceptions and functions of play and real fighting in early adolescence. *Child Development*, 74(5), 1522–33.

Pellegrini, A. (2009). *The Role of Play in Human Development*. Oxford, UK and New York: Oxford University Press.

Pellegrini, A. & Bartini, M. (2000). A longitudinal study of bullying, victimizations and peer affiliation during the transition from primary school to middle school. *American Educational Research Journal*, 37(3), 699–725.

Pellegrini, A. & Bartini, M. (2001). Dominance in early adolescent boys: Affiliative and aggressive dimensions and possible functions. *Merrill-Palmer Quarterly*, 47 (1), 142–63.

Pellegrini, A. & Long, J. (2002). A longitudinal study of bullying, dominance and victimization during the transition from primary school through secondary school. *British Journal of Developmental Psychology*, 20, 259–80.

Pellegrini, A. & Long, J. (2003). A sexual selection theory longitudinal analysis of sexual segregation and integration in early adolescence. *Journal of Experimental Child Psychology*, 85, 257–78.

Pellegrini, A. & Smith, P. K. (1998). Physical activity play: The nature and function of the neglected aspect of play. *Child Development*, 3, 577–98.

Pepler, D. & Craig, W. (1995). A peek behind the fence: Naturalistic observations of aggressive children with remote audiovisual recording. *Developmental Psychology*, 31(4), 548–53.

Pepler, D., Craig, W., & Roberts, W. (1998). Observations of aggressive and nonaggressive children on the school playground. *Merrill-Palmer Quaterfly*, 44, 55–76.

Pereira, B. (2008). *Para Uma Escola Sem Violência. Estudo E Prevenção Das Práticas Agressivas Entre Crianças* (2ª). Coimbra: Fundação Calouste Gulbenkian e Fundação para a Ciência e a Tecnologia, Ministério da Ciência e da Tecnologia.

Pereira, B., Mendonça, D., Neto, C., Valente, L., & Smith, P. K. (2004). Bullying in Portuguese schools. *School Psychology International*, 25(2), 207–22.

Pfister, G. (1994). Shaping up womanhood, gender and girl's physical education. *Women in Sport & Activity Journal*, 7(1), 45.

Plaza, M., Boiché, J., Brunel, L., & Ruchaud, F. (2017). Sport = male ... but not all sports: Investigating the gender stereotypes of sport activities at the explicit and implicit levels. *Sex Roles*, 76(3–4), 202–17.

Plummer, D. (2006). Sportophobia. Why do some men avoid sport? *Journal of Sport & Social Issues*, 30(2), 122–37.

Ponte, C. & Batista, S. (2019). EU Kids Online Portugal. Usos, competências, riscos e mediações da internet reportados por crianças e jovens (9–17 anos). EU Kids Online e NOVA FCSH. http://fabricadesites.fcsh.unl.pt/eukidsonline/wp-content/uploads/sites/36/2019/03/RELATO%CC%81RIO-FINAL-EU-KIDS-ONLINE.docx.pdf.

Pöyhönen, V. & Salmivalli, C. (2008). New directions in research and practice addressing bullying: Focus on defending behaviour (pp. 26–43). In W. Craig (Ed.). *An International Perspective on Understanding and Addressing Bullying*. Bloomington, IN: Author House.Bloom

Prevention of Sexualized Violence in Sports - Impulses for an Open, Secure and Sound Sporting Environment. (2012). *Prevention of Sexual and Gender Harassment and Abuse: Initiatives in Europe and Beyond*. Frankfurt am Main: Deutsche Sportjugend. https://www.iss-ffm.de/fileadmin/assets/veroeffentlichungen/downloads/Prevention_of_sexual_and_gender_harassment_and_abuse_in_sports.pdf.

Psaaji, R. & Schailée, H. (2019). Unsanctioned aggression and violence in amateur sport: A multidisciplinary synthesis. *Aggression and Violent Behavior*, 44, 36–46.

Randolph, J. (2010). Free-marginal multirater Kappa (multirater κfree): An alternative to Fleiss fixed-marginal multirater Kappa. *Advances in Data Analysis and Classification*, 4. https://pdfs.semanticscholar.org/799b/424118419cf7fc78ed1bc407e3af03aba01f.pdf

Raposo, A. (1976). *Desporto E Transformações Sociais*. Lisboa: DGD.

Rappaport, R. A. (1999). *Ritual and Religion in the Making of Humanity*. Cambridge: Cambridge University Press.

Rebolo Marques, A. & Neto, C. (2001). Changes in school playground and aggressive behaviour reduction (pp. 137–45). In M. Martinez (Ed.). *Prevention and Control of Aggression and the Impact on Its Victims*. Valencia: Kluwer Academic/Plenum Publishers.

Renfrew, C. (2017). Introduction: Play as the precursor of ritual in early human societies (pp. 9–19). In C. Renfrew, I. Morley & M. Boyd (Eds.). *Ritual, Play and Belief, in Evolution and Early Human Societies*. Cambridge, UK: Cambridge University Press.

Renson, R. (1976). The Flemish archery gilds from defense mechanisms to sports institution (pp. 135–59). In R. Renson, P. Paul de Nayer & M. Ostyn (Eds.). *The History of the Evolution and Diffusion of Sports and Games in Different Cultures*. Brussels: Bestuur voor de Lichamelijke Opvoeding, de Sport en het Openluchtleven.

Richard, J. F., Schneider, B. H., & Mallet, P. (2011). Revisiting the whole school approach to bullying: Really looking at the whole school. *School Psychology International*, 33, 263–84. DOI: 10.1177/0143034311415906.

Rigby, K. (1996). *Bullying in Schools*. Melbourne: Australian Coucil for Educational Research.

Rigby, K. (2005). Why do some children bully at school? The contributions of negative attitudes towards victims and the perceived expectations of friends, parents and teachers. *School Psychology International*, 26(2), 147–61.

Rivers, I. (2010). Bullying, homophobia and transphobia in sport: At what cost discrimination? (pp. 80–84). In C. H. Brackenridge & D. Rhind (Eds.). *Elite Child Athlete Welfare: International Perspectives*. London: Brunel University Press.

Rivers, I., Poteat, V. P., Noret, N., & Ashurst, N. (2009). Observing bullying at school: The mental health implications of witness status. *School Psychology Quarterly*, 24, 211–23.

Roberts, B. (2008). Invisible difference in space: The role of different spaces in homophobic bullying in schools. *Journal of LGBT Youth*, 5(13), 11–33.

Roland, E. & Idsoe, T. (2001). Aggression and bullying. *Aggressive Behavior*, 27, 446–62.

Rosen, N. L. & Nofzlger, S. (2018). Boys, bullying and gender roles: How hegemonic masculinity shapes bullying behavior. *Gender Issues*. DOI: 10.1007/s12147-018-9226-0.

Ross, S. R. & Shinew, K. J. (2008). Perspectives of women college athletes on sport and gender. *Gender Roles*, 58, 40–57. DOI: 10.1007/s11199-007-9275-4.

Sáenz Ibáñez, A., Gimeno Marco, F., Gutiérrez Pablo, H., & Garay Ibáñez de Elejalde, B. (2012). Prevención de la agresividad y la violencia en el deporte en edad escolar: Um estudio de revision. *Cuadernos De Psicología Del Deporte*, 12, 57–72.

Salmivalli, C. (2010). Bullying and the peer group: A review. *Aggression and Violent Behavior*, 15, 112–20.

Salmivalli, C. & Isaacs, J. (2005). Prospective relations among victimization, rejection, friendlessness, and children's self- and peer-perceptions. *Child Development*, 76, 1161–71.

Salmivalli, C., Kärnä, A., & Poskiparta, E. (2010). From peer putdowns to peer support: A theoretical model and how it translated into a national anti-bullying program (pp. 441–54). In S. Jimerson, S. Swearer & D. Espelage (Eds.). *Handbook of Bullying in Schools: An International Perspective*. New York: Routledge.

Salmivalli, C., Kaukiainen, A., Kaistaniemi, L., & Lagerspetz, K. (1999). Self-evaluated self-esteem, peer-evaluated self-esteem, and defensive egotism as predictors of adolescents' participation in bullying situations. *Personality and Social Psychology Bulletin*, 25, 1268–78.

Salmivalli, C., Lagerspetz, K., Björkqvist, K., Österman, K., & Kaukiainen, A. (1998). Bullying as a group process: Participant roles and their relations to social status within the group. *Aggressive Behavior*, 22(1), 1–15.

Salmivalli, C. & Voeten, M. (2004). Connections between attitudes, group norms, and behaviour in bullying situations. *International Journal of Behavioral Development*, 28, 246–58. DOI: 10.1080/01650250344000488.

Schmalz, D. & Kerstetter, D. (2006). Girlie girls and manly men: Children's stigma consciousness of gender in sports and physical activities. *Journal of Leisure Research*, 38(4), 536–57.

Schott, R. & Sondergaard, D. (2014). *School Bullying: New Theories in Context*. Cambridge, UK: Cambridge University Press.

Schwartz, D., Dodge, K., Hubbard, J., Cillessen, A., Lemerise, E., & Bateman, H. (1998). Social-cognitive and behavioural correlates of aggression and victimization in boys' play groups. *Journal of Abnormal Child Psychology*, 26, 431–40.

Schwartz, D., Proctor, L., & Chien, D. (2001). The aggressive victim of bullying: Emotional and behavioural dysregulation as a pathway to victimization by peers (pp. 147–74). In J. Juvonen & S. Graham (Eds.). *Peer Harassment in School. The Plight of the Vulnerable and Victimized*. New York: Guilford Press.

Scott, J. C. (2018). The Phoenicians and the formation of the western world. *Comparative Civilizations Review*, 78, Article 4, 25–40. https://scholarsarchive.byu.edu/ccr/vol78/iss78/4.

Sebastião, J. (2009). Violência na escola: Uma questão sociológica. *Interacções*, 13, 35–62. Ch3, P.1.

Seixas, S. (2009). Diferenças de género nos comportamentos de bullying: Contributos da neurobiologia. *Interacções*, 13, 63–97. CH1.

Seixas, S., Coelho, J., & Nicolas-Fischer, G. (2013). Bullies, victims and bully-victims. Impact on health profile. *Educação, Sociedade E Culturas*, 38, 53–75, CH1.

Sesar, K., Barisic, M., Pandza, M., & Dodag, A. (2012). The relationship between difficulties in psychological adjustment in young adulthood and exposure to bullying behaviour in childhood and adolescence. *Acta Medica Academica*, 41, 131–44.

Sherif, M. (1958). Superordinate goals in the reduction of intergroup conflict. *American Journal of Sociology*, 63(4), 349–56.

Shields, D., Bredemeier, B., LaVoi, N., & Power, F. (2005). The sport behavior of youth, parents, and coaches: The good, the bad, and the ugly. *Journal Research Character Education*, 3(1), 43–59.

Smith, M. (1976). Hostile outbursts in sport (pp. 203–5). In A. Yannakis, M. Melnick & R. McIntyre (Eds.). *Sport Sociology: Contemporary Themes* (4th ed.). Iowa: Kendall Hunt.

Smith, P. K. (2003). *Violence in Schools: The Response in Europe*. London: Routledge Falmer.

Smith, P. K. (2014). *Understanding School Bullying: Its Nature and Prevention Strategies*. London: Sage Publications.

Smith, P. K. (2016). School-based interventions to address bullying. *Estonian Journal of Education*, 4, 142–64.

Smith, P. K. (2019a). *The Psychology of School Bullying*. London: Routledge.

Smith, P. K. (Ed.). (2019b). *Making an Impact on School Bullying: Interventions and Recommendations*. London: Routledge.

Smith, P. K. et al. (2018). Issues in cross-national comparisons and the meaning of words for bullying in different languages (pp. 61–80). In P. K. Smith, S. Sundaram, B. Spears, C. Blaya, M. Schäfer & D. Sandhu (Eds.). *Bullying, Cyberbullying and Pupil Well-being in Schools: Comparing European, Australian and Indian Perspectives*. Cambridge: Cambridge University Press.

Smith, P. K. et al. (2002). Definitions of bullying: A comparison of terms used, and age and sex differences, in a 14-country international comparison. *Child Development*, 73(4), 1119–33.

Smith, P. K., Kwak, K., & Toda, Y. (Eds.). (2016). *School Bullying in Different Cultures: Eastern and Western Perspectives*. Cambridge: Cambridge University Press.

Smith, P. K., López-Castro, L., Robinson, S., & Görzig, A. (2019). Consistency of gender differences in bullying in different cross-cultural surveys. *Aggression and Violent Behavior*, 45, 33–40.

Smith, P. K., Madsen, K. C., & Moody, J. C. (1999). What causes the age decline in reports of being bullied? Towards a developmental analysis of risks of being bullied. *Educational Research*, 41, 267–85.

Smith, P. K. & Sharp, S. (Eds.). (1994). *School Bullying. Insights and Perspectives*. London: Routledge.

Smith, P. K., Talamelli, L., Cowie, H., Naylor, P., & Chaua, P. (2004). Profiles of non-victims, escaped victims, continuing victims and new victims of school bullying. *British Journal of Educational Psychology*, 74, 565–81.

Steinfeldt, J., Vaughan, E., LaFollete, J., & Steinfeldt, M. (2012). Bullying among adolescent football players: Role of masculinity and moral atmosphere. *Psychology of Men & Masculinity*, 13(4), 340–53. DOI: 10.1037/a0026645.

Stirling, A. E. (2009). Definition and constituents of maltreatment in sport: Establishing a conceptual framework for research practitioners. *British Journal of Sports Medicine*, 43, 1091–99. DOI: 10.1136/bjsm.2008.051433.

Stirling, A. E. (2013). Understanding the use of emotionally abusive coaching practices. *International Journal of Sports Science & Coaching*, 8(4), 625–39.

Stirling, A. E., Bridges, E., Cruz, L., & Mountjoy, M. (2011). Canadian Academy of Sport and Exercise Medicine position paper: Abuse, harassment and bullying in sport. *Clinical Journal of Sport Medicine*, 21, 385–91.

Stirling, A. E. & Kerr, G. (2007). Elite female swimmers' experiences of emotional abuse over time. *Journal of Emotional Abuse*, 7(4), 89–113.

Stirling, A. E. & Kerr, G. (2008). Child protection in sport: Implications of an athlete-centered philosophy. *Quest*, 60, 307–23.

Stirling, A. E. & Kerr, G. (2009). Abused athletes' perceptions of coach-athlete relationship. *Sport in Society*, 12(2), 227–39.

Stirling, A. E. & Kerr, G. (2010). Sport psychology consultants as agents of child protection. *Journal of Applied Sport Psychology*, 22, 305–19.

Stirling, A. E. & Kerr, G. (2013). The perceived effects of elite athletes' experiences of emotional abuse in the coach–athlete relationship. *International Journal of Sport and Exercise Psychology*, 11(1), 87–100.

Stirling, A. E. & Kerr, G. (2014). Initiating and sustaining emotional abuse in the coach–Athlete relationship: An ecological transactional model of vulnerability. *Journal of Aggression, Maltreatment & Trauma*, 23, 116–35.

Stonewall. (2016). Homophobic views still prevalent in sport, 20 September 2016. www.stonewall.org.uk/media-centre/media-release/homophobic-views-sport

Stubbe, J. H., Boomsma, D. I., & De Geus, E. J. C. (2005). Sports participation during adolescence: A shift from environmental to genetic factors. *Medicine and Science in Sports and Exercise*, 37, 563–70. Ch2, P.13.

Sullivan, K., Cleary, M., & Sullivan, G. (2003). *Bullying in Secondary Schools*. London: Paul Chapman.

Swigonski, N. L., Enneking, B. A., & Hendrix, K. S. (2014). Bullying behavior by athletic coaches. *Pediatrics*, 133(2), 273–75. DOI: 10.1542/peds.2013-3146.

Tagg, B. (2015). Macho men in a girl's game: Masculinities and the Otago men's netball team. *Sport in Society: Cultures, Commerce, Media, Politics*, 19(7), 906–22. DOI: 10.1080/17430437.2015.1067782.

Teräsahjo, T. & Salmivalli, C. (2003). "She is not actually bullied". The discourse of harassment in student groups. *Aggressive Behavior*, 29, 134–54.

Thornberg, R. (2011). "She's weird!" – The social construction of bullying in school: A review of qualitative research. *Children & Society*, 25, 258–67.

Tilindiene, I., Rastauskiné, G., Zalys, L., & Valantiniené, I. (2008). The influence of gender and sports on the expression of bullying experienced by teenagers between 12–15 years old and their bullying peers. *Socialiniai tyrimai/Social Research*, 3(13), 179–85.

Tomlinson, A. & Yorganci, I. (1997). Male coach/female athlete relations: Gender and power relations in competitive sport. *Journal of Sport and Social Issues*, 21(2), 134–55.

Trautmann, A. (2008). Maltrato entre pares o "bullying". Una visión actual. *Revista Chilena De Pediatría*, 79(1), 13–20.

Trochim, W. (2001). *Research Methods: Knowledge Base*. Cincinnati: Atomic Dog.

Ttofi, M., Farrington, D., & Losel, F. (2011). Health consequences of school bullying. *Journal of Aggression, Conflict and Peace Research*, 3(2), 60–62.

Twemlow, S., Biggs, B., Nelson, T., Vernberg, E., Fonagy, P., & Twemlow, S. (2008). Effects of participation in a martial arts-based antibullying program in elementary schools. *Psychology in Schools*, 45(10), 947–59.

Twemlow, S. & Sacco, F. (1998). The application of traditional martial arts practice and theory to the treatment of violent adolescents. *Adolescence*, 33(131), 505–18.

UNICEF. (2005). *UN Human Rights Standards and Mechanisms to Combat Violence against Children*. Florence: UNICEF Innocenti Research Centre. www.unicef-irc.org/research/pdf/unstandards-flier.pdf.

UNICEF. (2010). *Protecting Children from Violence in Sport. A Review with a Focus on Industrialized Countries*. Florence: UNICEF Innocenti Research Centre. www.unicef-irc.org/publications/pdf/violence_in_sport.pdf.

Unnever, J. D. & Cornell, D. G. (2004). Middle school victims of bullying. Who reports being bullied? *Aggressive Behavior*, 30, 373–88. DOI: 10.1002/ab.20030.

Van Roekel, E., Scholte, R. H. J., & Didden, R. (2009). Bullying among adolescents with autism spectrum disorders: Prevalence and perception. *Journal of Autism and Developmental Disorders*, 40, 63–73.

Ventura, C., Prat, M., Ríos, X., Flores, G., Lleixà, T., & Soler, S. (2019). Bullying i ciberbullying al futbol formatiu a Catalunya. In *Col·lecció Fundació*. Barcelona: Fundació Barça.

Vertommen, T., Veldhoven, N., Wouters, K., Kampen, J., Brackenridge, C., Rhind, D., Neels, K., & Van Den Eede, F. (2016). Interpersonal violence against children in sport in the Netherlands and Belgium. *Child Abuse & Neglect*, 51, 223–36.

Vichery, S. (1998). Let's not overlook content validity. *Decision Line*, 1, 10–13.

Volk, A. & Lagzdins, L. (2009). Bullying and victimization among adolescent girl athletes. *Athletic Insight*, 1(1), 15–25.

Waldron, J., Lynn, Q., & Krane, V. (2011). Duct tape, icy hot & paddles: Narratives of initiation onto US male sport teams. *Sport, Education and Society*, 16(1), 111–25. DOI: 10.1080/13573322.2011.531965.

Wang, C., Berry, B., & Swearer, S. M. (2013). The critical role of school climate in effective bullying prevention. *Theory Into Practice*, 52, 296–302. DOI: 10.1080/00405841.2013.829735.

Whitney, I. & Smith, P. K. (1993). A survey of the nature and extent of bullying in junior/middle and secondary schools. *Educational Research*, 35(1), 3–25.

Witvliet, M., Olthof, T., Hoeksma, J., Smits, M., Koot, H., & Goossens, F. (2009). Peer group affiliation of children: The role of perceived popularity, likeability, and behavioral similarity in bullying. *Social Development*, 19(2), 285–303.

Wolke, D., Lee, K., & Guy, A. (2017). Cyberbullying: A storm in a teacup? *European Child & Adolescent Psychiatry*, 26(8), 899–908.

Wolke, D. & Lereya, S. T. (2015). Long-term effects of bullying. *Archives of Disease in Childhood*, 100, 879–85.

Wolke, D. & Sapouna, M. (2008). Big men feeling small: Childhood bullying experience, muscle dysmorphia and other mental health problems in body builders. *Psychology of Sport and Exercise*, 9, 595–604.

Woolger, C. & Power, T. G. (1993). Parent and sport socialization: Views from the achievement literature. *Journal of Sport Behavior*, 16, 171–89.

World Health Organization. (1999). *Report of the Consultation on Child Abuse Prevention*. Geneva: WHO.

Yao, Z. (2009). Discussion of sports exhibition on the development of leisure sports. *Consumption Guide*, 9, 18–19.

Yoneyama, S. & Naito, A. (2003). Problems with the paradigm: The school as a factor in understanding bullying (with special reference to Japan). *British Journal of Sociology of Education*, 24(3), 315–30.

Zhang, Z. J. & Pan, S. L. (2011). Investigation on the leisure sports culture in Ancient China. *Everyone*, 136, 128–29.

Zhaojin & Aiping. (2015). A study on the historical development of China's sports dream. *Cross-Cultural Communication*, 11(1), 1–4.

Zimmer-Gembeck, M., Lees, D., & Skinner, E. (2011). Children's emotions and coping with interpersonal stress as correlates of social competence. *Australian Journal of Psychology*, 63, 131–41.

Appendix I

SPORT VIOLENCE STUDY AND PREVENTION QUESTIONNAIRE: BULLYING IN SPORT

Sport:
Age: School year:
How long have you practised this sport?

In this questionnaire, you will find questions about your life in the youth sports club (training, competition, informal meetings). There are several possible answers for each question, which are marked by a letter. In most of the questions, you can answer by circling the option selected by you, while in other questions you can circle more than one possible answer.

You should not put your name on this questionnaire: it's totally anonymous and nobody will be able to identify your answers. You will never suffer any consequences, based on your answers. The researcher is the only person who is going to read the questionnaires and personal information will not be shared with others. It is important that you answer honestly and truthfully. If you have any questions, raise your hand and they will be answered individually, respecting your privacy.

1. Are you a juvenile, junior or cadet? Juvenile A Junior B Cadet C
   If you are a juvenile, circle A, if you are a junior, circle B and if you are a cadet, circle C.

2. How many good friends do you have in your team? Circle <u>only one</u> answer.

   A. None.
   B. I have 1 good friend in my team.
   C. I have 2 or 3 good friends in my team.
   D. I have 4 or 5 good friends in my team.
   E. I have more than 5 good friends in my team.

ABOUT BEING <u>VICTIMIZED BY OTHERS</u> IN THE SPORTS CLUB (TRAINING OR COMPETITION)

3. **How frequently have you been victimized in the sports club since last season?**
Circle **only one** answer.

   A. I haven't been victimized in the sports club since last season.
   B. 1 or 2 times.
   C. 3 to 6 times.
   D. Once a week.
   E. Many times a week.
   F. Other. Say how frequently:_____

<u>NOTE:</u> If you have <u>never</u> been victimized, you can go directly to question 15.

4. **In what way have you been victimized in the sports club since last season?** Circle **one or more** answers.

   A. I haven't been victimized in the sports club since last season.
   B. They have punched, kicked and pushed me.
   C. I have been threatened.
   D. They have taken my money or other belongings or damaged them.
   E. They have gossiped, mocked or insulted me based on my skin colour or race.
   F. They have mocked or insulted me for other reasons. Why? _____
   G. Peers have hidden my belongings on purpose, excluded me from the peer group or totally ignored me.
   H. Peers have told lies or spread rumours about me, and/or tried to make others dislike me.
   I. They have gossiped and showed/shared uncomfortable photographs and/or videos of me through email, social networks (Facebook, Twitter, etc.).
   J. Others. Say how:_____

5. **For how long has victimization lasted in the sports club?** Circle **only one** answer.

   A. I haven't been victimized in the sports club since last season.
   B. One week.
   C. Several weeks.
   D. All this season.
   E. Since many seasons ago.
   F. Other. Say how long:_____

6. Where have you been victimized in the sports club? Circle <u>one or more</u> answers.

   A. I haven't been victimized in the sports club since last season.
   B. Training area.
   C. Competition setting.
   D. Halls and areas outside training area.
   E. Changing room or WC.
   F. Through the internet (websites, chats, social networks, emails) or via mobile phone (text messages, videos).
   G. Other location inside or outside the sports club. Which one? _____

7. Are you usually victimized by one or more peers? Circle <u>only one</u> answer.

   A. I haven't been victimized in the sports club since last season.
   B. Mostly by one peer.
   C. 2–3 peers.
   D. 4–9 peers.
   E. The whole group.
   F. I don't know/I don't want to say how many.
   G. Other. Say how many:_____

8. In which of these activities have you been victimized in the sports club since last season? Circle <u>one or more</u> answers.

   A. I haven't been victimized in the sports club since last season.
   B. Training.
   C. Competition.
   D. Other activity inside or outside the sports club. Say which one: _____

9. How have you felt when you have been victimized in the sports club since last season? Circle <u>one or more</u> answers.

   A. I haven't been victimized in the sports club since last season.
   B. Angry.
   C. Sad.
   D. Helpless, nobody could help me.
   E. Humiliated.
   F. Scared, frightened.
   G. Annoyed.
   H. Nothing.
   I. Worried about what others were thinking about me.
   J. Other. How did you feel?_____

10. What have you usually done when you have been victimized in the sports club since last season? Circle <u>one or more</u> answers.

    A. I haven't been victimized in the sports club since last season.
    B. Cried.
    C. Run away.
    D. Ignored them.
    E. Told them to stop.
    F. Asked my peers for help.
    G. Asked my coach for help (coaches, other sports agents, etc.).
    H. Defended myself.
    I. Others. Say how: _____

11. Who have you spoken with about being victimized in the sports club since last season? Circle <u>one or more</u> answers.

    A. I haven't been victimized in the sports club since last season.
    B. I haven't spoken with anybody, although I have been victimized.
    C. I have spoken with other peers.
    D. I have spoken with my coach or another adult.
    E. I have spoken with my parents.
    F. I have spoken with my siblings.
    G. I have spoken with my friends.
    H. Others. Who did you speak with?_____

12. Has your coach tried to stop others victimizing you in the sports club since last season? Circle <u>only one</u> answer.

    A. I haven't been victimized in the sports club since last season.
    B. No, because he doesn't know I have been victimized.
    C. No, he hasn't tried anything.
    D. Yes, he has tried but the victimization has increased.
    E. Yes, he has tried but nothing has changed.
    F. Yes, he has tried and the victimization has decreased.
    G. Yes, he has tried and the victimization has stopped.
    I. Other. Say what has happened:_____

13. Has someone from your family spoken with your coach in order to stop others victimizing you in the sports club since last season? Circle <u>only one</u> answer.

    A. I haven't been victimized in the sports club since last season.
    B. No, because they don't know I have been victimized.
    C. No, they haven't spoken with the coach.
    D. Yes, they have spoken but the victimization has increased.
    E. Yes, they have spoken but nothing has changed.

F. Yes, they have spoken and the victimization has decreased.
G. Yes, they have spoken and the victimization has stopped.
H. Other. Say what has happened:_____

14. Have some of your peers tried to stop others victimizing you in the sports club since last season? Circle **only one** answer.

    A. I haven't been victimized in the sports club since last season.
    B. No, because they don't know I have been victimized.
    C. No, they haven't tried anything.
    D. Yes, they have tried but the victimization has increased.
    E. Yes, they have tried but nothing has changed.
    G. Yes, they have tried and the victimization has decreased.
    H. Yes, they have tried and the victimization has stopped.
    I. Other. Say what has happened:_____

ABOUT BULLYING EPISODES YOU HAVE SEEN IN THE SPORTS CLUB (TRAINING OR COMPETITION)

15. In what way have your peers been victimized in the sports club since last season? Circle **one or more** answers.

    A. I haven't seen any peers being victimized in the sports club since last season.
    B. They have been punched, kicked and pushed.
    C. They have been threatened.
    D. They have had their money or other belongings taken or damaged.
    E. They have been gossiped about, mocked or insulted based on their skin colour or race.
    F. They have been mocked or insulted for other reasons. Why?_____
    G. Peers have hidden their belongings on purpose, excluded them from the peer group or totally ignored them.
    H. Peers have told lies or spread rumours about them, and/or tried to make others dislike them.
    I. They have been gossiped about and uncomfortable photographs and/or videos of them have been shown/shared through email, social networks (Facebook, Twitter, etc.).
    J. Others. Say how:_____

16. How did you feel when you saw other peers being victimized? Circle **one or more** answers.

    A. I've never seen anybody being victimized.
    B. Angry.

C. I was afraid it could also happen to me.
D. Sad.
E. I felt sorry for the victim.
F. I pretended I hadn't seen anything.
G. I didn't feel anything.
H. I felt good.
I. Other. Say how you felt:_____

17. **What have you done when you have seen somebody being victimized in the sports club since last season?** Circle <u>one or more</u> answers.

    A. I've never seen anybody being victimized.
    B. Very often, I have been the one who started it.
    C. I have also been victimized.
    D. Very often, I have helped others victimize some of my peers.
    E. I have been made to help victimize other peers.
    F. I haven't helped the perpetrator, but have enjoyed watching.
    G. I have tried not to take sides.
    H. I have told the perpetrators to stop.
    I. I have asked for help from an adult (coach, employees, etc.) to stop the victimization.
    J. I have helped the colleague who was being victimized.
    K. Other. Say what you have done:_____

18. **Why do you think some peers victimize others?** Circle <u>one or more</u> answers.

    A. I don't know.
    B. My peers don't victimize others.
    C. Because the others play better.
    D. Because victims deserve what is happening to them.
    E. Because victims have complained to the coach or other adults.
    F. Because victims have complained to other peers.
    G. Because they are provoked.
    H. Because the victims are different from others.
    I. To feel superior.
    J. Because they feel envy.
    K. Because they have problems and/or feel bad.
    L. Other reasons. Say which ones: _____

ABOUT <u>BULLYING OTHERS</u> IN THE SPORTS CLUB (TRAINING OR COMPETITION)

19. How frequently have you bullied others in the sports club since last season?
Circle <u>only one</u> answer.

   A. I haven't bullied other peers since last season.
   B. 1 or 2 times.
   C. 3 to 6 times.
   D. Once a week.
   E. Many times a week.
   F. Other. Say how frequently:_____

20. When you bullied other peers, did you do it alone or with other peers? Circle <u>only one</u> answer.

   A. I haven't bullied other peers since last season.
   B. Usually I did it alone.
   C. Usually I did it with 1 or 2 peers.
   D. Usually I did it with 3 to 8 peers.
   E. Usually I did it with more than 8 peers.
   F. Other. Say how many:_____

21. Have you bullied other peers in any of these ways since last season? Circle <u>one or more</u> answers.

   A. I haven't bullied other peers since last season.
   B. I have punched, kicked and pushed them.
   C. I have threatened them.
   D. I have taken their money or other belongings, or damaged them.
   E. I have insulted them based on their skin colour or race.
   F. I have insulted or mocked them in other ways. Which ones?_____
   G. I have excluded some peers on purpose, by keeping them apart from the peer group and ignoring them.
   H. I have spread rumours about some peers and/or tried to get others to dislike them.
   I. I have gossiped and showed/shared uncomfortable photographs and/or videos of them through email, social networks (Facebook, Twitter, etc.).
   J. Others. Say how: _____

22. What have you felt if you have bullied other peers in the sports club since last season? Circle **one or more** answers.

   A. I haven't bullied other peers since last season.
   B. I felt great.
   C. It was funny.
   D. I felt they deserved what was happening to them.
   E. I didn't feel anything.
   F. I was worried about what they could say to my coach or parents.
   G. I'm sure they would have done the same to me.
   H. I felt bad.
   I. I felt sorry for them.
   J. Other. What did you feel?_____

23. Who has talked with you about bullying others since last season? Circle **one or more** answers.

   A. I haven't bullied other peers since last season.
   B. Nobody has talked to me, although I have bullied other peers.
   C. The teammates.
   D. The coach.
   E. My parents.
   F. My siblings.
   G. My friends.
   H. Other. Say who: _____

THANK YOU VERY MUCH FOR ANSWERING THIS QUESTIONNAIRE.

Appendix 2

Interview script (STUDY 2)
Concerning the bullying definition provided before, have you ever been involved in bullying episodes in a sports setting?

1. Have you suffered from bullying in your sports club?
2. Have you inflicted bullying on your colleagues?
3. Have you seen bullying episodes between your colleagues?

Victims

Categories	Sub-categories	Questions
Circumstances	Types	What happened?
	Location	Where did it take place?
	Participants (number of athletes involved)	Were bullying episodes performed by a single athlete or by more colleagues?
	Reasons	Why do you think bullying exists? Why do you think others choose you to be targeted? Have you ever also got involved as a perpetrator? If so, why did you do it?
	Social settings	Does bullying involvement occur exclusively in the sports club or also in other social settings (school, other peer group, etc.)? (If exclusively in the sports club), why do you think it only happens in the sports setting?
Roles	Profiles	**Victims** How would you describe yourself as an individual and as an athlete (good and bad)? How would you like to be? How would you like to be seen by others? **Perpetrators** How would you describe perpetrators as individuals and as athletes (good and bad)?

(Continued)

(Cont.)

	Sociometry (social status)		How are perpetrators perceived by your colleagues?
	Coach		What do you think is your coach's opinion about you? What do you think is your coach's opinion about perpetrators?
Practical implications	Interventions		How do you think bullying could be efficiently tackled? What interventions should be done with perpetrators? What would you like to change? What have you done to change things?

Bullies

Categories	Sub-categories	Questions
Circumstances	Types	What happened?
	Location	Where did it take place?
	Participants (number of athletes involved)	Did you get involved alone or with some colleagues?
	Reasons	Why do you think bullying exists? Why did you choose certain colleagues as targets?
	Social settings	Does bullying involvement occur exclusively in the sports club or also in other social settings (school, other peer group, etc.)? (If exclusively in the sports club), why do you think it only happens in the sports setting?
Roles	Profiles	**Perpetrators** How would you describe yourself as an individual and as an athlete (good and bad)? How would you like to be? How would you like to be seen by others? **Victims** How would you describe victims as individuals and as athletes (good and bad)?
	Sociometry (social status)	How are victims seen by your colleagues?
	Coach	What do you think is your coach's opinion about you? What do you think is your coach's opinion about victims?

(Continued)

(Cont.)

Practical implications	Empathy	What do you think victims feel when they are the target of bullying?
	Behavioural inhibiting mechanisms	Do you feel bad about your involvement in bullying episodes? Have you ever stopped bullying because you felt bad about it?

Bystanders

Categories	Sub-categories	Questions
Circumstances	Types	What happened?
	Location	Where have you seen bullying episodes?
	Participants (number of athletes involved)	Were the bullying episodes observed performed by a single perpetrator or by more colleagues?
	Reasons	Why do you think bullying exists? Why do perpetrators choose specific athletes as targets?
	Social settings	Does bullying occur exclusively in the sports club or also in other social settings (school, other peer group, etc.)? (If exclusively in the sports club), why do you think it only happens in the sports setting?
Roles	Profiles	**Perpetrators** How would you describe perpetrators as individuals and as athletes (good and bad)? **Victims** How would you describe victims as individuals and as athletes (good and bad)?
	Sociometry (social status)	How are perpetrators and victims seen by your colleagues?
	Coach	What do you think is your coach's opinion about perpetrators? What do you think is your coach opinion's about victims?
Practical implications	Intervention	How do you think bullying issues could be efficiently tackled? What interventions should be done with perpetrators? What would you like to change? What have you done to change things?

Appendix 3

Interview script (STUDY 3)

Coaches

Categories	Sub-categories	Questions
Conceptual issues	Aggressiveness in sport	How might aggressiveness be important in the sports setting?
	Bullying or banter?	When different athletes are involved in the same social interaction, some of them describe it as banter, while others consider it bullying. What do you think?
Circumstances	Types	What happened?
	Reasons	Why do you think bullying exists? When the team is having bad results, bullying behaviours tend to occur more often. Do you agree?
	Crucial moments	Some coaches stated that when a younger athlete is integrated into an already existing group of older athletes, the probability of being targeted increases. What do you think?
	Hazing rituals	Are there any hazing rituals in your group? Can you give some examples? What is the purpose? What do you think of this?
	Changes over time	Do you think bullying behaviours differ at different ages (frequency, type of bullying, etc.)? How do you think it changes over the years?
	Social settings	Do you have any knowledge of whether bullying occurs exclusively in the sports club or also in other social settings (school, other peer group, etc.)?
		(If exclusively in the sports club), why do you think it only happens in the sports setting?

(Continued)

(Cont.)

Roles	Profiles	**Perpetrators** How would you describe perpetrators as individuals and as athletes (good and bad)? **Victims** How would you describe victims as individuals and as athletes (good and bad)?
	Sociometry (social status)	How are perpetrators and victims seen by their colleagues?
Practical implications	Prevention/Intervention	How do you think bullying could be efficiently tackled?

Appendix 4

Interview script (STUDY 4)

Interview script: ex-elite athletes (recall study)

Topic	Objective	Questions
1. Involvement in bullying episodes	To know if the participant got involved in bullying episodes and the role played.	During your sporting career, have you ever got involved in bullying episodes? (Option 1 or Option 2)
• **Option 1:** In case of a **negative** answer to question 1, move to questions 2, 3 and 4.		
2. Opinion	To know the opinion of the participant about bullying in the sport he practised.	What do you think about bullying in youth sports training?
3. Importance	To know the importance given by the participant to the topic being studied.	How important do you think this topic is?
4. Burnout	Ask the participant to comment on the possible relation between early sports abandonment and victimization.	Do you consider a possible relation between early sports abandonment and victimization?
• **Option 2:** In case of an **affirmative** answer to question 1 (about involvement in bullying episodes in the sports setting), move to question 5.		
5. Role	To know which role the participant played in bullying episodes.	Concerning bullying episodes you reported, did you get involved as victim, perpetrator or bystander? (Option 1, Option 2 or Option 3)
• **Option 1:** In case the participant has answered getting involved as **victim** to question 5, move to question 6.		

(Continued)

(Cont.)

6. Report	To collect narratives about victimization, trying to include the sub-questions above. If a topic wasn't covered by the participant's speech, ask directly about it.	Based on your sporting career, can you give examples of victimization?
6.1. Frequency	To collect information about the frequency of victimization.	How frequently have you been targeted?
6.2. Location	To collect information about the location of victimization.	Where did the episodes take place?
6.3. Types	To collect information about the types of bullying.	In which ways have you been targeted by your colleagues?
6.4. Participants (number of athletes involved)	To collect information about the peers involved.	Were bullying episodes performed by a single athlete or by more colleagues?
6.5. Profiles	To describe perpetrators and victims.	Please describe perpetrators and victims.
6.6. Feelings	To collect information about feelings towards bullying.	What did you feel when you were targeted by your colleagues?
6.7. Reasons	To explore the beliefs of the participant about the existence of bullying.	Why do you think there is bullying in sport?
6.8. Social settings	To collect information about the social settings in which bullying episodes occurred.	Was bullying involvement restricted to the sports setting or did it also happen in other social settings?
6.9. Intervention	To understand which strategies athletes consider to be more efficient to deal with bullying.	How do you think bullying in sport can be dealt with?

- **Option 2:** In case the participant has answered getting involved as **perpetrator** to question 5, move to question 7.

7. Report	To collect narratives about bullying others, trying to include the sub-questions above. If a topic wasn't covered by the participant's speech, ask directly about it.	Based on your sporting career, can you give examples of bullying others?
7.1. Frequency	To collect information about the frequency of bullying.	How frequently have you bullied others?
7.2. Location	To collect information about the location of bullying.	Where did the episodes take place?

(Continued)

(Cont.)

7.3. Types	To collect information about the types of bullying.	In which ways have you bullied your colleagues?
7.4. Participants (number of athletes involved)	To collect information about the peers involved.	Were bullying episodes performed individually or by more colleagues?
7.5. Profiles	To describe perpetrators and victims.	Please describe victims and bystanders.
7.6. Feelings	To collect information about feelings towards bullying.	What did you feel when you bullied your colleagues?
7.7. Reasons	To explore the beliefs of the participant about the existence of bullying.	Why do you think there is bullying in sport?
7.8. Social settings	To collect information about the social settings in which bullying episodes occurred.	Was bullying involvement restricted to the sports setting or did it also happen in other social settings?
7.9. Victims' feelings	Explore the perception of the perpetrator concerning victims' feelings.	What do you think victims feel when you bully them?

- **Option 3:** In case the participant has answered getting involved as **bystander** to question 5, move to question 8.

8. Report	To collect narratives about bullying episodes observed, trying to include the sub-questions above. If a topic wasn't covered by the participant's speech, ask directly about it.	Based on your sporting career, can you give examples of bullying episodes you observed?
8.1. Frequency	To collect information about the frequency of bullying.	How frequently have you observed bullying episodes?
8.2. Location	To collect information about the location of bullying.	Where did the episodes take place?
8.3. Types	To collect information about the types of bullying.	In which ways have you seen your colleagues being bullied?
8.4. Participants (number of athletes involved)	To collect information about the peers involved.	Were bullying episodes performed individually or by more colleagues?
8.5. Profiles	To describe perpetrators and victims.	Please describe perpetrators and victims.

(Continued)

(Cont.)

8.6. Feelings	To collect information about feelings towards bullying.	What did you feel when you saw your colleagues being bullied?
8.7. Reasons	To explore the beliefs of the participant about the existence of bullying.	Why do you think there is bullying in sport?
8.8. Social settings	To collect information about the social settings in which bullying episodes occurred.	Did bullying episodes occur only in the sports setting or did they also happen in other social settings?
8.9. Intervention	To understand which strategies the athletes consider to be more efficient to deal with bullying.	How do you think bullying in sport could be efficiently tackled?

Index

Page numbers in **bold** denote a table. Page numbers in *italics* denote a figure.

abuse 1, 6, 9, 10, 14, 16, 28, 40–41, 46, 52–3, 59, 64, 71, 77, 130–31, 140–41, 147–50, 157, 173, 176, 183, 192, 198, 211, 213–31, 233, 239, 240–42, 261–63
anti-bullying program 11, 14, 22, 32, 65, 123, 201, 251–52
athlete welfare 41, 71, 235

BIRNAW 41
bully 4, *98*; ringleader 18, 247
bullying: athlete-to-athlete 5, 197, 208, 214, 242, 247, 251, 260; bias/prejudice-based 15–16, 80; coach-to-athlete 64, 214, 221, 260–61; cyberbullying 10, 14, 16, 20, 58, 102, **110**, 118, 190, 211–12, 250, 257; direct 13, 17–19, 21, 29, 32, 34–35, 37, 39, 91, 144, 160, 164, 169, 175, 179, 187, 190, 193, 197, 199, 201, 206, 212, 234, 235–37, 244, 248, 257–58; hostile 17, 215; indirect 11–14, 17, 19–20, 56, 193, 217, 234, 255; instrumental 17, 147, 218; physical 11, 16–17, 19–20, 22, 27, 29–30, 35, 37, 43, 46, 72, 83–84, 102, **104**, 118, 125, 127–29, 131, 133–35, 137, 140, 142, 145, 151, 153, 159–60, 162, 164–65, 174, 182, 188–93, 208–09, 211, 215–17, 222, 224–28, 247, 261–63; pro-active 18, 29, 60, 62, 108, 114, 123, 138, 139, 144–45, 207, 234; reactive 18, 143, 233, 237, 251, 253, 255; social 4, 5, 9, 12–13, 16–17, 19, 21–30, 32, 40–41, 52, 54–55, 58–59, 61–64, 66, 77, 83–84, 88, 90–92, 94, 98–102, **104**, 107, 114, 117–18, 125, 127–31, 134–36, 139, 140–51, 153, 155, 157, 159, 162–69, 171–75, 179–83, 185–86, 188–96, 200, 203, 205, 207–11, 215–17, 219, 221–23, 226–32, 233–36, 241–42, 247, 248, 250–51, 254–55, 257, 261–62; verbal 11, 16–17, 19–20, 46, 58–60, 83–84, 102, **104**, 116–18, 125, 127–29, 140, 142, 145, 148, 157, 160, 164–66, 171, 175, 180, 188–90, 193–94, 208–09, 211, 215–17, 221, 224–25, 258
bystander 4, 5, 12–14, 18–20, 28, 32, 60, 62, 77, 79, 84, 86, 90–92, 97–98, 102, **104**–06, 116, 120–21, 123–28, 130, 137–41, 144–45, 147, 162, 164–66, 170–71, 174–75, 180, 184, 187, 195–96, 200–01, 204–06, 208, 211–12, 219, 225, 227, 231, 233–34, 238, 247, 250, 256, 259, 260, 293, 296, 298; defender 13, 19, 170, 188, 206, 234; outsider 19, 45, 90, 146, 158, 174, 180, 195

Canadian Red Cross 215
changes over time 147, 151, 158, 294
circumstances 101, 106, 107–09, 117, 124–25, 127, 140, 146, 148, 157, 161–62, 164–65, 170, 191, 199, 291–94; frequency 4, 18, 41; location

3–5, 55, 58–59, 79, 83–85, 90–92, 105–**110**, 125, 129, 140, 162, 164, 166, 172, 194–95, 211, 285, 291–93, 297–98; number athletes 4–5, 84, 105–06, 115–17, 119, 125, 130, 136, 141, 162, 164, 166, 170–71, 184, 291–93, 297–98; types bullying 3–4, 13–14, 17, 19–20, 58, 79, 84–85, 90, 97, 105, 116–17, 125, 127–28, 140, 146, 148, 157–58, 162, 164–65, 171,188, 190, 193, 211–12, 297–98
coach 3–6, 14, 25, 32–33, 39, 44, 48, 51, 53, 56, 58, 60, 64–65, 67, 69–71, 74, 77, 84, 86–88, 90, 92, 95–96, 99, 105, 109, **111**–12, 116, 120, 125–26, 129–32, 136–37, 139–41, 143, 145–61, 163–64, 167–72, 175, 179–180, 182–84, 186–99, 201–06, 209–240, 242–46, 249, 251–54, 256, 260–64; action 148, 153; artificial selection 136–37, 143, 153, 159; equal opportunities 136, 159, 197
coach-athlete relationship 53, 58, 60, 213, 224, 227, 240
conceptual issues; banter 51, 52, 60, 102, 116, 124–29, 133, 135, 139, 145–48, 153, 156, 160–62, 166–67, 170, 174–75, 179, 181, 189, 191–92, 204, 210, 215, 241, 245, 247–48, 251, 294; aggression 1, 2, 10–13, 19, 24, 28, 32, 51, 53, 57–58, 60, 62, 79, 98, 128–30, 132, 137, 140, 141, 143–44, 162–66, 171, 174–75, 180–82, 184, 186, 189–90, 195, 209, 211, 215, 217, 230, 241, 242, 259; aggressiveness 3, 24, 27, 47, 48, 62, 63, 146–47, 155–56, 181–82, 189, 294; assertiveness 24, 133, 159, 181, 233, 257; coach abuse 6, 64, 71, 215, 218, 220, 262; coach bullying 56, 212, 214–21, 228–29, 260–63; emotional abuse 214–15, 218–19, 231; encouragement 27, 36, 156, 211, 215–16, 221, 228, 260, 263; hazing 40, 50, 52, 59, 90, 147, 151, 158, 160, 171, 182–83, 219, 225; initiation 52; intellectualized justifications 59, 219–20; interpersonal violence 41, 53, 64, 71, 74, 88, 161, 164, 168; mobbing 11; normalization 156, 161–62, 172, 182, 184, 188, 214, 216, 221, 228, 234, 242, 263; play 18, 23, 26, 28, 34–35, 38, 45–47, 49, 51, 54–55, 58, 62, 65, 67, 74, 78, 90, 111, 121, 125–130, 136–37, 142, 145, 147, 149, 151–52, 154–55, 158, 163–66, 168–69, 171–72, 175, 180–84, 186, 189, 192–95, 197, 199–203, 213, 217, 222–23, 225, 231, 240, 243, 251, 254, 256, 261, 264; regular sports aggression 32, 52–53, 184; rough and tumble 35, 180, 181
consequences 2–3, 5, 9–10, 15, 19, 31–32, 52–53, 58, 61, 64, 88, 117, 125, 134, 137–38, 141, 144, 147–48, 153–56, 160, 162, 164, 168–69, 175, 180, 193, 203–04, 207–212, 216, 219, 221–23, 227–30, 247, 256–59, 263; anti-social behaviour 32, 55, 63, 80, 85, 92, 147, 255; depression 26, 31, 222, 228, 233; long-term 32, 52, 61, 78, 107, 193, 210, 221, 263; short-term 209, 216; suicide 10, 31
crucial moments 90, 146, 148, 150, 156–57, 162, 164, 166, 172, 194, 196, 211, 294
data: analysis 3, 78, 80, 85, 91, 93, 120, 140, 196–97; collection 33, 58, 66, 77–80, 82–83, 85–88, 90–92, 95, 184

desporto sem bullying 41, 49
discrimination 42, 45, 47, 49, 100, 183, 190, 233, 240–42
dominance 20, 25, 29–30, 48, 60, 128, 141, 173, 180–82, 188–89, 192, 196, 198–99, 216, 224, 231

ecological systems theory 3, 29, 34, 55, 57, 64, 231, 232; exo-system 56–57, 232; macro-system 29, 56, 57, 232; meso-system 56–57, 232; micro-system 55, 57, 232
ethical issues 95
ex-elite athlete 3, 5, 77, 86–87, 90–92, 95–96, 161–176, 179, 181, 184, 186, 188–89, 191, 193–96, 198–99, 202, 209, 211–12, 218, 296
expert panel 81, 88–89

homophobia 42, 45–46, 48, 183, 189, 225

integration 128, 133–34, 138–39, 142, 145, 147, 148, 150–51, 154–55, 158, 160, 163, 183, 192, 194, 196, 211, 233, 235–36, 243, 251, 254
International Olympic Committee 38, 40, 223
intervention program 1–2, 10, 66, 102, 187, 218, 230, 233–34
intervention strategies 5, 29, 90, 137, 154, 159, 169, 174, 206, 253, 256
interview 4–5, 33, 46, 51, 78, 80, 86–96, 99, 124, 126, 129, 141, 146, 148, 153, 155–56, 161, 175, 179–180, 184, 186, 189, 191, 194, 196, 198, 200–02, 209, 211–12, 218, 233, 237–38; script 86, 88–91, 96, 146, 148, 153, 196, 211

key concepts in SHA 225; risk factors 21–22, 30, 124, 127, 202, 218, 226–29, 242; sexual exploitation 225; sexual harassment 17; sexual abuse 223; sexual harassment and abuse 6, 40, 214–15, 222–23, 225, 229; silence 2, 31, 59–60, 84, 101, 108, 111–19, 123, 140, 144, 186, 203–04, 221–22, 226–27, 238, 243–44, 252, 256

masculine hegemony 48
mentality: sport culture 49, 219, 228; sport mentality 57, 192; tough mentality 32, 41, 52, 59, 159, 192, 203, 219, 221, 228
methods 3–4, 77, 79, 81, 83; quantitative 3, 4, 11, 33, 77–78, 82, 93, 95, 97, 188, 193–94, 208, 212; qualitative 3–4, 11, 33, 77–78, 80, 82, 86, 88, 94–95, 102, 124, 188, 193, 204, 205, 212
multi-level approach 21, 30, 55, 230; group dynamics approach 28, 55; individual traits approach 3, 19, 22–23, 54, 55, 77, 173; social environment 3, 21.22, 25, 27, 29, 30, 54, 57, 63, 77, 128, 150–51, 157, 159, 167, 169, 173, 182, 186, 191–93, 199, 209, 231, 234, 241, 248, 251, 262

NSPCC 41, 265

Olympic Games 34, 36–39; Ancient Greece 35–36, 49; Middle Ages 37–38; Modern Ages 38; Renaissance 37; Roman Empire 37, 49

Paralympics 46
parents 5–6, 20, 24, 26–27, 31, 56, 61, 88, 91, 95, 109, **111**, 129, 155, 160, 162, 164, 168, 175, 184, 187, 209–210, 213, 215–221, 226, 228–230, 232–33, 239, 242, 244–46, 249, 251–53, 259–63
peer nomination 12
peer pressure 77, 130–32, 141, 145, 157, 167, 173, 176, 193, 196, 198–99, 211
performance 2, 24, **30**, 34, 37, 39, 42–44, 50, 55, 61, 71, 74, 127, 131, 133–36, 142–43, 145, 147, 149, 150–53, 155, 158–59, 160, 162, 164–65, 168–69, 172–74, 176, 182, 186–87, 191–92, 196 -200, 202, 209–210, 213, 216, 219, 220–22, 227–28, 242, 251, 254, 260, 263
pilot test 82, 88–90
power dynamics 25, 32, 58, 198, 210, 264
practical implications 5–6, 87, 90, 125, 137, 144, 146–47, 159, 161–62, 164, 169, 174, 177, 196, 201, 230–31, 292–93, 295; consequences of prevention and intervention strategies 90, 137, 154, 159, 169
prevention 12, 22, 40, 66, 81, 90, 125, 137, 147, 154, 159, 162, 164, 169, 174–75, 187, 202, 227, 230–31, 233, 240, 242, 253, 263
Profiles 5, 12, 19, 23–24, 26, **30**, 70, 90–91, 125, 134, 143, 145, 147, 149, 152, 159, 162, 164, 168, 173, 191, 196, 211, 230; social status 17, 28–30, 36–37, 40, 49, 52, 90, 107, 125, 130–32, 135, 141, 143, 145, 147, 149, 150, 153, 159, 162, 164–65, 168–69, 171–74, 181, 192, 196, 198, 200, 203, 205, 221

questionnaire 11–13, 33, 65–66, 74, 77–83, 85–86, 88, 95–97, 107, 198, 212; coping 3–5, 19, 30–31, 84, 88, 90–91, 105, 107–08, 111–13, 114, 120–21, 123, 137–38, 144–45, 147, 160, 162, 193, 203, 206–07, 222, 227, 233; support sources 4, 31, 79, 84, 105, 107–08, 111–12, 115, 204, 224, 251

racism 42, 47, 184
Reasons 4–5, 21, 38, 78–79, 84, 90–92, 94, 105, 116, 120–22, 124–25, 127, 130–32, 141, 145, 148–150, 155, 157, 160–64, 167, 173, 176, 186, 189, 191–92, 198–99, 203, 209, 211, 218, 221, 228, 248; divergence from accepted standard 198–99; fundamental abuse of perceived power 130, **131**, 141, 148–49, 157, 173, 176, 198; envy **131**–32, 141, 148–49, 152, 157, 160, 167, 198; hierarchy **131**, 141, 148, 150, 157, 160, 162, 167, 173, 176, 198–99; individual characteristics **55**, 130–**31**, 133–34, 142, 145, 198, 202, 211; body issues 30, 127, **131**, 133, 135, 145, 169, 191, 198, 202; low sports performance 127, **131**, 133–34, 142, 150, 153, 198, 202; personality **131**, 133, 142, 155, 157, 167–68, 173, 192–93, 197–98, 202, 238; peer pressure 9, 14, 19, 28, 30, 54, 77, 130–32, 141, 145, 157, 167, 173, 176, 193, 196, 198–200, 211; imitation **131**–32, 141, 198–200, 212, 217–18, 255; rivalry **131**–32, 141, 148–150, 157, 167, 173, 176, 198; victims' responsibility **131**, 133, 138, 141, 144, 162
research 1–4, 6, 9–16, 19, 21, 23–25, 28, 30–34, 39–41, 48, 50–55, 58–63, 65–66, 68, 74, 75, 77–86, 88–95, 99, 100, 102, 107, 109, 114, 115, 121, 126, 128–131, 136–37, 139–142, 144, 149, 151–52, 159, 171–75, 179, 182, 184–88, 190, 192–97, 199–200, 204–05, 208, 210–12, 214, 215, 217, 218, 222–23, 226, 230–31, 240, 242, 251
risk factors 21–22, 30, 124, 127, 202, 218, 226–29, 242

roles 2, 5, 13, 18–19, 23, 28–29, 47, 49, 51, 54–55, 79, 86–87, 90, 92, 97–98, 102, 104, 124–25, 127, 134, 140, 143, 145–47, 149, 152, 157, 159, 161–62, 164, 168, 173, 180–81, 184, 194, 196–97, 233, 239, 251, 256

sample 11, 46, 58, 77, 78, 81–83, 87, 89, 94–95, 97–98, 100–02, 107, 114, 159, 170, 184, 187–88, 193, 212
sexual harassment and abuse 6, 40, 214–15, 222–23, 225, 229
sexual stereotypes 3, 20, 34, 47–48, 57, 63, 184, 242; femininity 48, 59; masculinity 24, 45, 48, 50, 52, 59, 143, 156, 173–74, 182–83, 188–89, 191–92, 203, 231
social settings 2, 5, 23, 25, 27, 32, 50–52, 54, 56, 63–64, 125, 134, 142, 145–46, 149, 157, 162, 164, 167–68, 173, 179, 185, 192, 197, 211, 227, 291–95, 297–99
sexuality 3, 46–47, 77, 80, 189
sport club **55**, 217, 219, 221–23, 225, 227
sports: athletics 43–44, **72**–73, 82, 85, 87, 99–100, 155, 161, 164, 209; football 43–47, 49, 50, 54, 58, **72**–73, 82, 85, 87, 99–100, 127–28, 136–37, 149, 154, 161–63, 169, 175, 182, 184, 189, 199, 202, 209, 220, 222–23; gymnastics 43, 50, **72**–73, 82, 85, 87, 99–100, 134, 149, 161, 163, 198, 200, 222; handball **72**–73, 82, 85, 87, 99, 100, 129, 152, 155, 161, 164–65, 168, 194, 200, 208, 209; judo **72**–73, 82, 85, 87, 99–100, 156, 161–64, 209; rugby 43, 46–47, 50, **72**, 73, 82, 85, 87, 99, 100, 161, 164, 165, 182, 199, 202, 206, 209; swimming 44, 46, 50, **72**–73, 82, 85, 87, 99–100, 161–62, 164, 222–23; volleyball 43, 45, 50, **72**–73, 82, 85, 87, 99–100, 161, 164, 200–01; wrestling 63, **72**–73, 82, 85, 87, 99–100, 161, 164–66, 169
stakeholders 40, 43–44, 46–48, 52, 68, 78, 86, 95–96, 137, 156, 160, 164, 169–170, 175, 179, 181–82, 187, 212, 216, 218, 222–23, 228, 230–35,

240, 242, 252, 255, 261, 263

test-retest 82
training 1–5, 32–34, 37, 39, 51, 53, 62–63, 66, 71, 75, 77–80, 84–86, 93, 97–98, 101, 106–07, 109–111, 114, 124, 128–130, 132, 135, 137, 140, 46, 149, 150, 153, 155–56, 158, 161, 165–66, 170, 172, 175, 189–190, 194–95, 200, 209–10, 212–13, 215–16, 219–20, 222, 224, 226–27, 233–36, 239, 243, 248, 253–54, 257, 261–64
translation 2, 15, 81, 241

UEFA 47, 49
UNICEF 41, 223, 230

validation 3–4, 81, 86, 88–90, 96
victim: bully-victim 18–19, 23, 26, 28, 31, 97–98, 207; provocative victim 18, 237, 257
violence 1, 3, 17, 19, 25, 32, 34, 37, 40–42, 47, 51, 53, 55–58, 63–64, 71, 74, 81, 88, 154, 161, 164, 168, 188–89, 199, 227, 230, 233, 239–42, 259

world health organisation 215, 227

youth 1, 3–5, 23, 29, 32–34, 41–42, 51, 53, 55, 57–61, 63–69, 74, 75, 77–79, 86, 90–91, 93–94, 97, 102, 124, 127, 137, 143, 146, 148, 153, 156, 158–161, 167–68, 170–71, 179, 182–88, 211–15, 219, 221–22, 226, 229–31, 240–41, 251, 253, 263